ANGEL &FAITH™

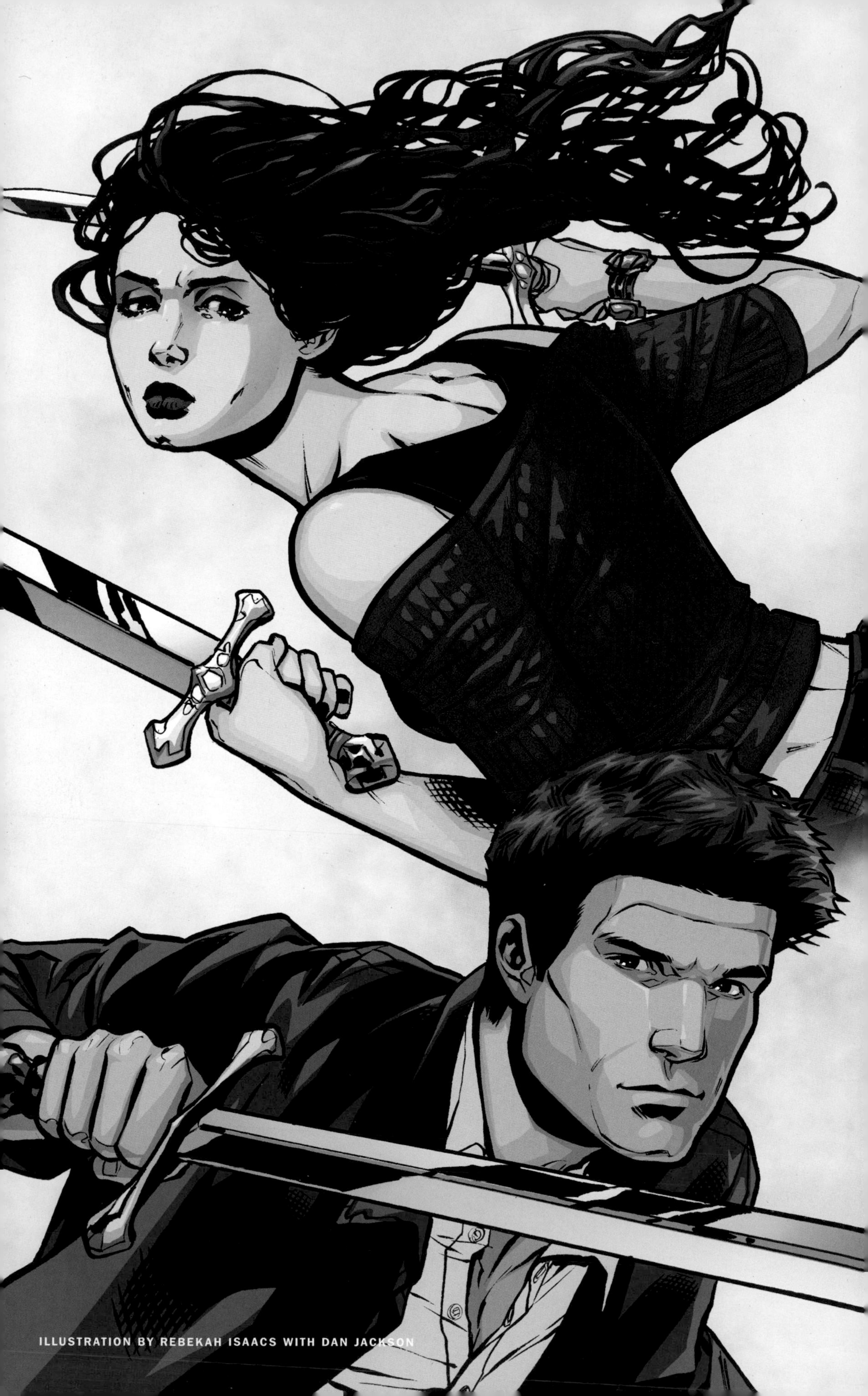

ILLUSTRATION BY REBEKAH ISAACS WITH DAN JACKSON

ANGEL &FAITH™

SEASON 9 · VOLUME 2

SCRIPT
CHRISTOS GAGE

DADDY ISSUES

ART
REBEKAH ISAACS

COLORS
DAN JACKSON

WOMEN OF A CERTAIN AGE

ART
CHRIS SAMNEE

COLORS
JORDIE BELLAIRE

LETTERS
RICHARD STARKINGS & Comicraft's
JIMMY BETANCOURT

COVER ART
STEVE MORRIS

EXECUTIVE PRODUCER
JOSS WHEDON

DARK HORSE BOOKS

PRESIDENT & PUBLISHER
MIKE RICHARDSON

EDITORS
SCOTT ALLIE & SIERRA HAHN

ASSISTANT EDITOR
FREDDYE LINS

COLLECTION DESIGNER
JUSTIN COUCH

Published by Dark Horse Books
A division of Dark Horse Comics, Inc.
10956 SE Main Street
Milwaukie, OR 97222

DarkHorse.com

To find a comics shop in your area, call the
Comic Shop Locator Service toll-free at
(888) 266-4226.

First edition: November 2012
ISBN 978-1-59582-960-3

10 9 8 7 6 5 4 3 2 1

This story takes place during *Buffy the Vampire Slayer* Season 9, created by Joss Whedon.

Special thanks to Lauren Valencia at Twentieth Century Fox and Daniel Kaminsky.

NEIL HANKERSON Executive Vice President • TOM WEDDLE Chief Financial Officer • RANDY STRADLEY
Vice President of Publishing • MICHAEL MARTENS Vice President of Book Trade Sales • ANITA NELSON
Vice President of Business Affairs • DAVID SCROGGY Vice President of Product Development • DALE
LaFOUNTAIN Vice President of Information Technology • DARLENE VOGEL Senior Director of Print, Design,
and Production • KEN LIZZI General Counsel • MATT PARKINSON Vice President of Marketing • DAVEY
ESTRADA Editorial Director • SCOTT ALLIE Senior Managing Editor • CHRIS WARNER Senior Books Editor •
DIANA SCHUTZ Executive Editor • CARY GRAZZINI Director of Print and Development • LIA RIBACCHI Art
Director • CARA NIECE Director of Scheduling

This volume reprints the comic-book series *Angel & Faith* #6–#10 from Dark Horse Comics.

ANGEL & FAITH ™

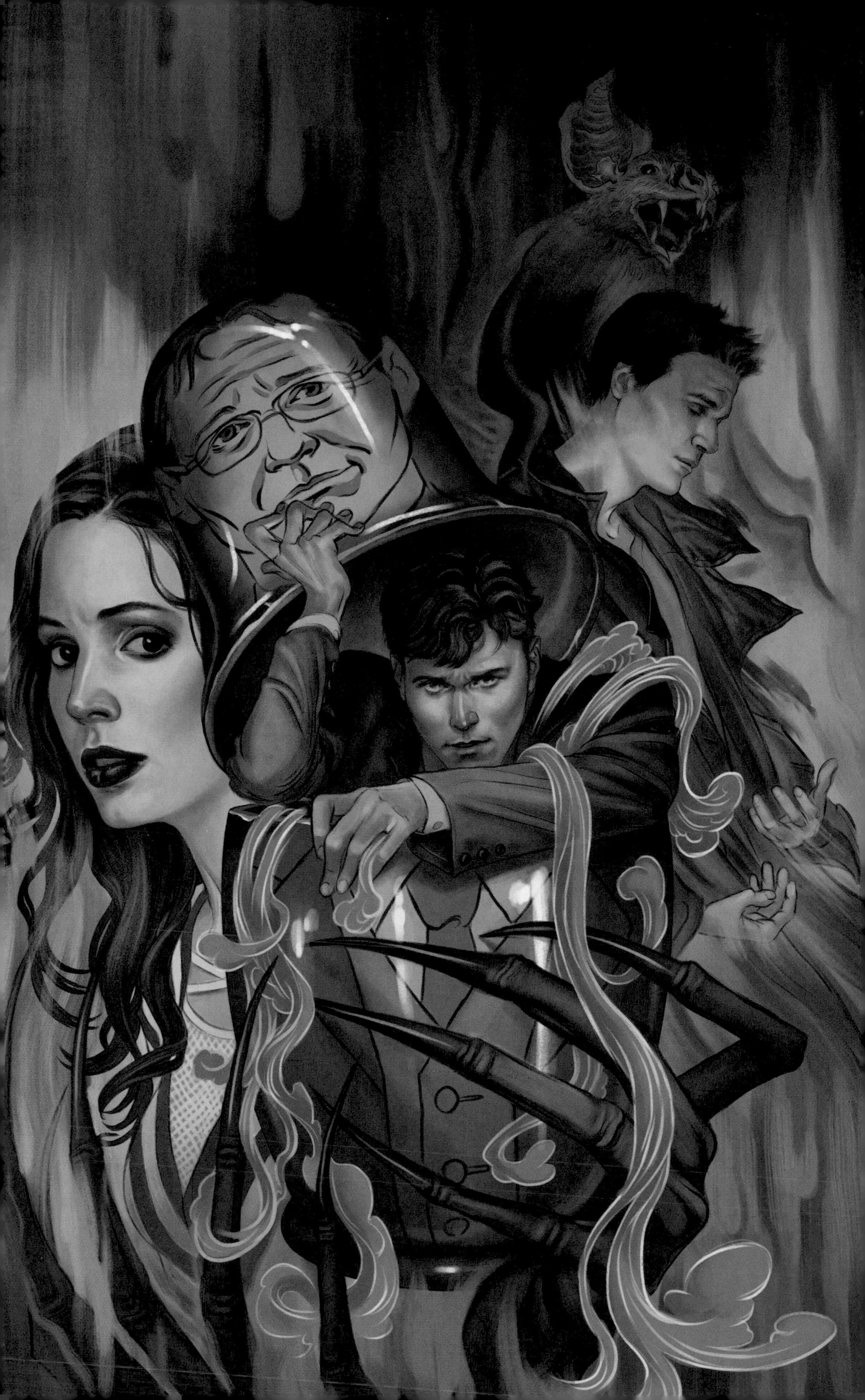

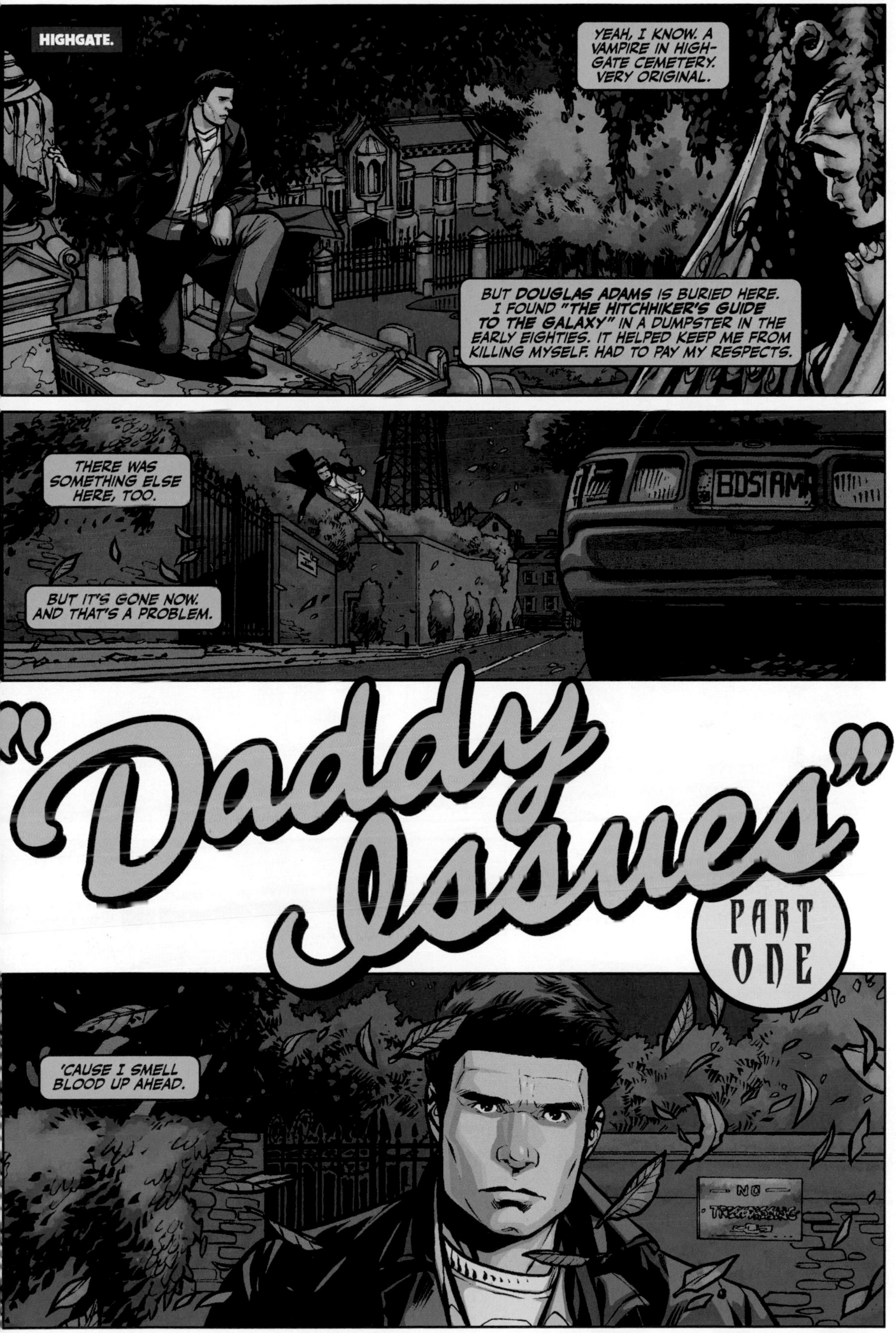
HIGHGATE.
YEAH, I KNOW. A VAMPIRE IN HIGH-GATE CEMETERY. VERY ORIGINAL.
BUT DOUGLAS ADAMS IS BURIED HERE. I FOUND "THE HITCHHIKER'S GUIDE TO THE GALAXY" IN A DUMPSTER IN THE EARLY EIGHTIES. IT HELPED KEEP ME FROM KILLING MYSELF. HAD TO PAY MY RESPECTS.
THERE WAS SOMETHING ELSE HERE, TOO.
BUT IT'S GONE NOW. AND THAT'S A PROBLEM.
"Daddy Issues"
PART ONE
'CAUSE I SMELL BLOOD UP AHEAD.
NO
TRESPASSING

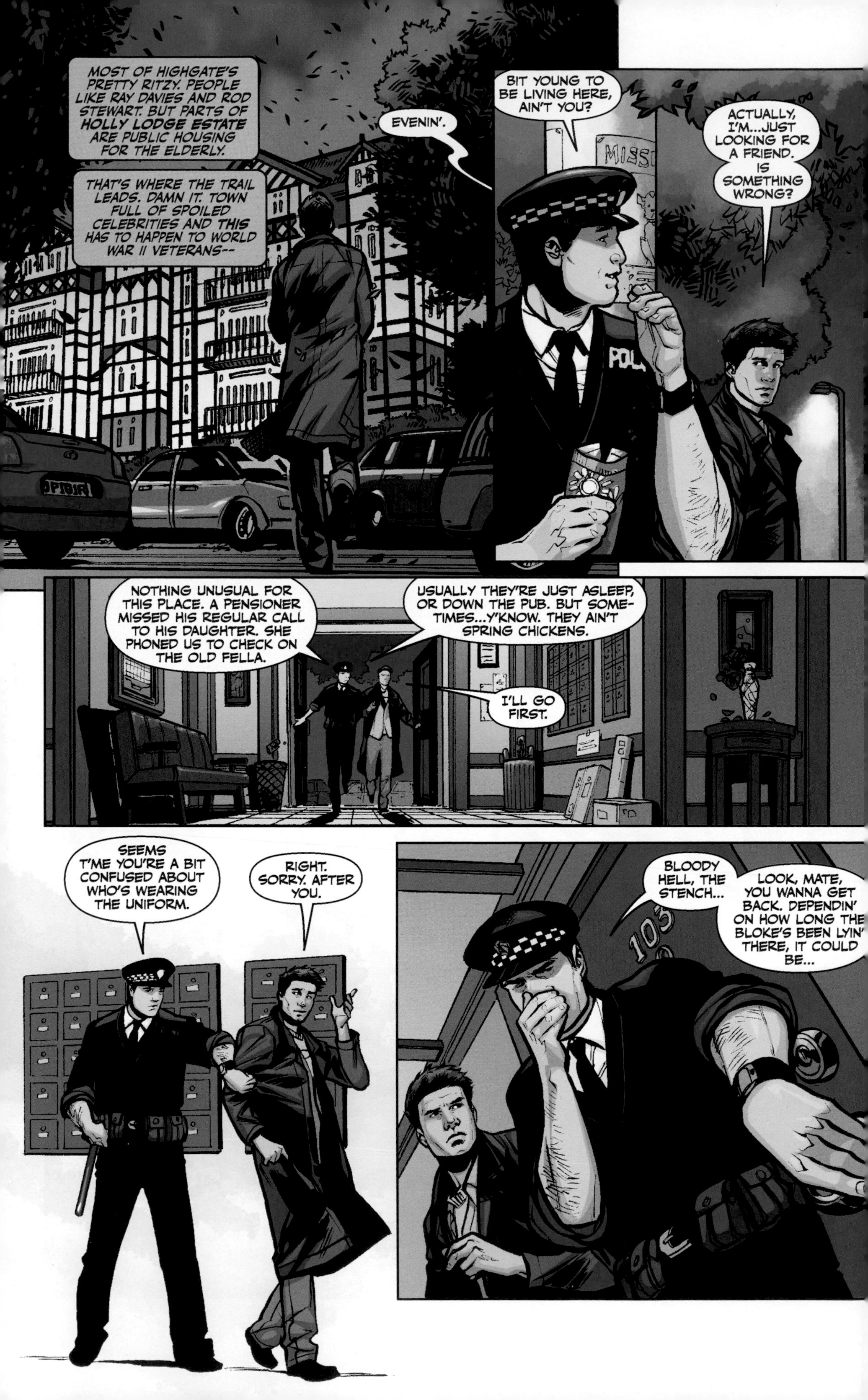
MOST OF HIGHGATE'S PRETTY RITZY. PEOPLE LIKE RAY DAVIES AND ROD STEWART. BUT PARTS OF HOLLY LODGE ESTATE ARE PUBLIC HOUSING FOR THE ELDERLY.
THAT'S WHERE THE TRAIL LEADS. DAMN IT. TOWN FULL OF SPOILED CELEBRITIES AND THIS HAS TO HAPPEN TO WORLD WAR II VETERANS--
EVENIN'.
BIT YOUNG TO BE LIVING HERE, AIN'T YOU?
ACTUALLY, I'M...JUST LOOKING FOR A FRIEND. IS SOMETHING WRONG?
NOTHING UNUSUAL FOR THIS PLACE. A PENSIONER MISSED HIS REGULAR CALL TO HIS DAUGHTER. SHE PHONED US TO CHECK ON THE OLD FELLA.
USUALLY THEY'RE JUST ASLEEP, OR DOWN THE PUB. BUT SOMETIMES...Y'KNOW. THEY AIN'T SPRING CHICKENS.
I'LL GO FIRST.
SEEMS T'ME YOU'RE A BIT CONFUSED ABOUT WHO'S WEARING THE UNIFORM.
RIGHT. SORRY. AFTER YOU.
BLOODY HELL, THE STENCH...
LOOK, MATE, YOU WANNA GET BACK. DEPENDIN' ON HOW LONG THE BLOKE'S BEEN LYIN' THERE, IT COULD BE...

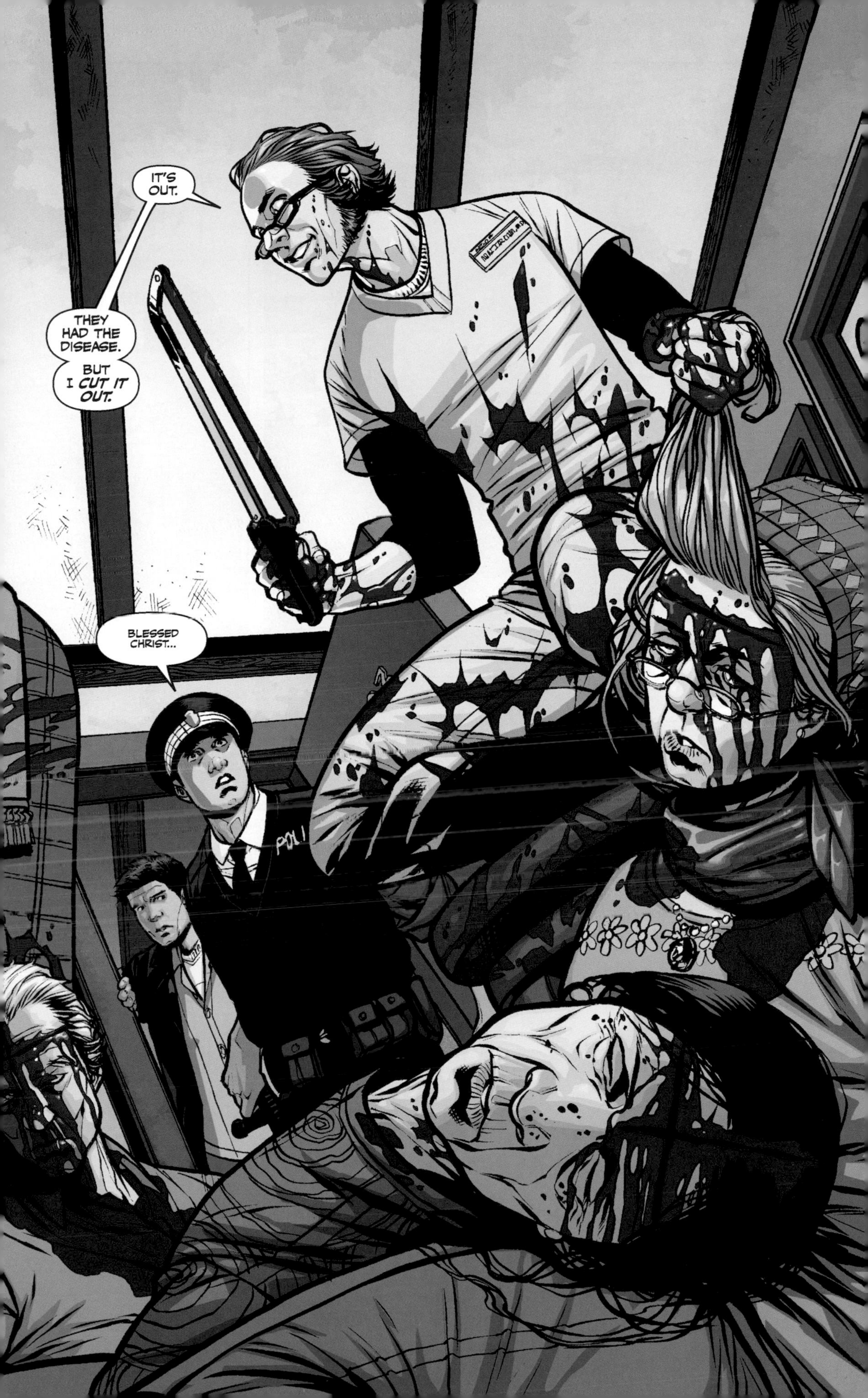
IT'S OUT.
THEY HAD THE DISEASE.
BUT I CUT IT OUT.
BLESSED CHRIST...

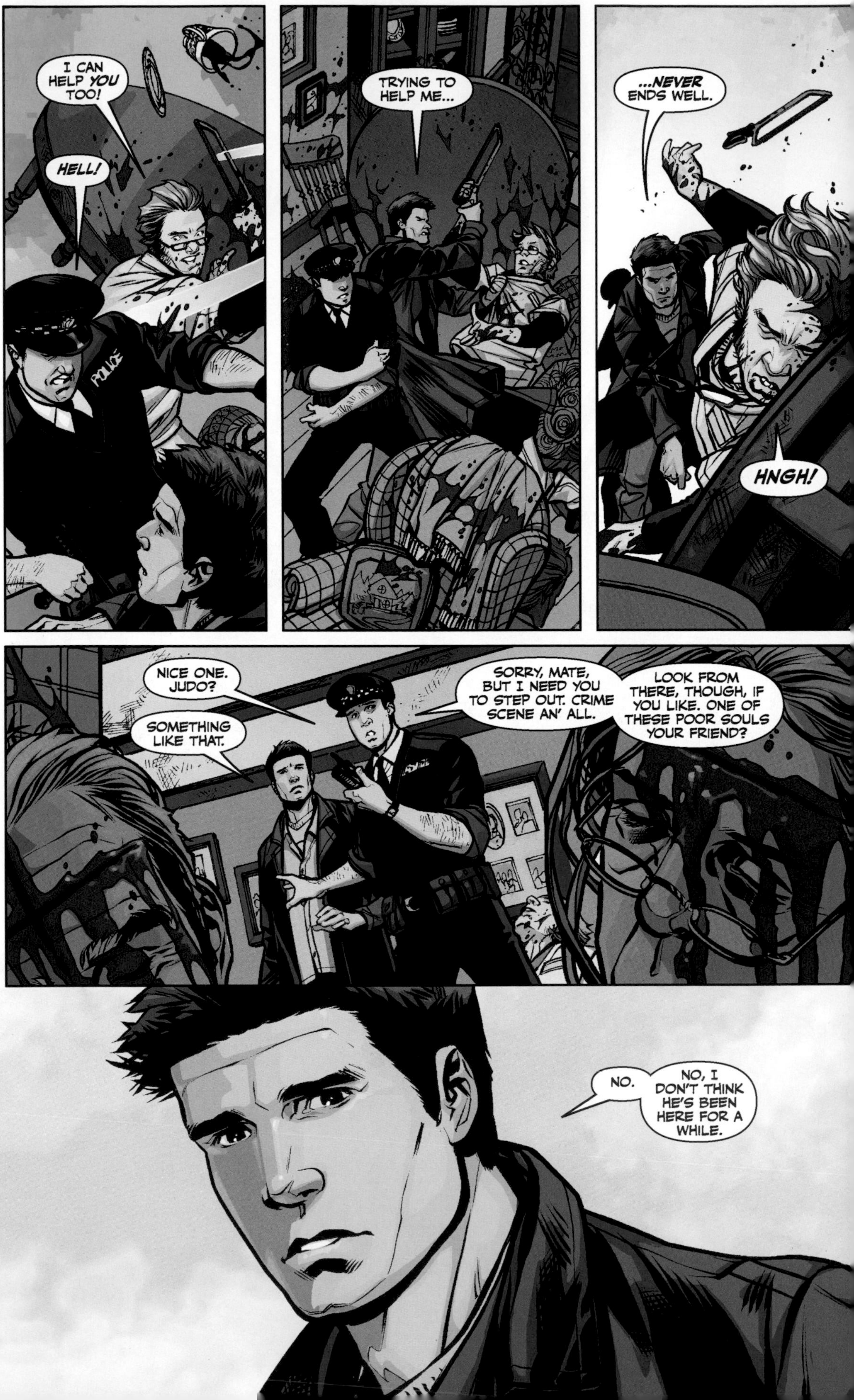
I CAN HELP *YOU* TOO!
HELL!
TRYING TO HELP ME...
...*NEVER* ENDS WELL.
HNGH!
NICE ONE. JUDO?
SOMETHING LIKE THAT.
SORRY, MATE, BUT I NEED YOU TO STEP OUT. CRIME SCENE AN' ALL.
LOOK FROM THERE, THOUGH, IF YOU LIKE. ONE OF THESE POOR SOULS YOUR FRIEND?
NO.
NO, I DON'T THINK HE'S BEEN HERE FOR A WHILE.

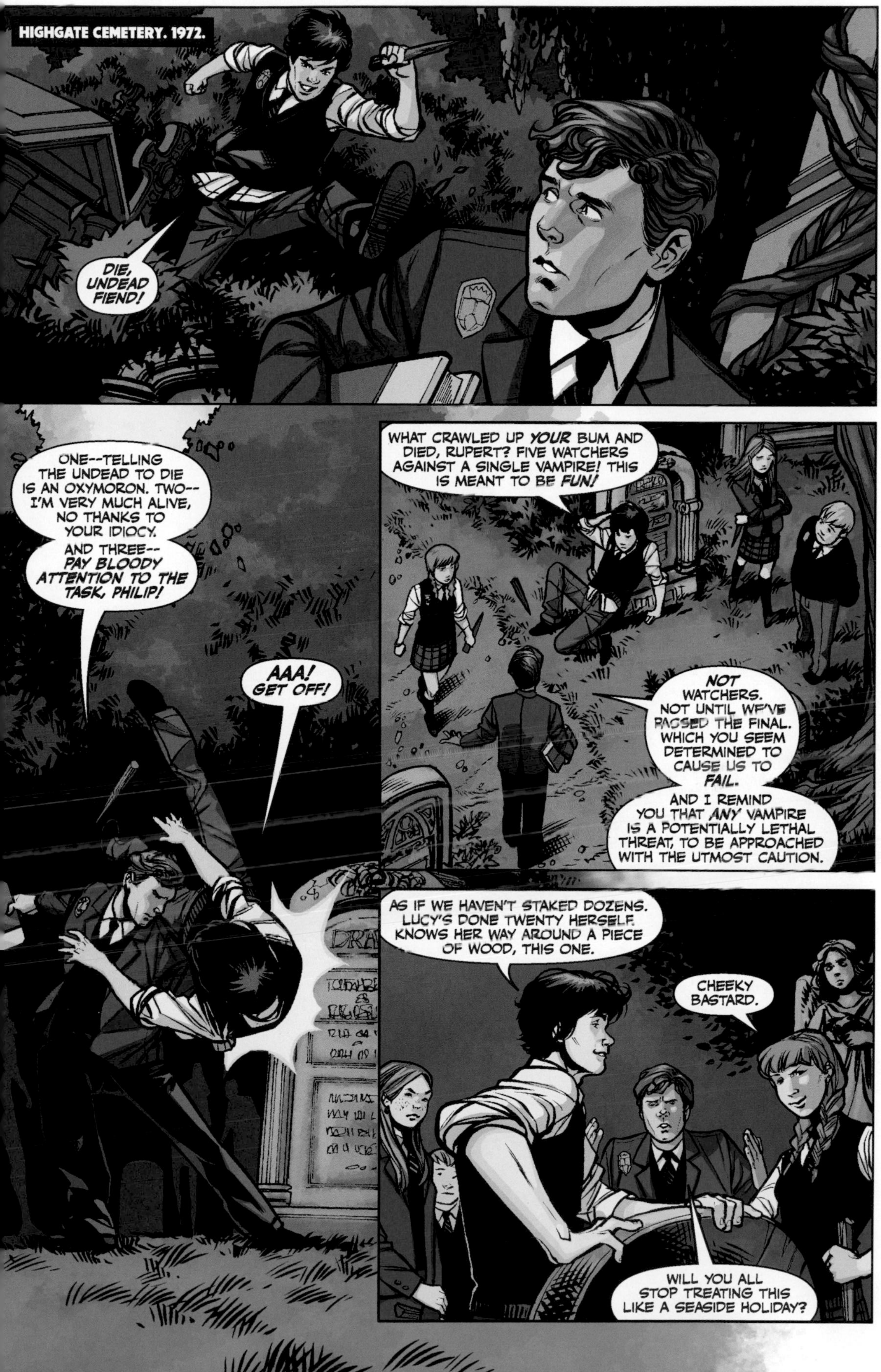
HIGHGATE CEMETERY. 1972.
DIE, UNDEAD FIEND!
ONE--TELLING THE UNDEAD TO DIE IS AN OXYMORON. TWO-- I'M VERY MUCH ALIVE, NO THANKS TO YOUR IDIOCY.
AND THREE-- PAY BLOODY ATTENTION TO THE TASK, PHILIP!
AAA! GET OFF!
WHAT CRAWLED UP YOUR BUM AND DIED, RUPERT? FIVE WATCHERS AGAINST A SINGLE VAMPIRE! THIS IS MEANT TO BE FUN!
NOT WATCHERS. NOT UNTIL WE'VE PASSED THE FINAL. WHICH YOU SEEM DETERMINED TO CAUSE US TO FAIL.
AND I REMIND YOU THAT ANY VAMPIRE IS A POTENTIALLY LETHAL THREAT, TO BE APPROACHED WITH THE UTMOST CAUTION.
AS IF WE HAVEN'T STAKED DOZENS. LUCY'S DONE TWENTY HERSELF. KNOWS HER WAY AROUND A PIECE OF WOOD, THIS ONE.
CHEEKY BASTARD.
WILL YOU ALL STOP TREATING THIS LIKE A SEASIDE HOLIDAY?

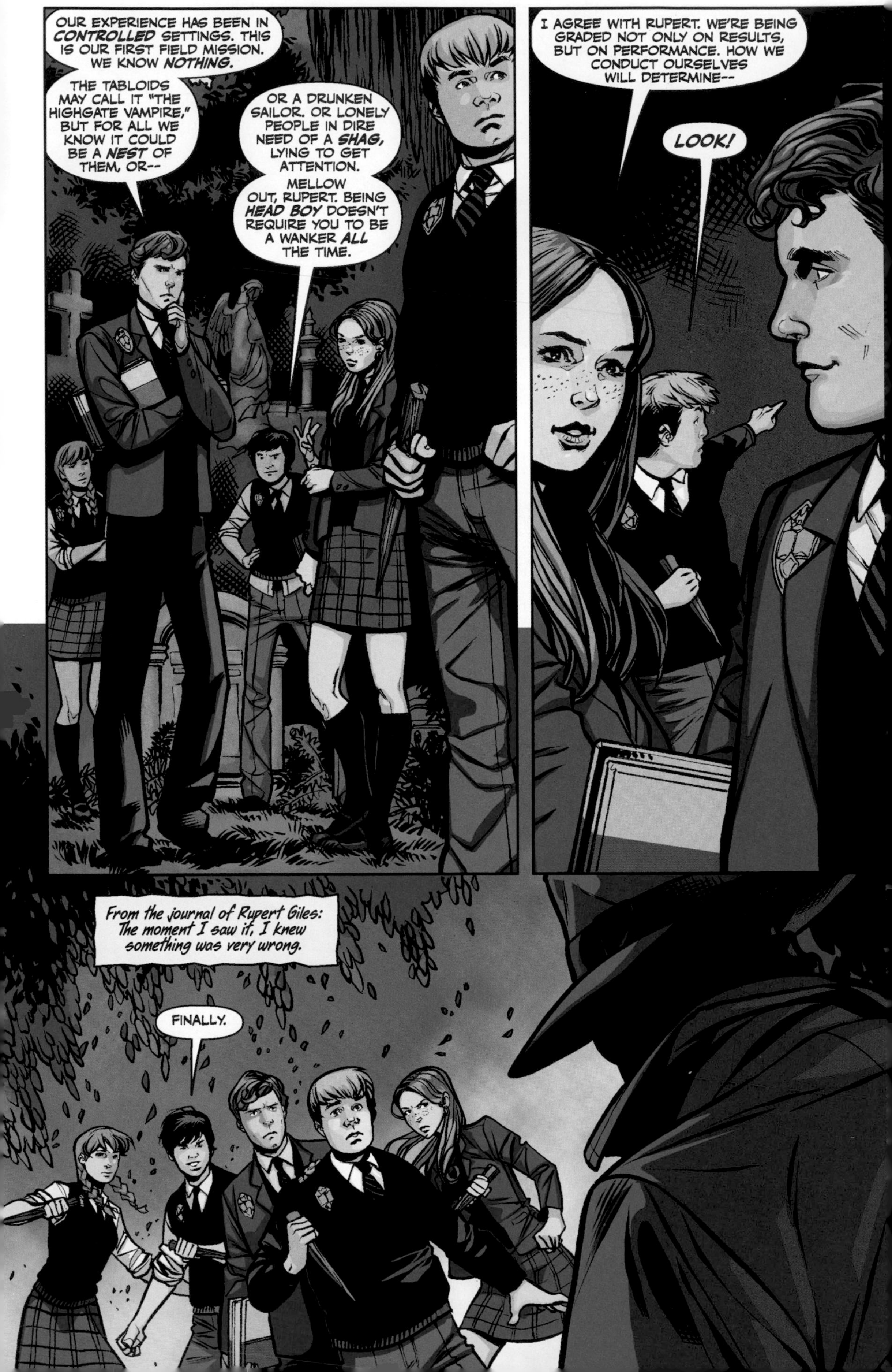
OUR EXPERIENCE HAS BEEN IN *CONTROLLED* SETTINGS. THIS IS OUR FIRST FIELD MISSION. WE KNOW *NOTHING.*
THE TABLOIDS MAY CALL IT "THE HIGHGATE VAMPIRE," BUT FOR ALL WE KNOW IT COULD BE A *NEST* OF THEM, OR--
OR A DRUNKEN SAILOR. OR LONELY PEOPLE IN DIRE NEED OF A *SHAG,* LYING TO GET ATTENTION.
MELLOW OUT, RUPERT. BEING *HEAD BOY* DOESN'T REQUIRE YOU TO BE A WANKER *ALL* THE TIME.
I AGREE WITH RUPERT. WE'RE BEING GRADED NOT ONLY ON RESULTS, BUT ON PERFORMANCE. HOW WE CONDUCT OURSELVES WILL DETERMINE--
LOOK!
From the journal of Rupert Giles: The moment I saw it, I knew something was very wrong.
FINALLY.

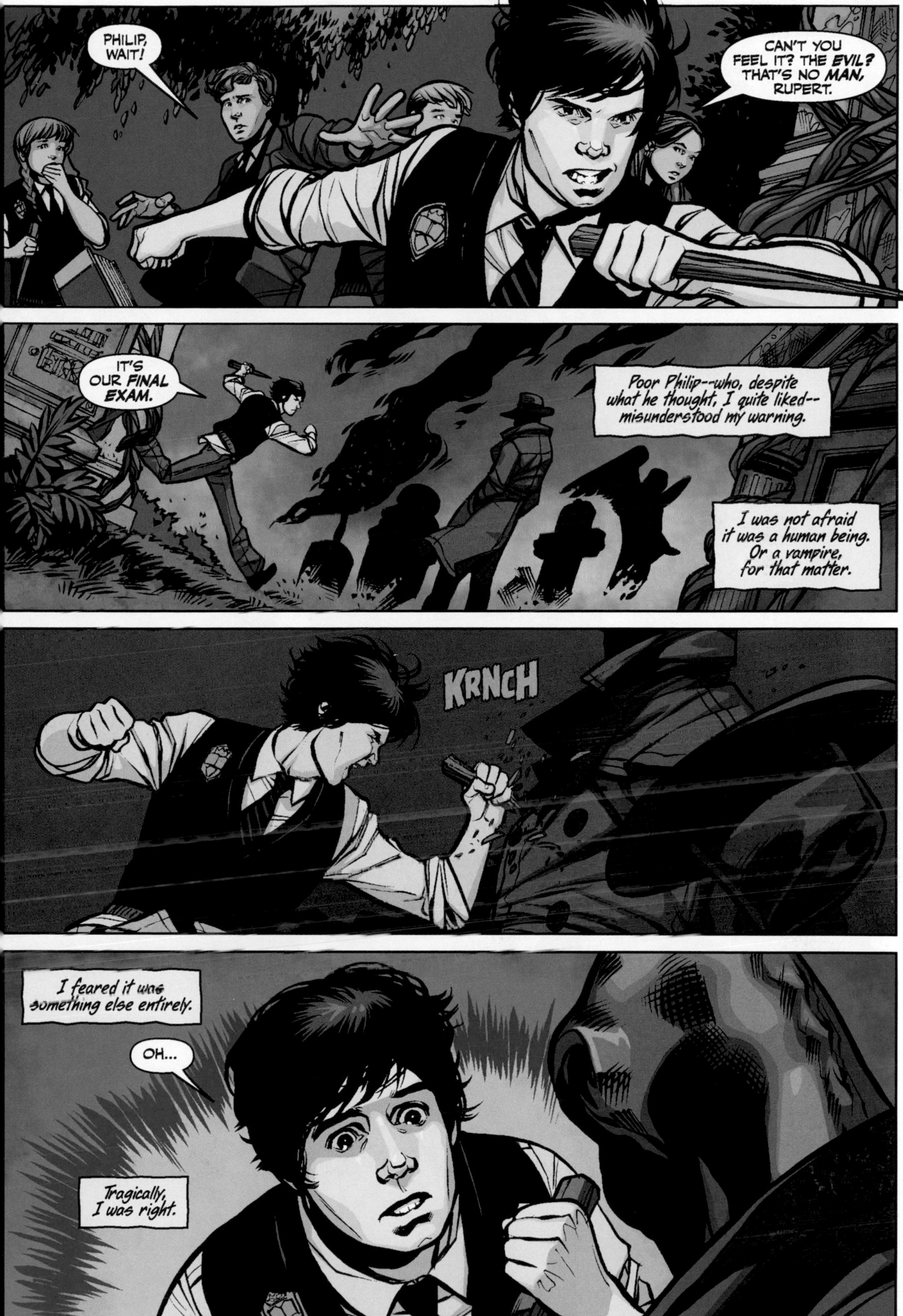
PHILIP, WAIT!
CAN'T YOU FEEL IT? THE EVIL? THAT'S NO MAN, RUPERT.
IT'S OUR FINAL EXAM.
Poor Philip--who, despite what he thought, I quite liked--misunderstood my warning.
I was not afraid it was a human being. Or a vampire, for that matter.
KRNCH
I feared it was something else entirely.
OH...
Tragically, I was right.

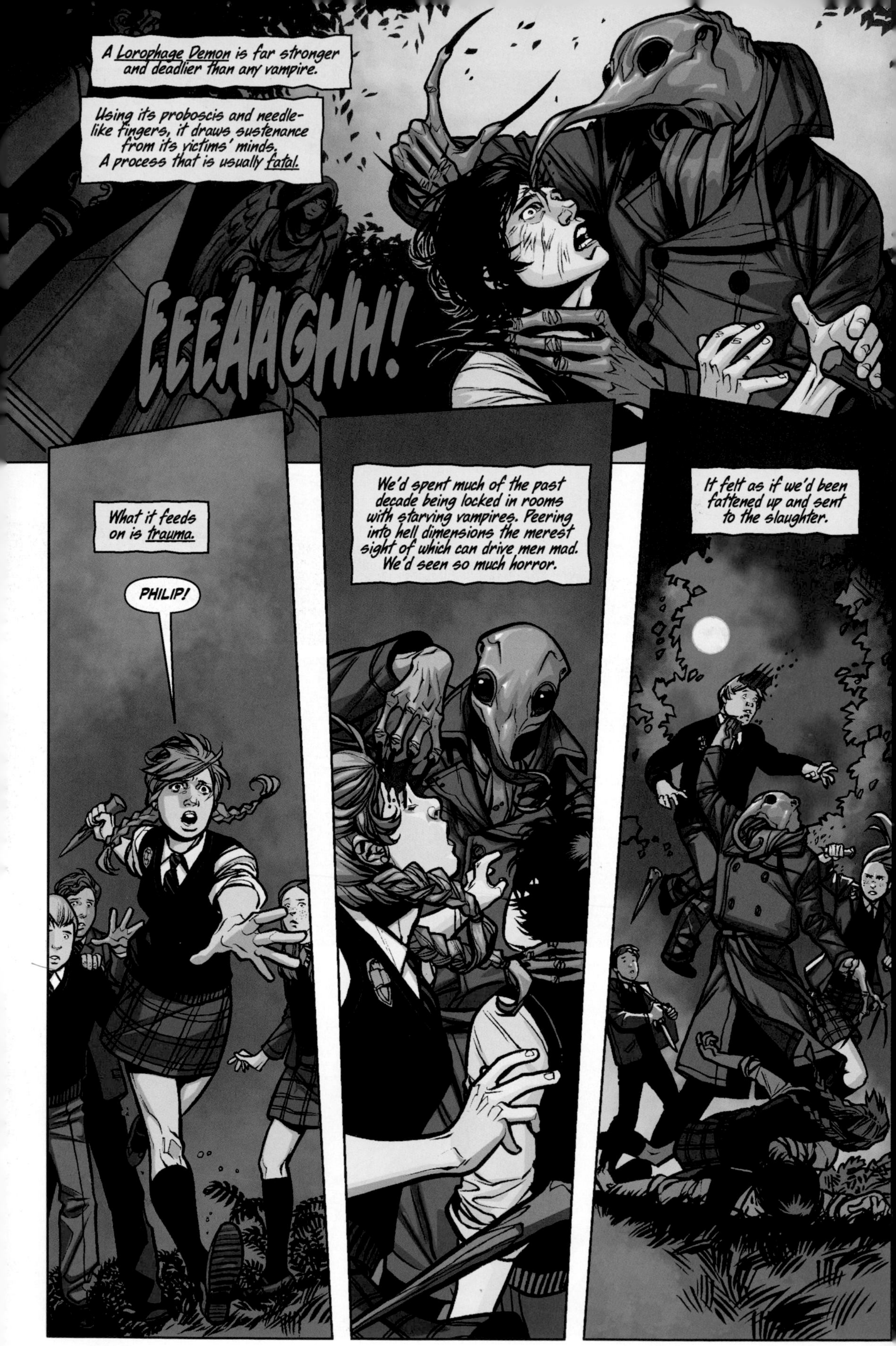
A Lorophage Demon is far stronger and deadlier than any vampire.
Using its proboscis and needle-like fingers, it draws sustenance from its victims' minds. A process that is usually fatal.
EEEAAGHH!
What it feeds on is trauma.
PHILIP!
We'd spent much of the past decade being locked in rooms with starving vampires. Peering into hell dimensions the merest sight of which can drive men mad. We'd seen so much horror.
It felt as if we'd been fattened up and sent to the slaughter.

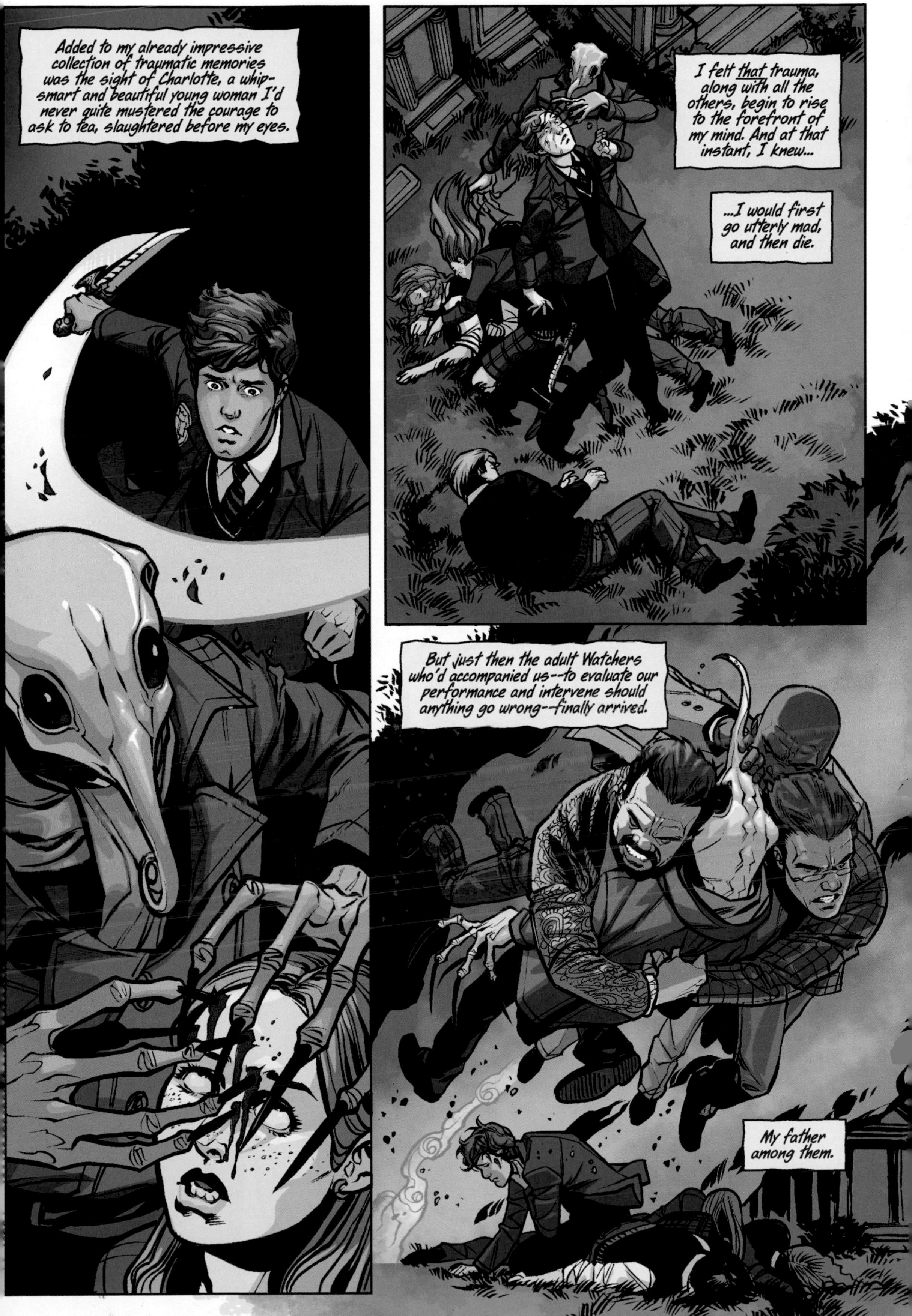
Added to my already impressive collection of traumatic memories was the sight of Charlotte, a whip-smart and beautiful young woman I'd never quite mustered the courage to ask to tea, slaughtered before my eyes.
I felt that trauma, along with all the others, begin to rise to the forefront of my mind. And at that instant, I knew...
...I would first go utterly mad, and then die.
But just then the adult Watchers who'd accompanied us--to evaluate our performance and intervene should anything go wrong--finally arrived.
My father among them.

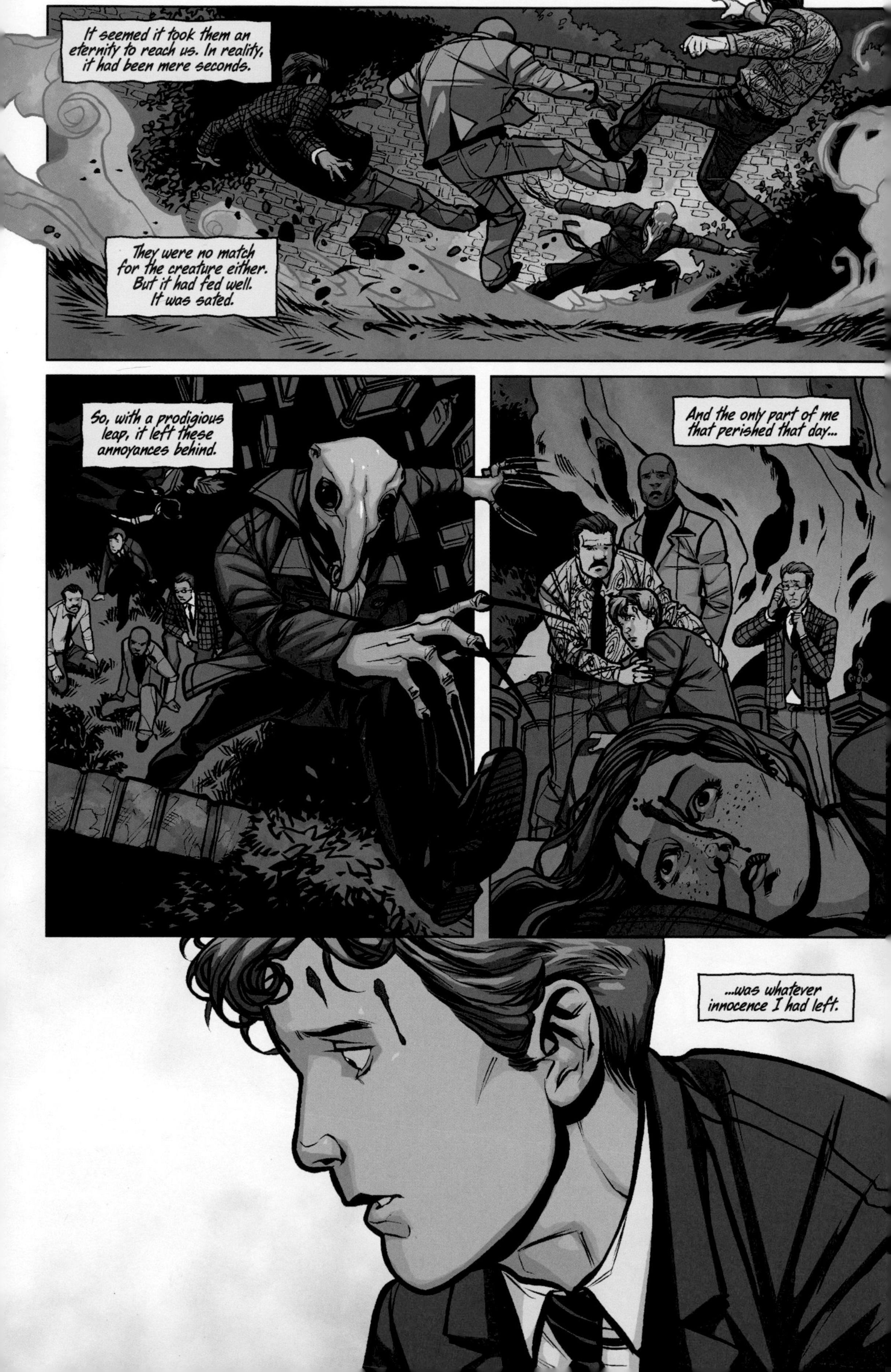
It seemed it took them an eternity to reach us. In reality, it had been mere seconds.
They were no match for the creature either. But it had fed well. It was sated.
So, with a prodigious leap, it left these annoyances behind.
And the only part of me that perished that day...
...was whatever innocence I had left.

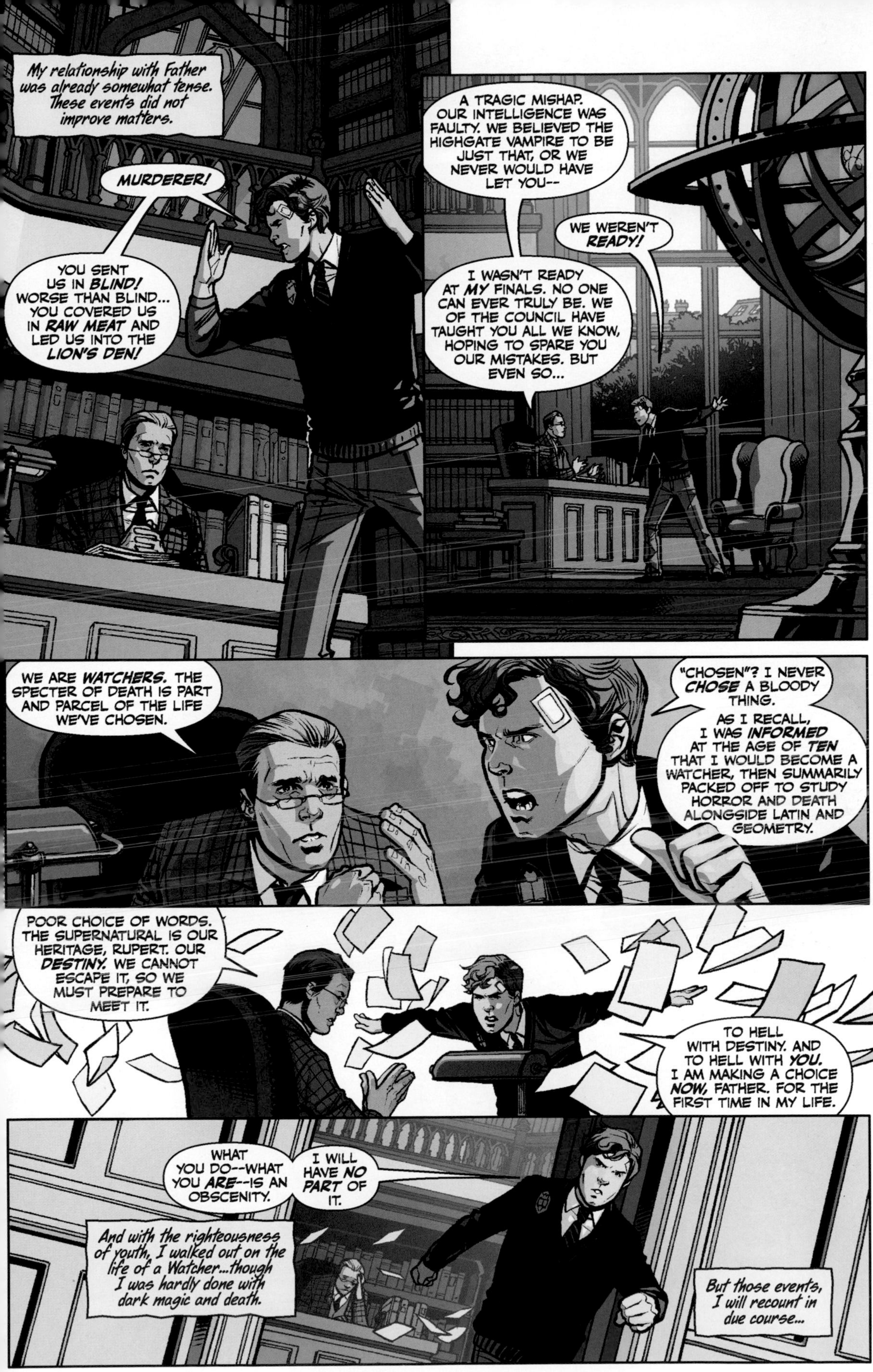

My relationship with Father was already somewhat tense. These events did not improve matters.
MURDERER!
YOU SENT US IN BLIND! WORSE THAN BLIND... YOU COVERED US IN RAW MEAT AND LED US INTO THE LION'S DEN!
A TRAGIC MISHAP. OUR INTELLIGENCE WAS FAULTY. WE BELIEVED THE HIGHGATE VAMPIRE TO BE JUST THAT, OR WE NEVER WOULD HAVE LET YOU--
WE WEREN'T READY!
I WASN'T READY AT MY FINALS. NO ONE CAN EVER TRULY BE. WE OF THE COUNCIL HAVE TAUGHT YOU ALL WE KNOW, HOPING TO SPARE YOU OUR MISTAKES. BUT EVEN SO...
WE ARE WATCHERS. THE SPECTER OF DEATH IS PART AND PARCEL OF THE LIFE WE'VE CHOSEN.
"CHOSEN"? I NEVER CHOSE A BLOODY THING.
AS I RECALL, I WAS INFORMED AT THE AGE OF TEN THAT I WOULD BECOME A WATCHER, THEN SUMMARILY PACKED OFF TO STUDY HORROR AND DEATH ALONGSIDE LATIN AND GEOMETRY.
POOR CHOICE OF WORDS. THE SUPERNATURAL IS OUR HERITAGE, RUPERT. OUR DESTINY. WE CANNOT ESCAPE IT, SO WE MUST PREPARE TO MEET IT.
TO HELL WITH DESTINY. AND TO HELL WITH YOU. I AM MAKING A CHOICE NOW, FATHER. FOR THE FIRST TIME IN MY LIFE.
WHAT YOU DO--WHAT YOU ARE--IS AN OBSCENITY.
I WILL HAVE NO PART OF IT.
And with the righteousness of youth, I walked out on the life of a Watcher...though I was hardly done with dark magic and death.
But those events, I will recount in due course...

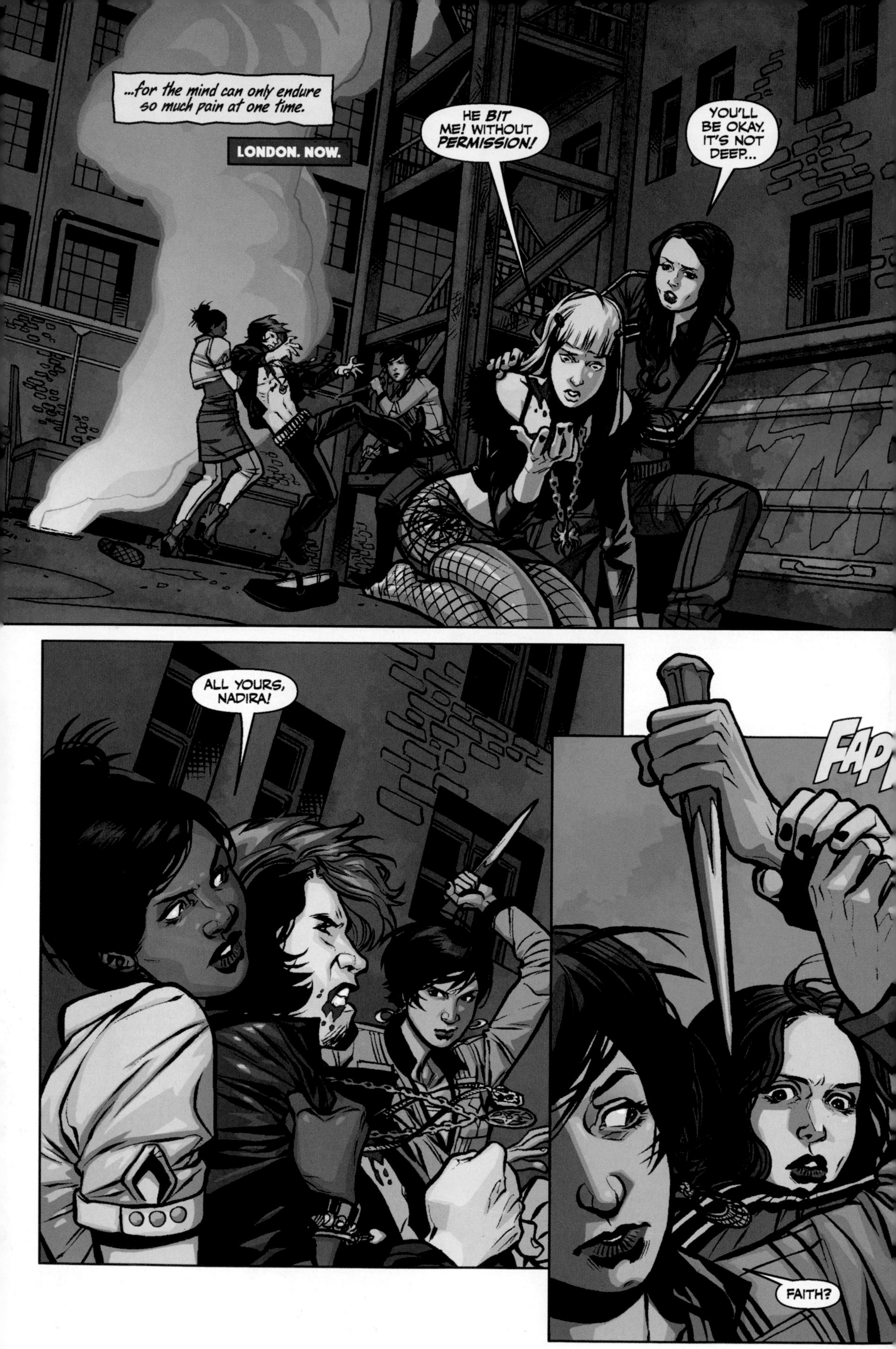

...for the mind can only endure so much pain at one time.
LONDON. NOW.
HE BIT ME! WITHOUT PERMISSION!
YOU'LL BE OKAY. IT'S NOT DEEP...
ALL YOURS, NADIRA!
FAP!
FAITH?

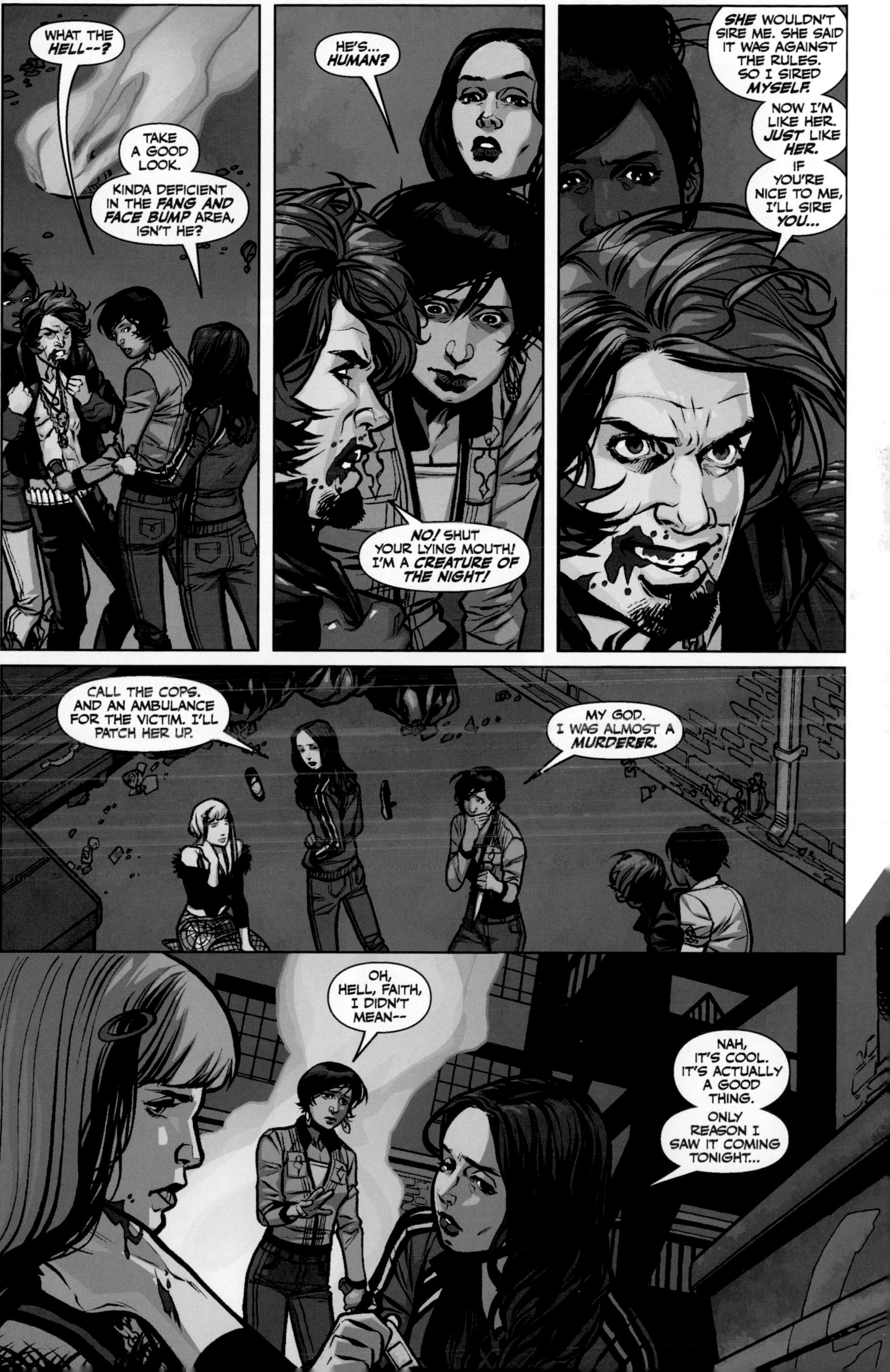

WHAT THE HELL--?
TAKE A GOOD LOOK.
KINDA DEFICIENT IN THE FANG AND FACE BUMP AREA, ISN'T HE?
HE'S... HUMAN?
NO! SHUT YOUR LYING MOUTH! I'M A CREATURE OF THE NIGHT!
SHE WOULDN'T SIRE ME. SHE SAID IT WAS AGAINST THE RULES. SO I SIRED MYSELF.
NOW I'M LIKE HER. JUST LIKE HER.
IF YOU'RE NICE TO ME, I'LL SIRE YOU...
CALL THE COPS. AND AN AMBULANCE FOR THE VICTIM. I'LL PATCH HER UP.
MY GOD. I WAS ALMOST A MURDERER.
OH, HELL, FAITH, I DIDN'T MEAN--
NAH, IT'S COOL. IT'S ACTUALLY A GOOD THING.
ONLY REASON I SAW IT COMING TONIGHT...

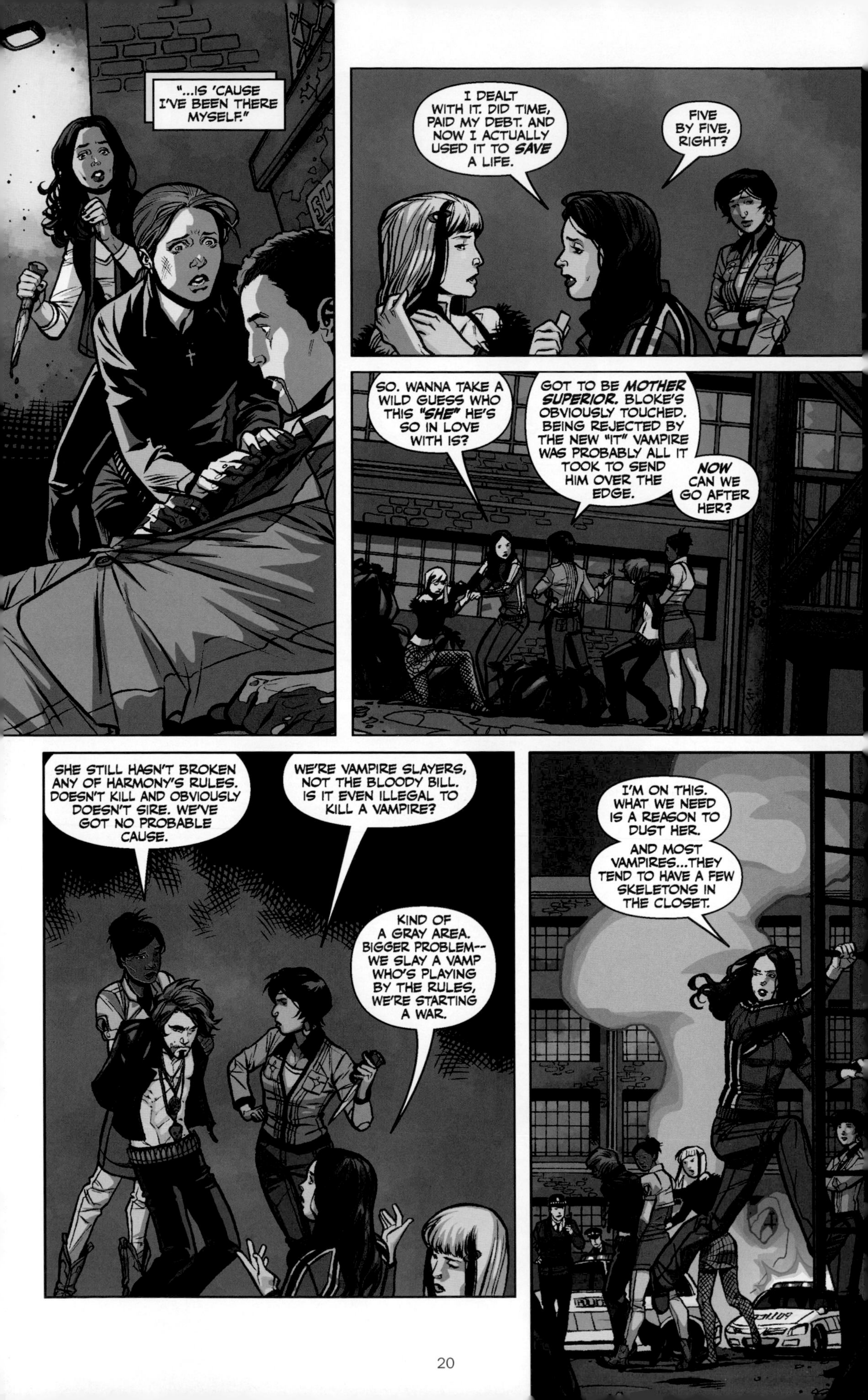
"...IS 'CAUSE I'VE BEEN THERE MYSELF."
I DEALT WITH IT. DID TIME, PAID MY DEBT. AND NOW I ACTUALLY USED IT TO *SAVE* A LIFE.
FIVE BY FIVE, RIGHT?
SO. WANNA TAKE A WILD GUESS WHO THIS *"SHE"* HE'S SO IN LOVE WITH IS?
GOT TO BE *MOTHER SUPERIOR.* BLOKE'S OBVIOUSLY TOUCHED. BEING REJECTED BY THE NEW "IT" VAMPIRE WAS PROBABLY ALL IT TOOK TO SEND HIM OVER THE EDGE.
NOW CAN WE GO AFTER HER?
SHE STILL HASN'T BROKEN ANY OF HARMONY'S RULES. DOESN'T KILL AND OBVIOUSLY DOESN'T SIRE. WE'VE GOT NO PROBABLE CAUSE.
WE'RE VAMPIRE SLAYERS, NOT THE BLOODY BILL. IS IT EVEN ILLEGAL TO KILL A VAMPIRE?
KIND OF A GRAY AREA. BIGGER PROBLEM-- WE SLAY A VAMP WHO'S PLAYING BY THE RULES, WE'RE STARTING A WAR.
I'M ON THIS. WHAT WE NEED IS A REASON TO DUST HER.
AND MOST VAMPIRES...THEY TEND TO HAVE A FEW SKELETONS IN THE CLOSET.

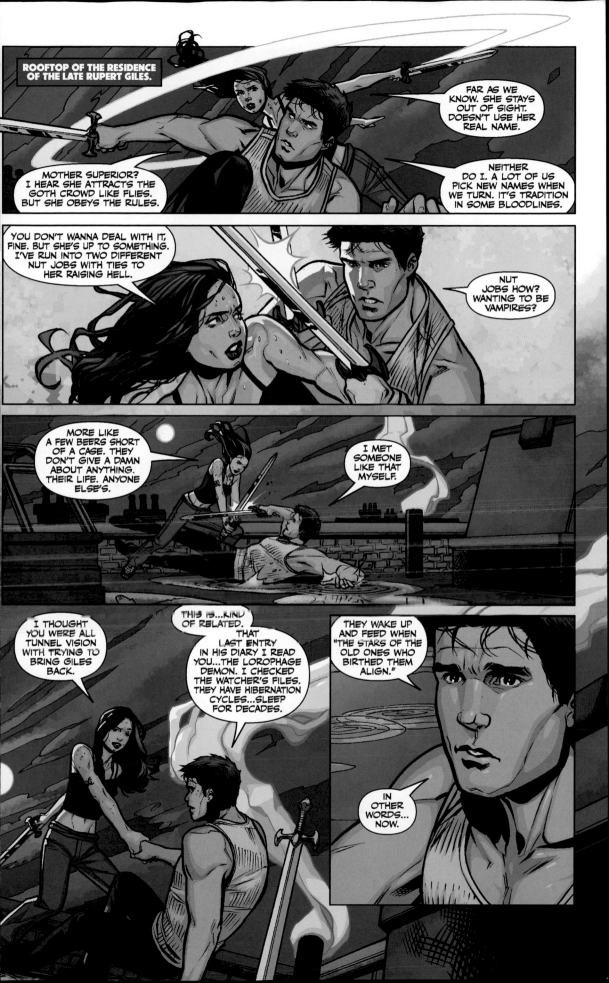

ROOFTOP OF THE RESIDENCE OF THE LATE RUPERT GILES.

FAR AS WE KNOW. SHE STAYS OUT OF SIGHT. DOESN'T USE HER REAL NAME.

MOTHER SUPERIOR? I HEAR SHE ATTRACTS THE GOTH CROWD LIKE FLIES. BUT SHE OBEYS THE RULES.

NEITHER DO I. A LOT OF US PICK NEW NAMES WHEN WE TURN. IT'S TRADITION IN SOME BLOODLINES.

YOU DON'T WANNA DEAL WITH IT, FINE. BUT SHE'S UP TO SOMETHING. I'VE RUN INTO TWO DIFFERENT NUT JOBS WITH TIES TO HER RAISING HELL.

NUT JOBS HOW? WANTING TO BE VAMPIRES?

MORE LIKE A FEW BEERS SHORT OF A CASE. THEY DON'T GIVE A DAMN ABOUT ANYTHING. THEIR LIFE. ANYONE ELSE'S.

I MET SOMEONE LIKE THAT MYSELF.

I THOUGHT YOU WERE ALL TUNNEL VISION WITH TRYING TO BRING GILES BACK.

THIS IS...KIND OF RELATED. THAT LAST ENTRY IN HIS DIARY I READ YOU...THE LOROPHAGE DEMON. I CHECKED THE WATCHER'S FILES. THEY HAVE HIBERNATION CYCLES...SLEEP FOR DECADES.

THEY WAKE UP AND FEED WHEN "THE STARS OF THE OLD ONES WHO BIRTHED THEM ALIGN."

IN OTHER WORDS... NOW.

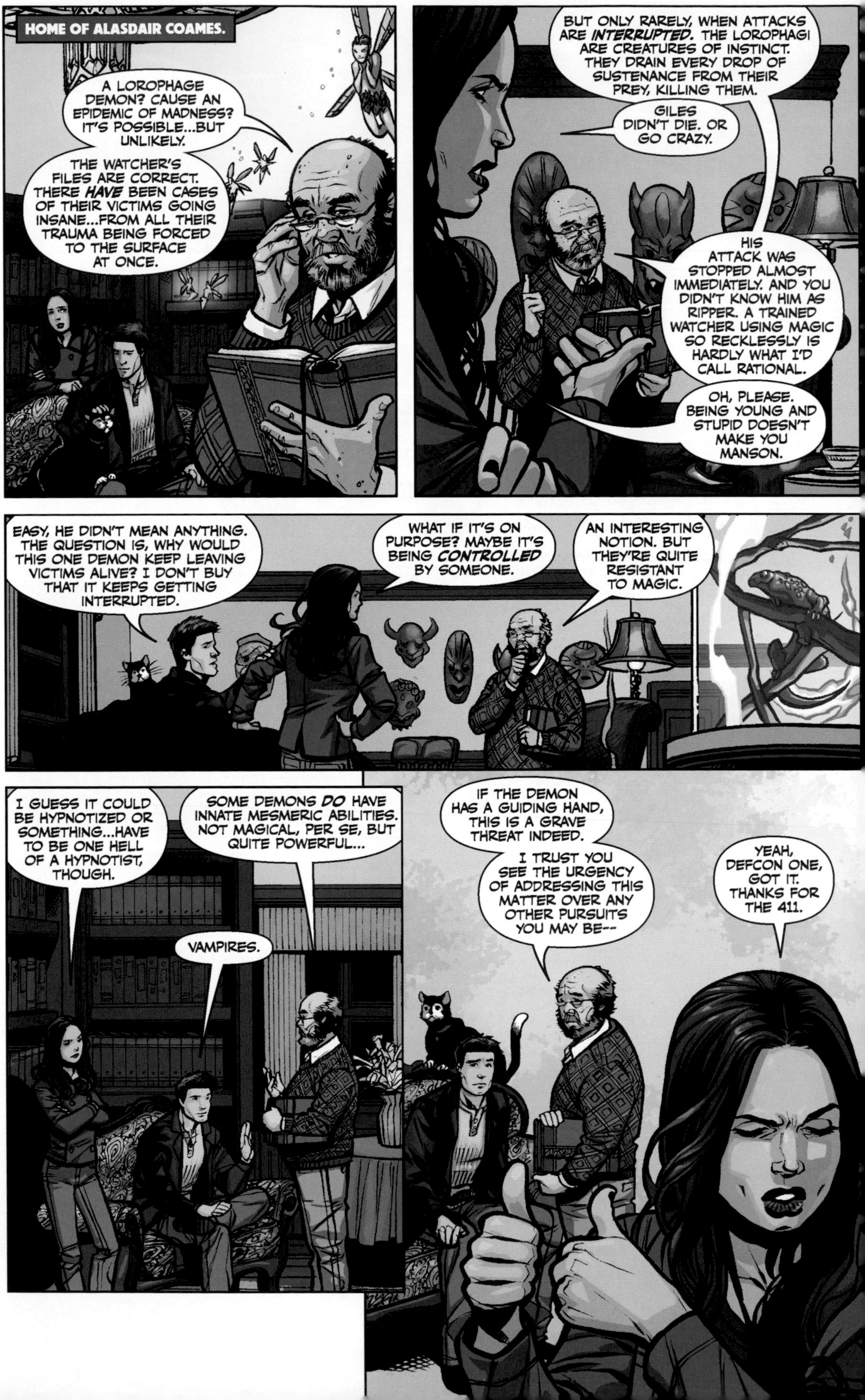
HOME OF ALASDAIR COAMES.
A LOROPHAGE DEMON? CAUSE AN EPIDEMIC OF MADNESS? IT'S POSSIBLE...BUT UNLIKELY.
THE WATCHER'S FILES ARE CORRECT. THERE HAVE BEEN CASES OF THEIR VICTIMS GOING INSANE...FROM ALL THEIR TRAUMA BEING FORCED TO THE SURFACE AT ONCE.
BUT ONLY RARELY, WHEN ATTACKS ARE INTERRUPTED. THE LOROPHAGI ARE CREATURES OF INSTINCT. THEY DRAIN EVERY DROP OF SUSTENANCE FROM THEIR PREY, KILLING THEM.
GILES DIDN'T DIE. OR GO CRAZY.
HIS ATTACK WAS STOPPED ALMOST IMMEDIATELY. AND YOU DIDN'T KNOW HIM AS RIPPER. A TRAINED WATCHER USING MAGIC SO RECKLESSLY IS HARDLY WHAT I'D CALL RATIONAL.
OH, PLEASE. BEING YOUNG AND STUPID DOESN'T MAKE YOU MANSON.
EASY, HE DIDN'T MEAN ANYTHING. THE QUESTION IS, WHY WOULD THIS ONE DEMON KEEP LEAVING VICTIMS ALIVE? I DON'T BUY THAT IT KEEPS GETTING INTERRUPTED.
WHAT IF IT'S ON PURPOSE? MAYBE IT'S BEING CONTROLLED BY SOMEONE.
AN INTERESTING NOTION. BUT THEY'RE QUITE RESISTANT TO MAGIC.
I GUESS IT COULD BE HYPNOTIZED OR SOMETHING...HAVE TO BE ONE HELL OF A HYPNOTIST, THOUGH.
SOME DEMONS DO HAVE INNATE MESMERIC ABILITIES. NOT MAGICAL, PER SE, BUT QUITE POWERFUL...
VAMPIRES.
IF THE DEMON HAS A GUIDING HAND, THIS IS A GRAVE THREAT INDEED.
I TRUST YOU SEE THE URGENCY OF ADDRESSING THIS MATTER OVER ANY OTHER PURSUITS YOU MAY BE--
YEAH, DEFCON ONE, GOT IT. THANKS FOR THE 411.

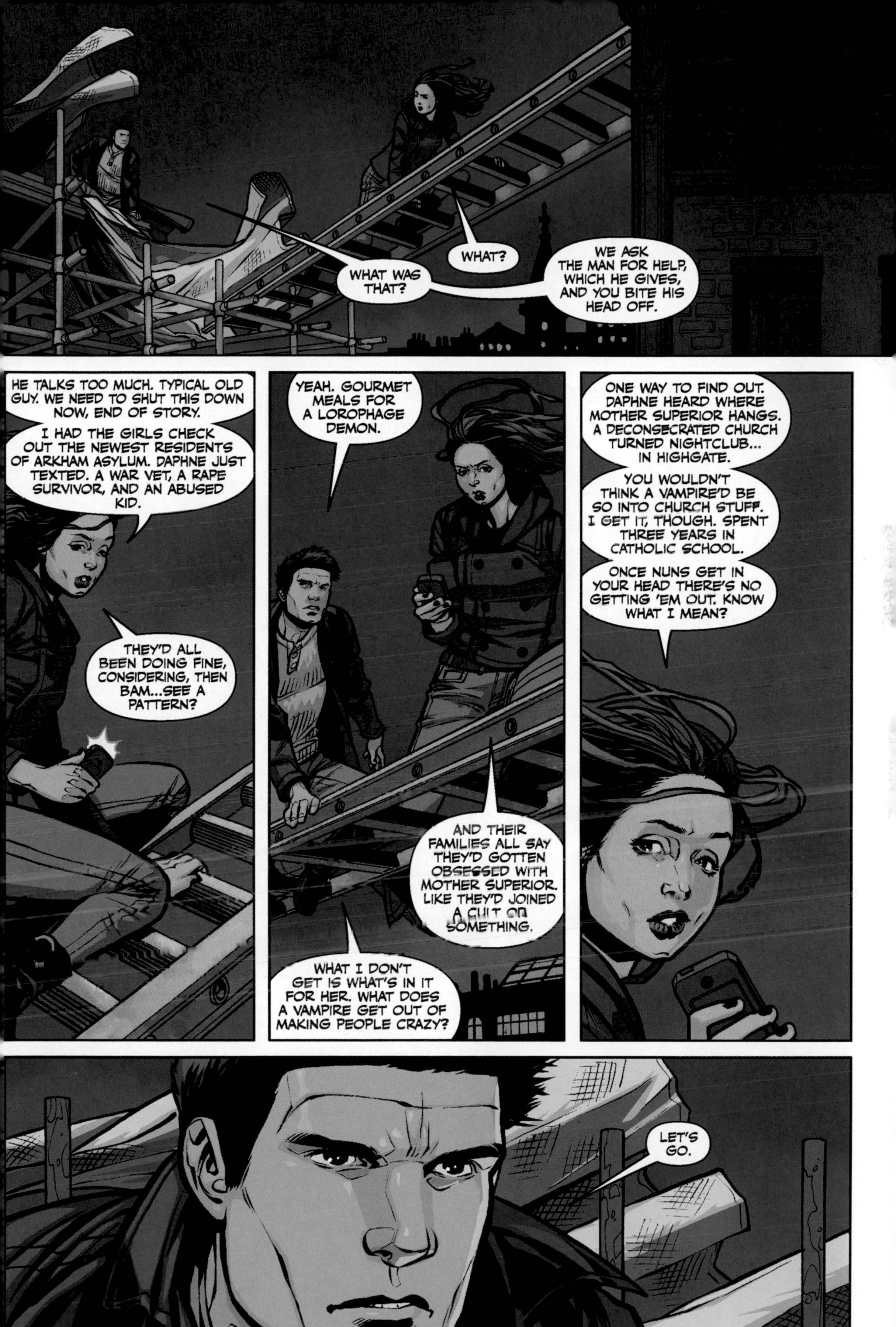
WHAT WAS THAT?
WHAT?
WE ASK THE MAN FOR HELP, WHICH HE GIVES, AND YOU BITE HIS HEAD OFF.
HE TALKS TOO MUCH. TYPICAL OLD GUY. WE NEED TO SHUT THIS DOWN NOW, END OF STORY.
I HAD THE GIRLS CHECK OUT THE NEWEST RESIDENTS OF ARKHAM ASYLUM. DAPHNE JUST TEXTED. A WAR VET, A RAPE SURVIVOR, AND AN ABUSED KID.
THEY'D ALL BEEN DOING FINE, CONSIDERING, THEN BAM...SEE A PATTERN?
YEAH. GOURMET MEALS FOR A LOROPHAGE DEMON.
AND THEIR FAMILIES ALL SAY THEY'D GOTTEN OBSESSED WITH MOTHER SUPERIOR. LIKE THEY'D JOINED A CULT OR SOMETHING.
WHAT I DON'T GET IS WHAT'S IN IT FOR HER. WHAT DOES A VAMPIRE GET OUT OF MAKING PEOPLE CRAZY?
ONE WAY TO FIND OUT. DAPHNE HEARD WHERE MOTHER SUPERIOR HANGS. A DECONSECRATED CHURCH TURNED NIGHTCLUB... IN HIGHGATE.
YOU WOULDN'T THINK A VAMPIRE'D BE SO INTO CHURCH STUFF. I GET IT, THOUGH. SPENT THREE YEARS IN CATHOLIC SCHOOL.
ONCE NUNS GET IN YOUR HEAD THERE'S NO GETTING 'EM OUT. KNOW WHAT I MEAN?
LET'S GO.

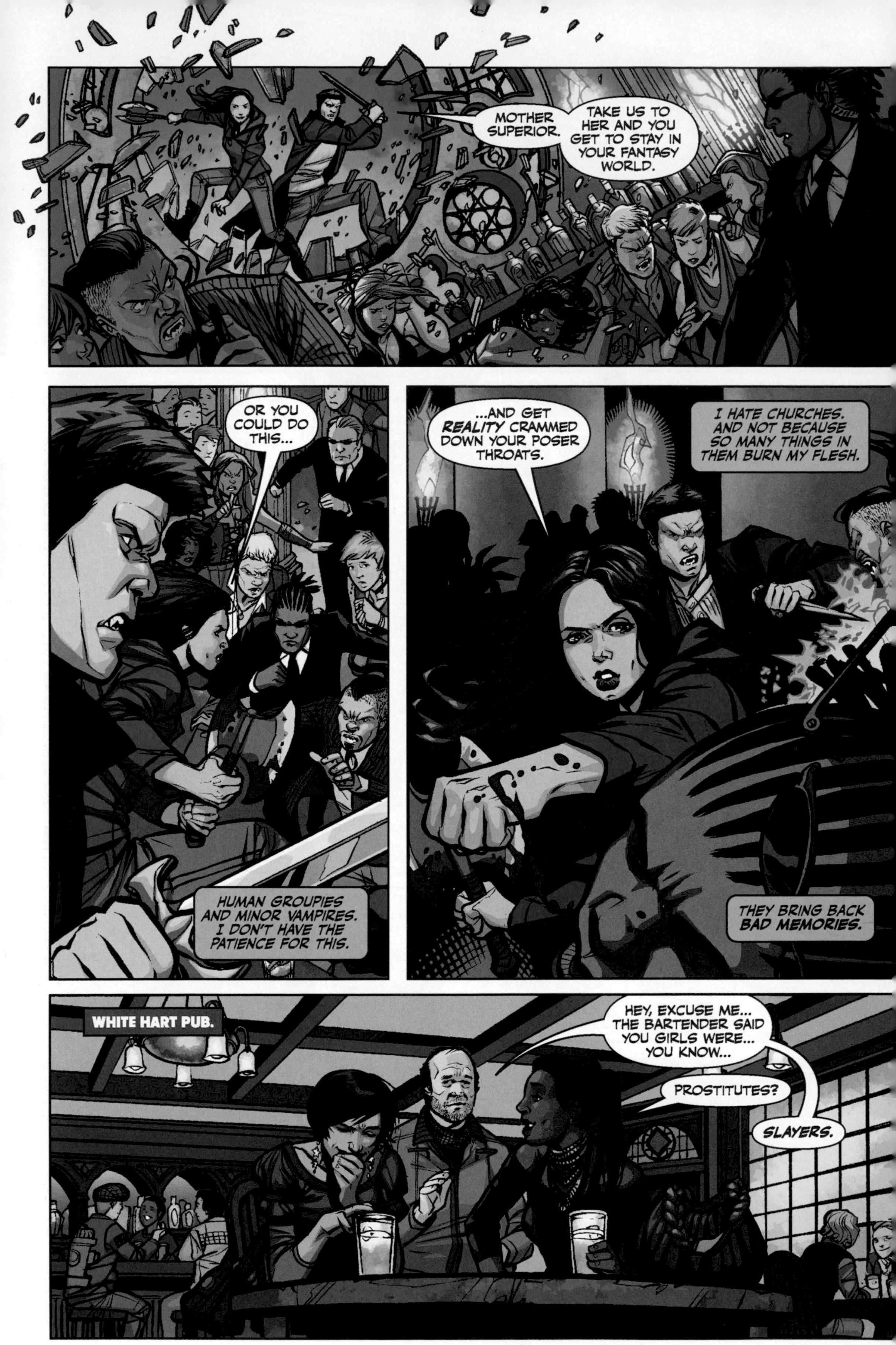
MOTHER SUPERIOR.
TAKE US TO HER AND YOU GET TO STAY IN YOUR FANTASY WORLD.
OR YOU COULD DO THIS...
HUMAN GROUPIES AND MINOR VAMPIRES. I DON'T HAVE THE PATIENCE FOR THIS.
...AND GET REALITY CRAMMED DOWN YOUR POSER THROATS.
I HATE CHURCHES. AND NOT BECAUSE SO MANY THINGS IN THEM BURN MY FLESH.
THEY BRING BACK BAD MEMORIES.
WHITE HART PUB.
HEY, EXCUSE ME... THE BARTENDER SAID YOU GIRLS WERE... YOU KNOW...
PROSTITUTES?
SLAYERS.

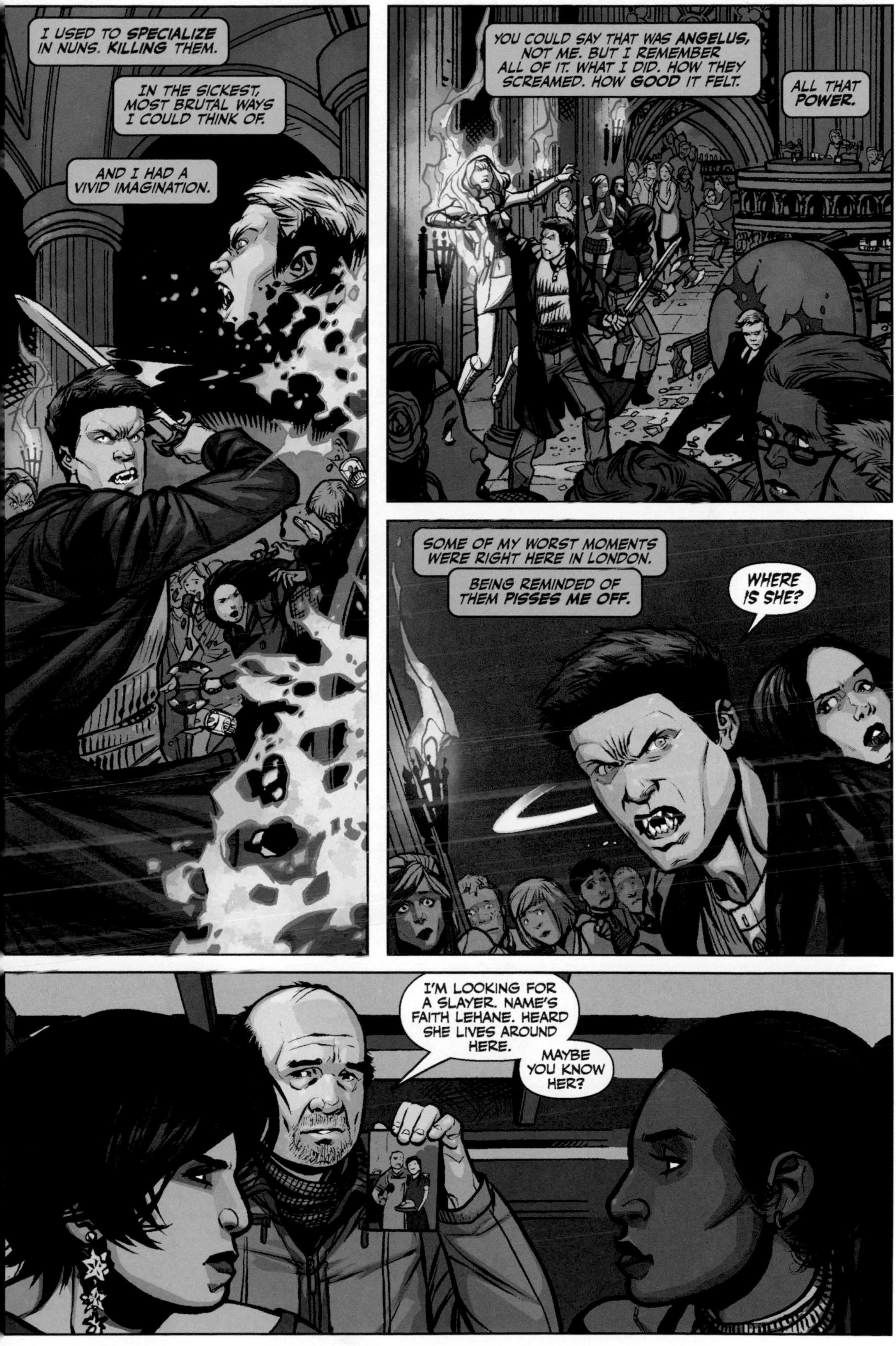
I USED TO SPECIALIZE IN NUNS. KILLING THEM.
IN THE SICKEST, MOST BRUTAL WAYS I COULD THINK OF.
AND I HAD A VIVID IMAGINATION.
YOU COULD SAY THAT WAS ANGELUS, NOT ME. BUT I REMEMBER ALL OF IT. WHAT I DID. HOW THEY SCREAMED. HOW GOOD IT FELT.
ALL THAT POWER.
SOME OF MY WORST MOMENTS WERE RIGHT HERE IN LONDON.
BEING REMINDED OF THEM PISSES ME OFF.
WHERE IS SHE?
I'M LOOKING FOR A SLAYER. NAME'S FAITH LEHANE. HEARD SHE LIVES AROUND HERE.
MAYBE YOU KNOW HER?

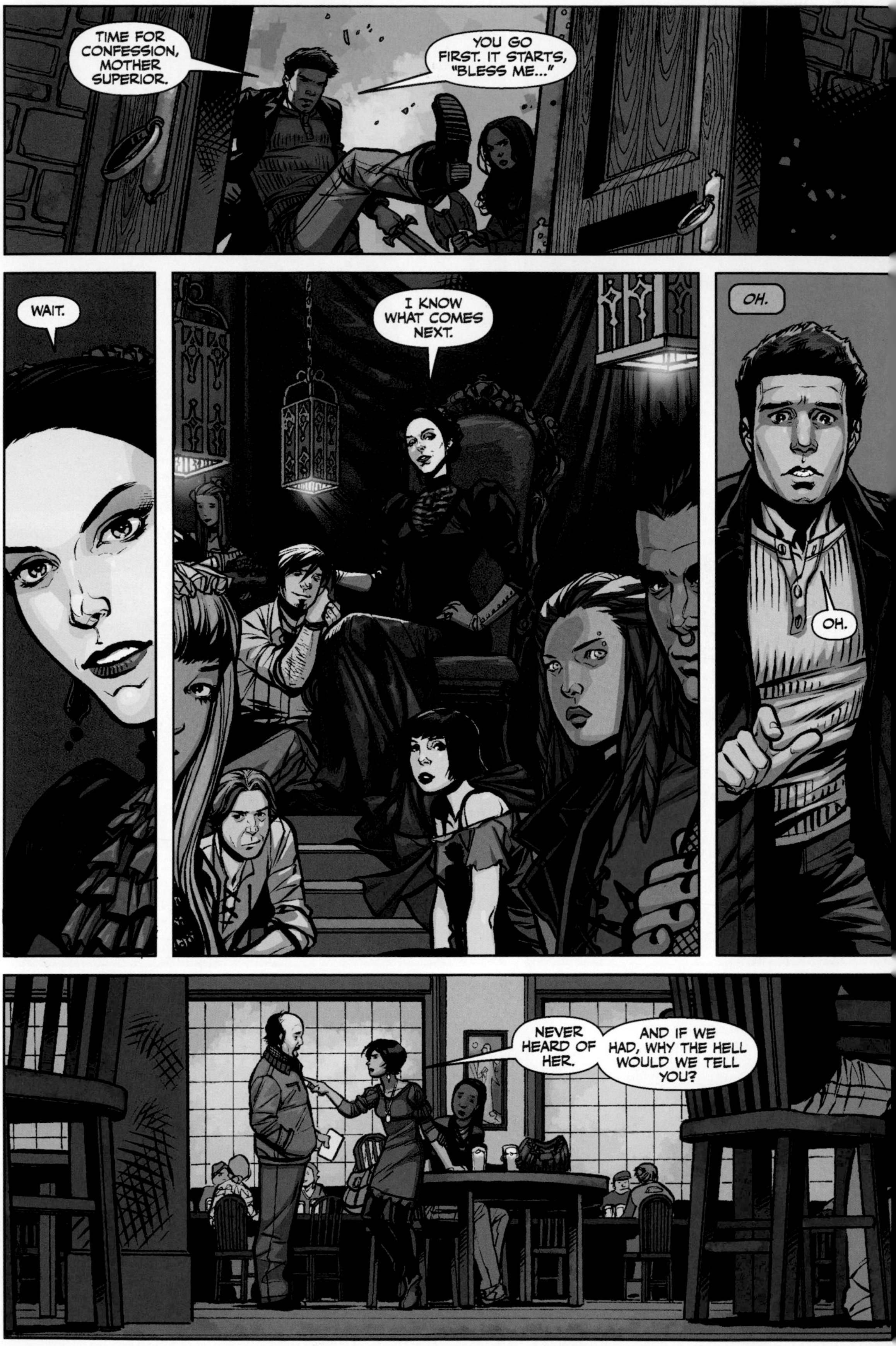
TIME FOR CONFESSION, MOTHER SUPERIOR.
YOU GO FIRST. IT STARTS, "BLESS ME..."
WAIT.
I KNOW WHAT COMES NEXT.
OH.
OH.
NEVER HEARD OF HER.
AND IF WE HAD, WHY THE HELL WOULD WE TELL YOU?

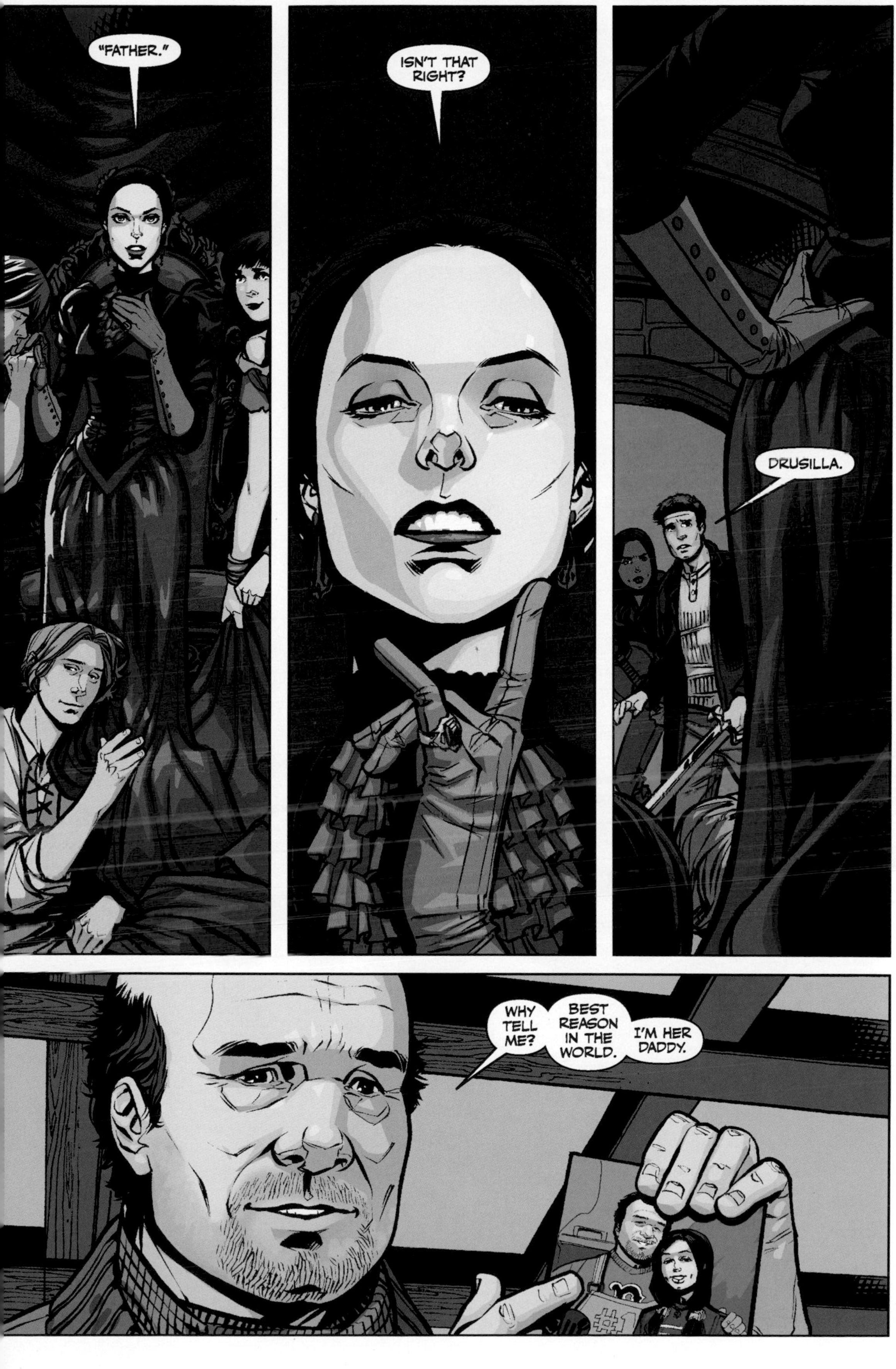
"FATHER."
ISN'T THAT RIGHT?
DRUSILLA.
WHY TELL ME?
BEST REASON IN THE WORLD.
I'M HER DADDY.
#1

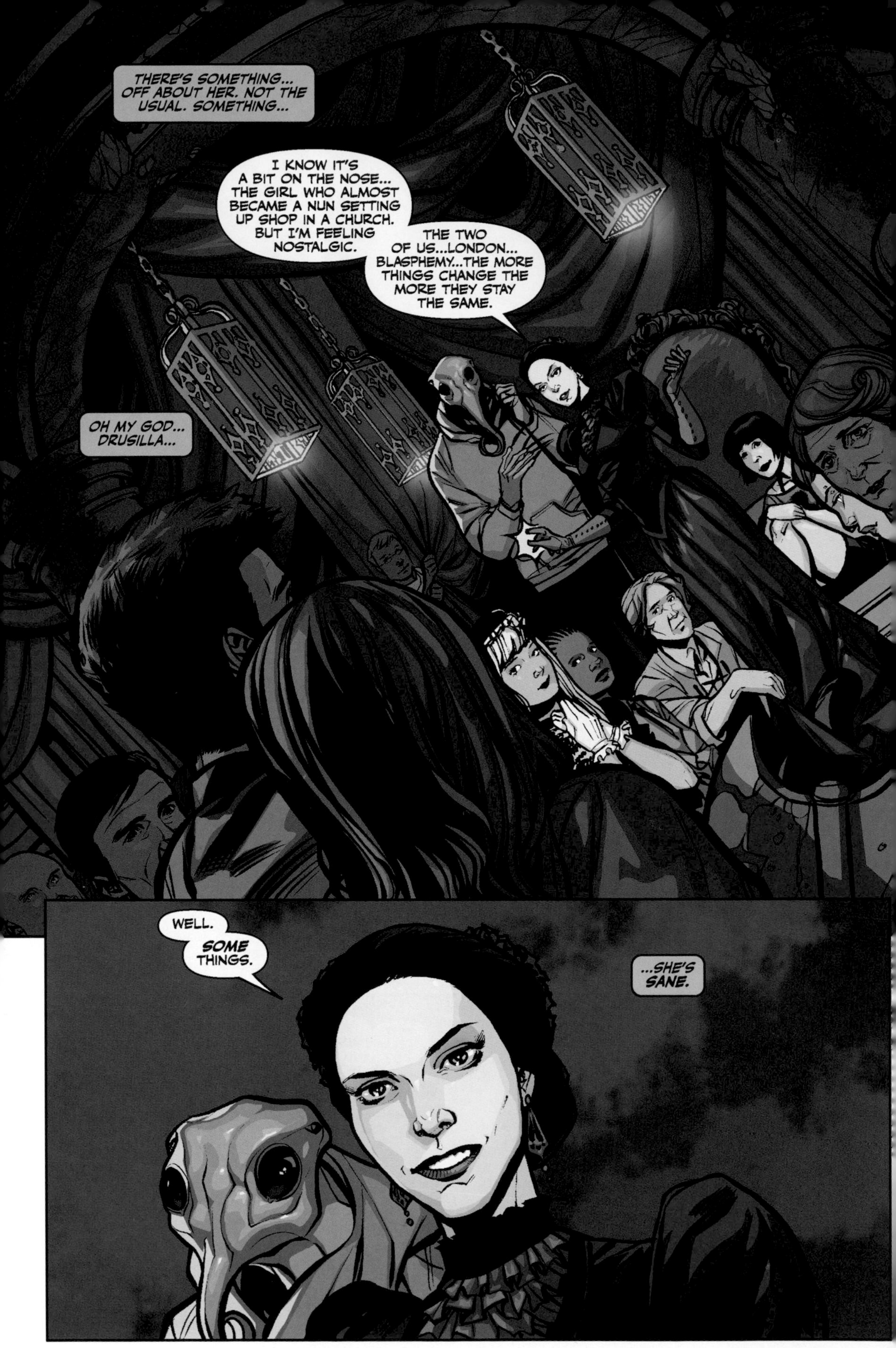
THERE'S SOMETHING... OFF ABOUT HER. NOT THE USUAL. SOMETHING...
I KNOW IT'S A BIT ON THE NOSE... THE GIRL WHO ALMOST BECAME A NUN SETTING UP SHOP IN A CHURCH. BUT I'M FEELING NOSTALGIC.
THE TWO OF US...LONDON... BLASPHEMY...THE MORE THINGS CHANGE THE MORE THEY STAY THE SAME.
OH MY GOD... DRUSILLA...
WELL. SOME THINGS.
...SHE'S SANE.

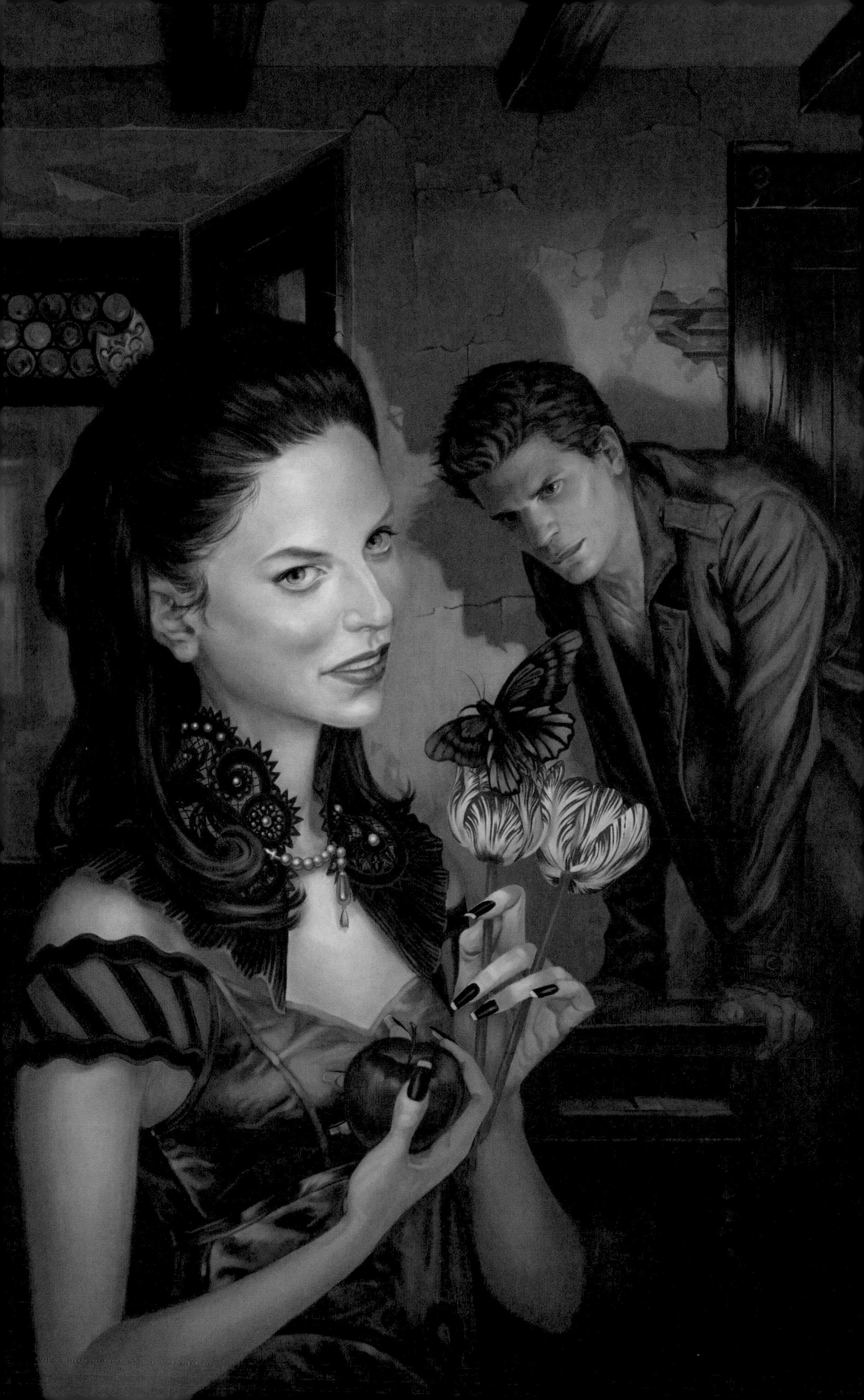

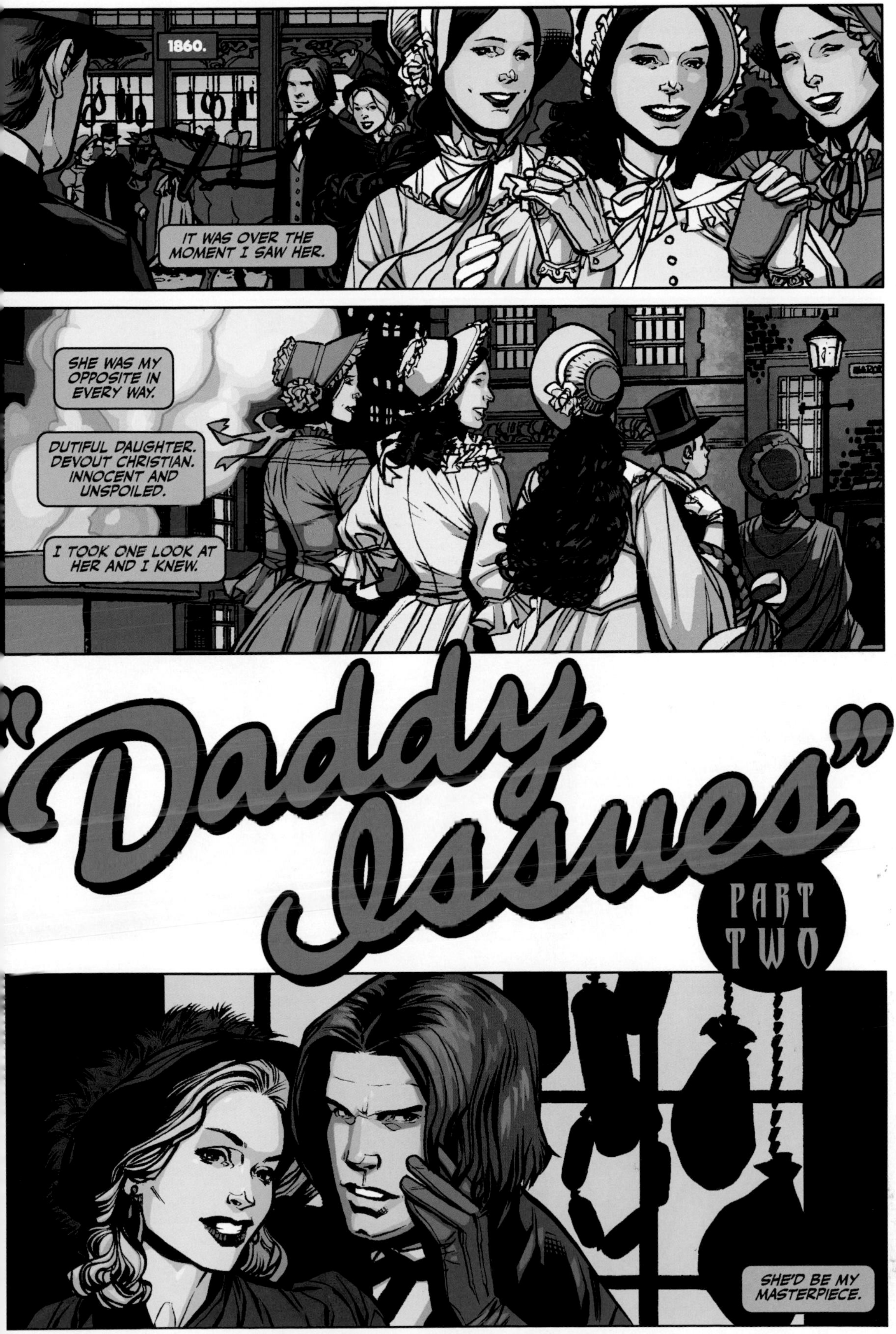
1860.
IT WAS OVER THE MOMENT I SAW HER.
SHE WAS MY OPPOSITE IN EVERY WAY.
DUTIFUL DAUGHTER. DEVOUT CHRISTIAN. INNOCENT AND UNSPOILED.
I TOOK ONE LOOK AT HER AND I KNEW.
"Daddy Issues"
PART TWO
SHE'D BE MY MASTERPIECE.

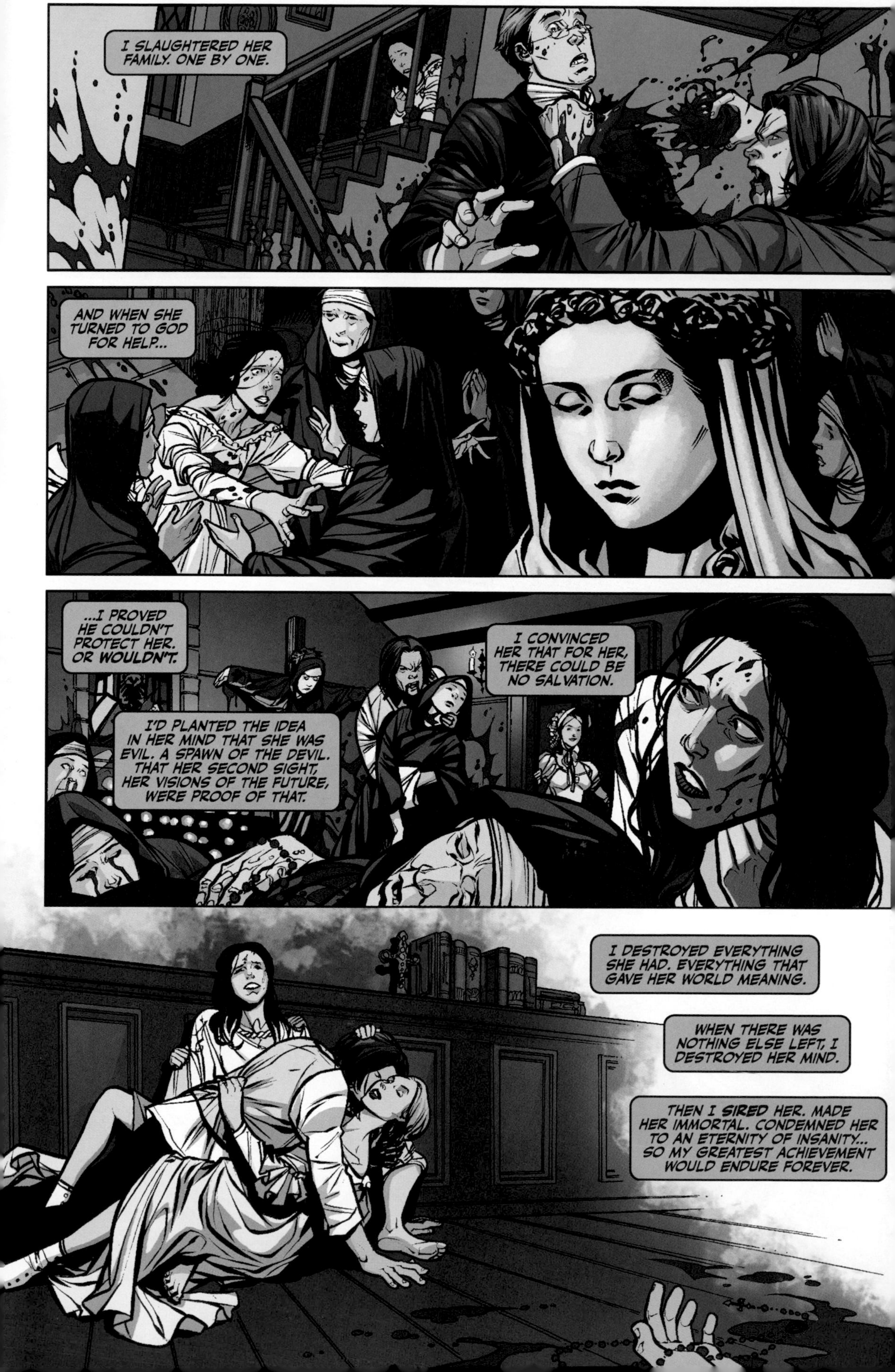
I SLAUGHTERED HER FAMILY. ONE BY ONE.
AND WHEN SHE TURNED TO GOD FOR HELP...
...I PROVED HE COULDN'T PROTECT HER. OR WOULDN'T.
I'D PLANTED THE IDEA IN HER MIND THAT SHE WAS EVIL. A SPAWN OF THE DEVIL. THAT HER SECOND SIGHT, HER VISIONS OF THE FUTURE, WERE PROOF OF THAT.
I CONVINCED HER THAT FOR HER, THERE COULD BE NO SALVATION.
I DESTROYED EVERYTHING SHE HAD. EVERYTHING THAT GAVE HER WORLD MEANING.
WHEN THERE WAS NOTHING ELSE LEFT, I DESTROYED HER MIND.
THEN I SIRED HER. MADE HER IMMORTAL. CONDEMNED HER TO AN ETERNITY OF INSANITY... SO MY GREATEST ACHIEVEMENT WOULD ENDURE FOREVER.

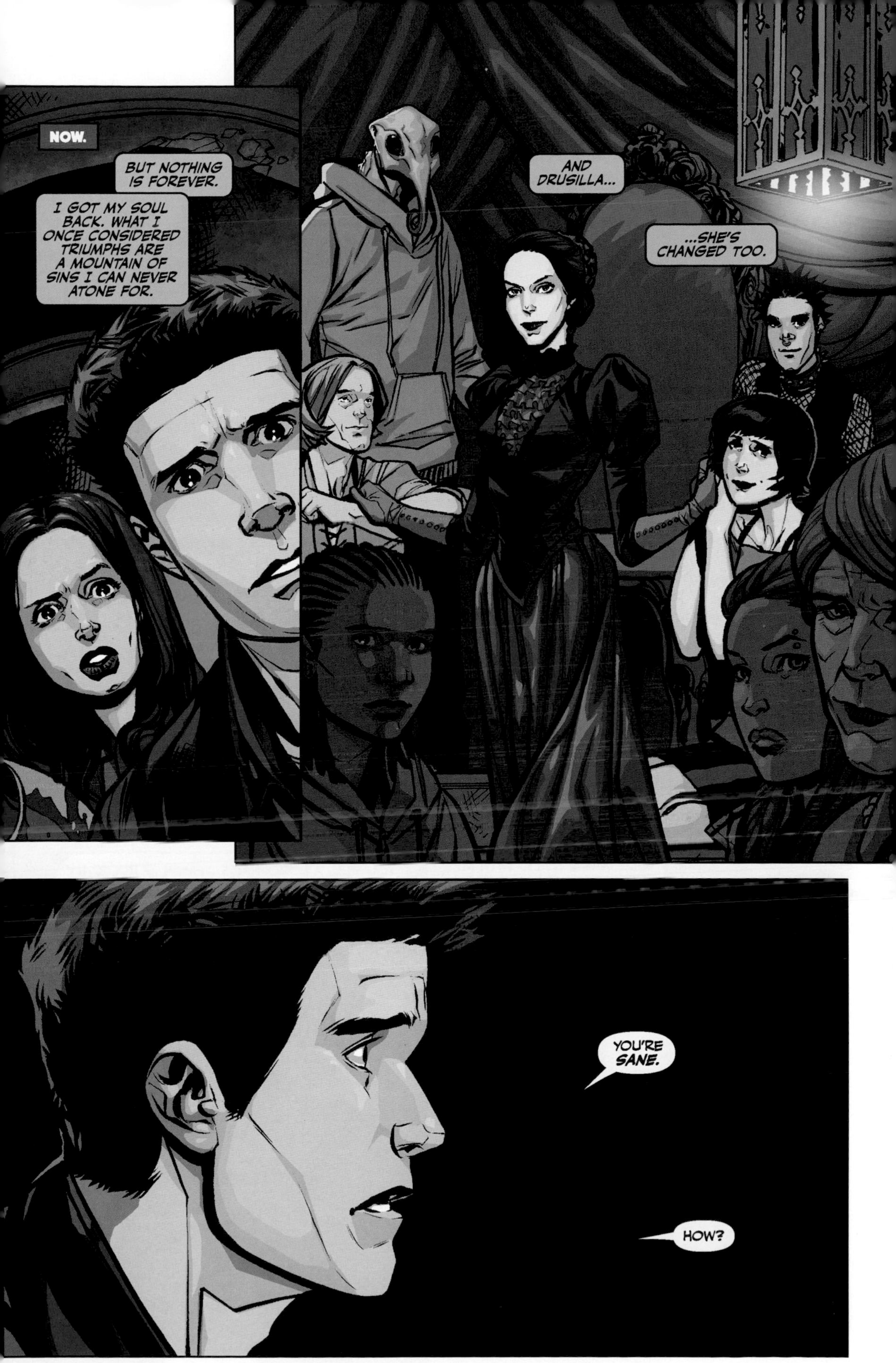
NOW.
BUT NOTHING IS FOREVER.
I GOT MY SOUL BACK. WHAT I ONCE CONSIDERED TRIUMPHS ARE A MOUNTAIN OF SINS I CAN NEVER ATONE FOR.
AND DRUSILLA...
...SHE'S CHANGED TOO.
YOU'RE SANE.
HOW?

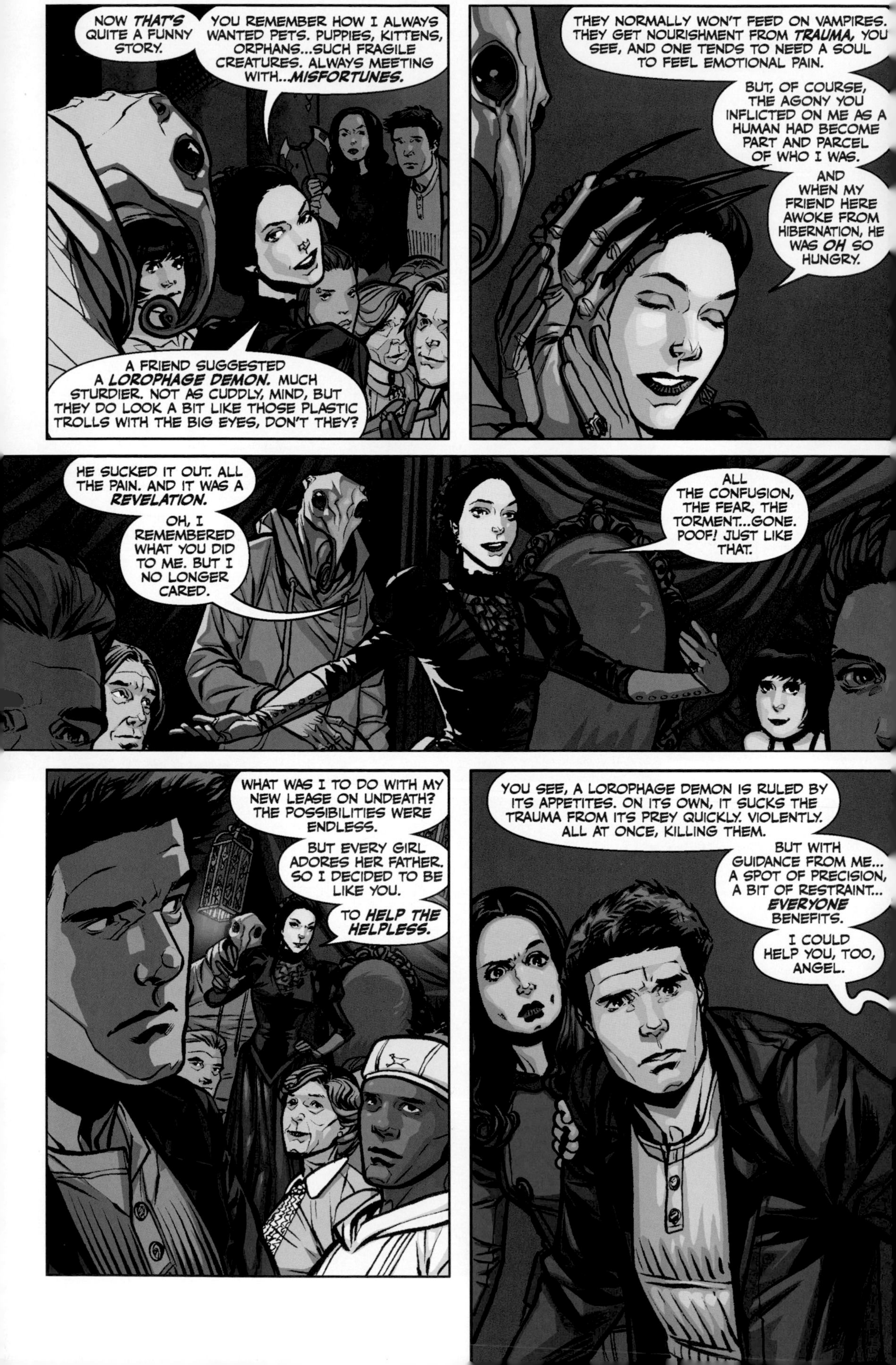
NOW THAT'S QUITE A FUNNY STORY.
YOU REMEMBER HOW I ALWAYS WANTED PETS. PUPPIES, KITTENS, ORPHANS...SUCH FRAGILE CREATURES. ALWAYS MEETING WITH...MISFORTUNES.
A FRIEND SUGGESTED A LOROPHAGE DEMON. MUCH STURDIER. NOT AS CUDDLY, MIND, BUT THEY DO LOOK A BIT LIKE THOSE PLASTIC TROLLS WITH THE BIG EYES, DON'T THEY?
THEY NORMALLY WON'T FEED ON VAMPIRES. THEY GET NOURISHMENT FROM TRAUMA, YOU SEE, AND ONE TENDS TO NEED A SOUL TO FEEL EMOTIONAL PAIN.
BUT, OF COURSE, THE AGONY YOU INFLICTED ON ME AS A HUMAN HAD BECOME PART AND PARCEL OF WHO I WAS.
AND WHEN MY FRIEND HERE AWOKE FROM HIBERNATION, HE WAS OH SO HUNGRY.
HE SUCKED IT OUT. ALL THE PAIN. AND IT WAS A REVELATION.
OH, I REMEMBERED WHAT YOU DID TO ME. BUT I NO LONGER CARED.
ALL THE CONFUSION, THE FEAR, THE TORMENT...GONE. POOF! JUST LIKE THAT.
WHAT WAS I TO DO WITH MY NEW LEASE ON UNDEATH? THE POSSIBILITIES WERE ENDLESS.
BUT EVERY GIRL ADORES HER FATHER. SO I DECIDED TO BE LIKE YOU.
TO HELP THE HELPLESS.
YOU SEE, A LOROPHAGE DEMON IS RULED BY ITS APPETITES. ON ITS OWN, IT SUCKS THE TRAUMA FROM ITS PREY QUICKLY. VIOLENTLY. ALL AT ONCE, KILLING THEM.
BUT WITH GUIDANCE FROM ME... A SPOT OF PRECISION, A BIT OF RESTRAINT... EVERYONE BENEFITS.
I COULD HELP YOU, TOO, ANGEL.

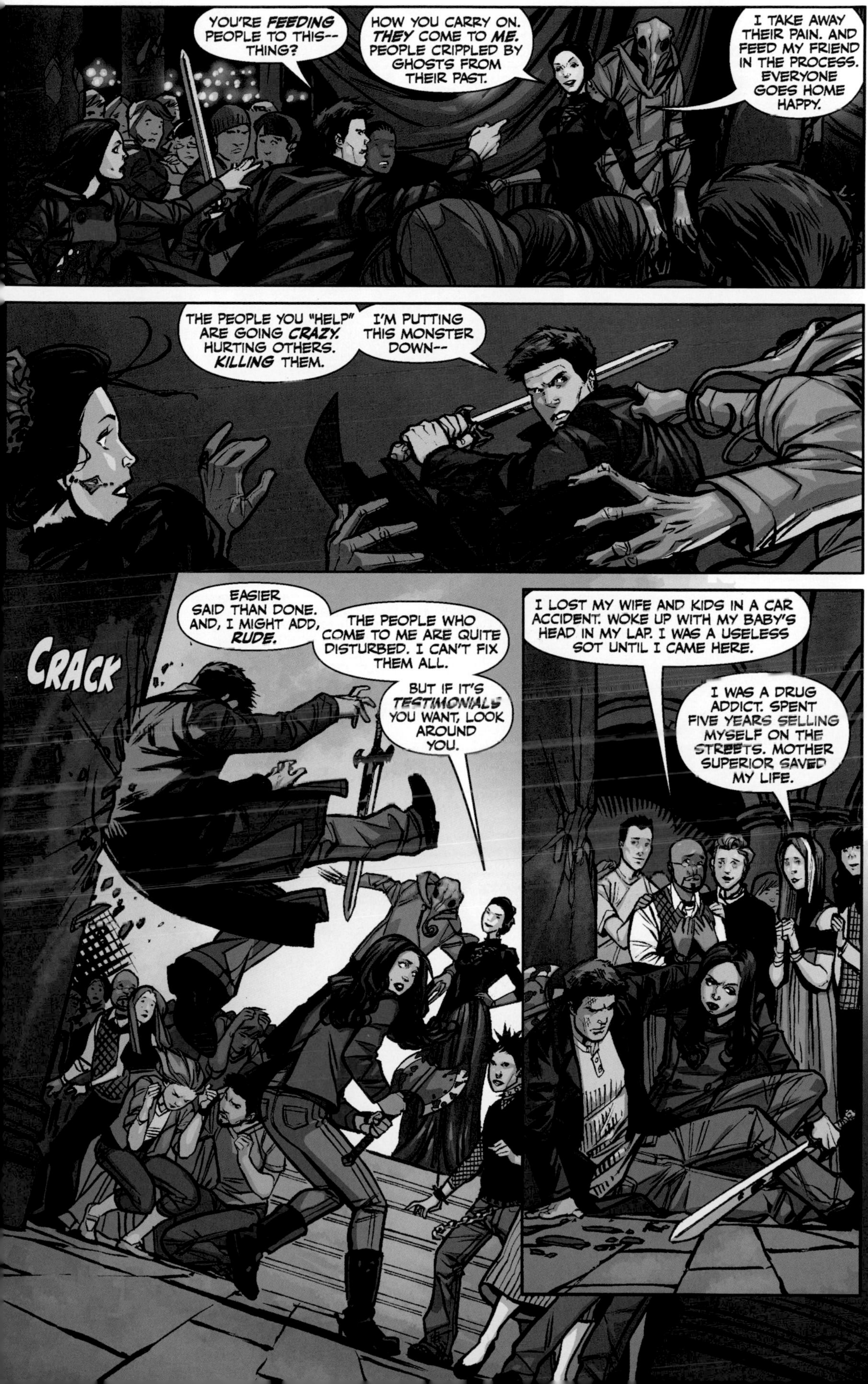
YOU'RE FEEDING PEOPLE TO THIS--THING?
HOW YOU CARRY ON. THEY COME TO ME. PEOPLE CRIPPLED BY GHOSTS FROM THEIR PAST.
I TAKE AWAY THEIR PAIN. AND FEED MY FRIEND IN THE PROCESS. EVERYONE GOES HOME HAPPY.
THE PEOPLE YOU "HELP" ARE GOING CRAZY. HURTING OTHERS. KILLING THEM.
I'M PUTTING THIS MONSTER DOWN--
CRACK
EASIER SAID THAN DONE. AND, I MIGHT ADD, RUDE.
THE PEOPLE WHO COME TO ME ARE QUITE DISTURBED. I CAN'T FIX THEM ALL.
BUT IF IT'S TESTIMONIALS YOU WANT, LOOK AROUND YOU.
I LOST MY WIFE AND KIDS IN A CAR ACCIDENT. WOKE UP WITH MY BABY'S HEAD IN MY LAP. I WAS A USELESS SOT UNTIL I CAME HERE.
I WAS A DRUG ADDICT. SPENT FIVE YEARS SELLING MYSELF ON THE STREETS. MOTHER SUPERIOR SAVED MY LIFE.

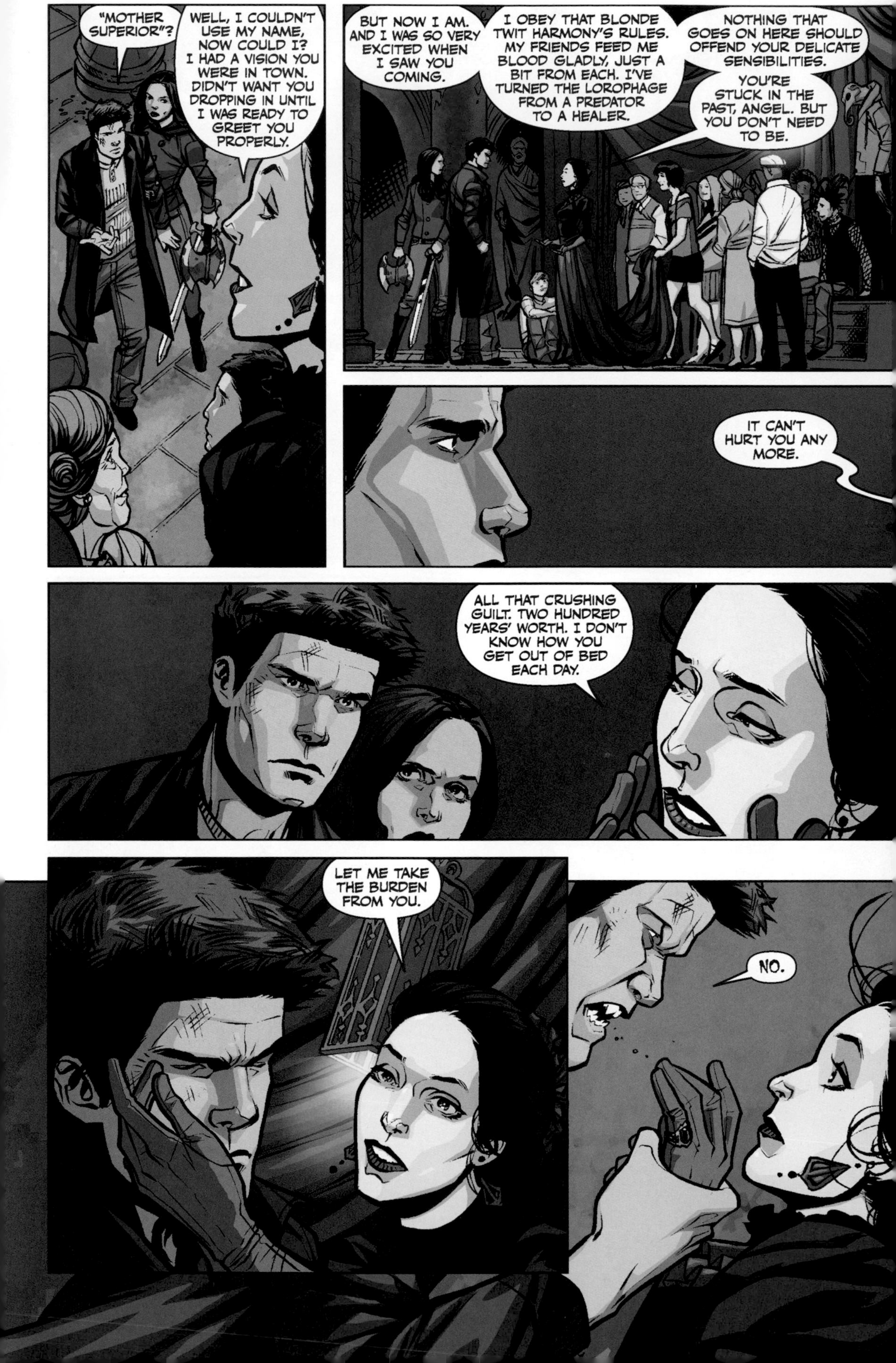
"MOTHER SUPERIOR"?
WELL, I COULDN'T USE MY NAME, NOW COULD I? I HAD A VISION YOU WERE IN TOWN. DIDN'T WANT YOU DROPPING IN UNTIL I WAS READY TO GREET YOU PROPERLY.
BUT NOW I AM. AND I WAS SO VERY EXCITED WHEN I SAW YOU COMING.
I OBEY THAT BLONDE TWIT HARMONY'S RULES. MY FRIENDS FEED ME BLOOD GLADLY, JUST A BIT FROM EACH. I'VE TURNED THE LOROPHAGE FROM A PREDATOR TO A HEALER.
NOTHING THAT GOES ON HERE SHOULD OFFEND YOUR DELICATE SENSIBILITIES.
YOU'RE STUCK IN THE PAST, ANGEL. BUT YOU DON'T NEED TO BE.
IT CAN'T HURT YOU ANY MORE.
ALL THAT CRUSHING GUILT. TWO HUNDRED YEARS' WORTH. I DON'T KNOW HOW YOU GET OUT OF BED EACH DAY.
LET ME TAKE THE BURDEN FROM YOU.
NO.

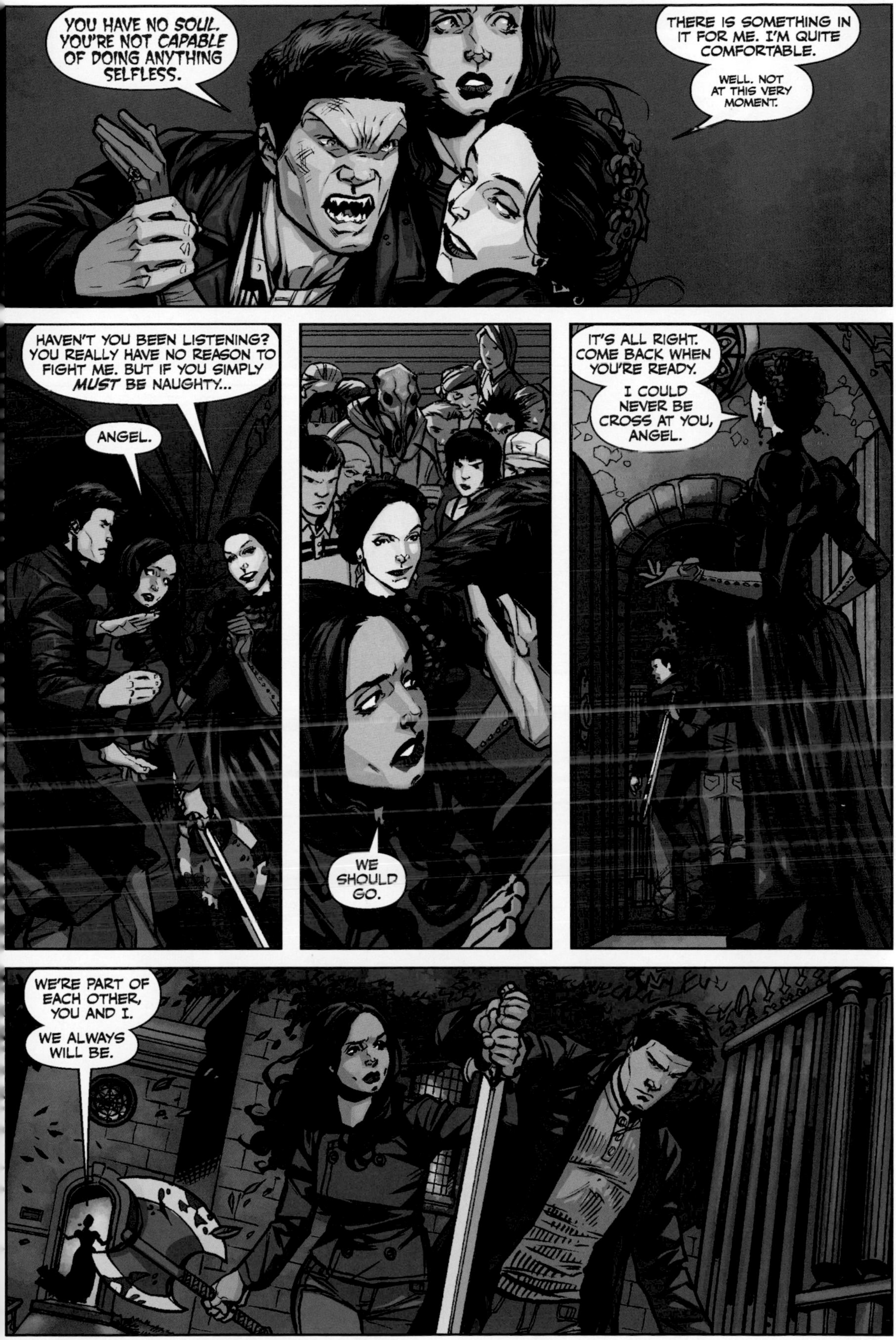
YOU HAVE NO SOUL. YOU'RE NOT CAPABLE OF DOING ANYTHING SELFLESS.
THERE IS SOMETHING IN IT FOR ME. I'M QUITE COMFORTABLE.
WELL. NOT AT THIS VERY MOMENT.
HAVEN'T YOU BEEN LISTENING? YOU REALLY HAVE NO REASON TO FIGHT ME. BUT IF YOU SIMPLY MUST BE NAUGHTY...
ANGEL.
WE SHOULD GO.
IT'S ALL RIGHT. COME BACK WHEN YOU'RE READY.
I COULD NEVER BE CROSS AT YOU, ANGEL.
WE'RE PART OF EACH OTHER, YOU AND I.
WE ALWAYS WILL BE.

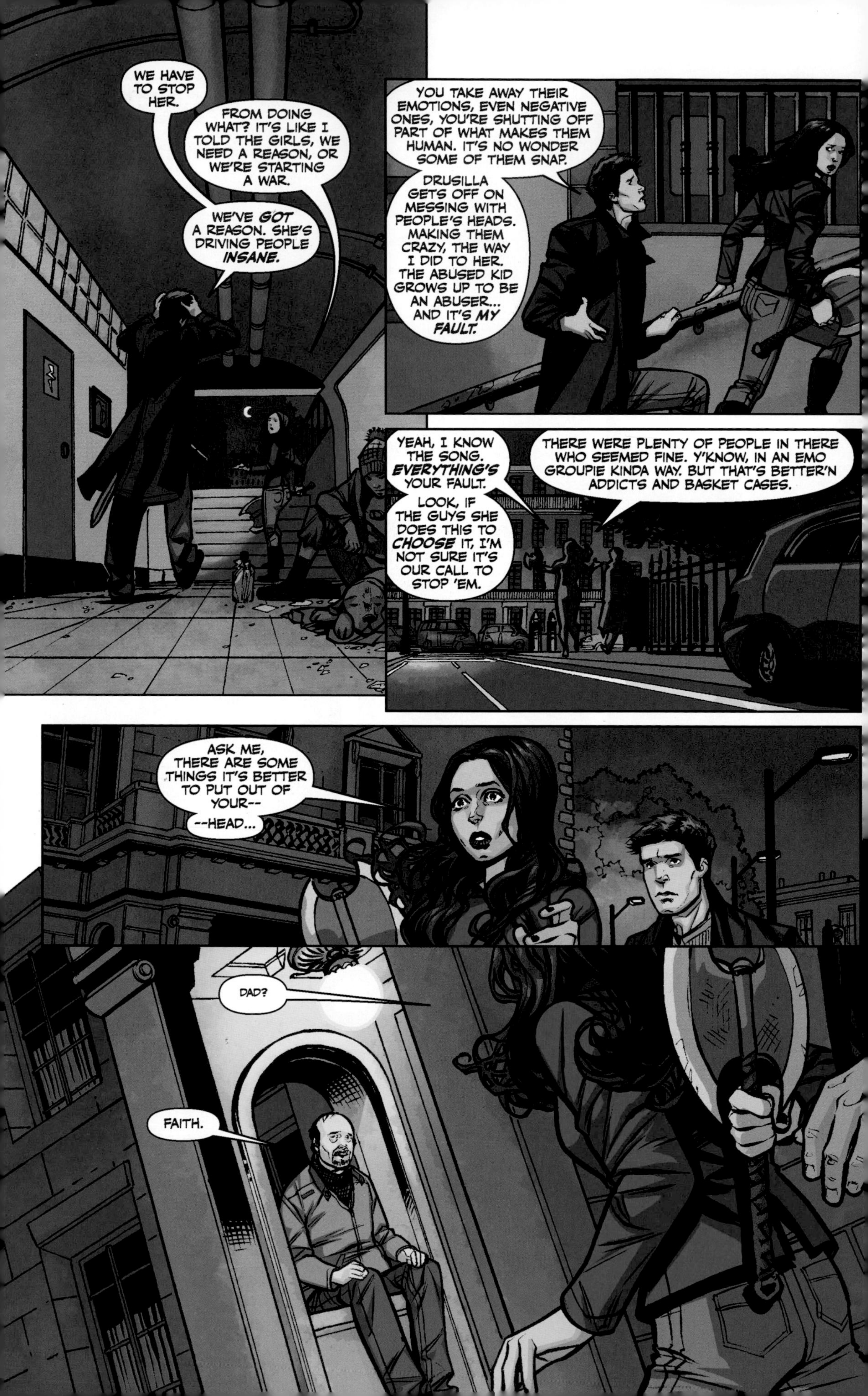
WE HAVE TO STOP HER.
FROM DOING WHAT? IT'S LIKE I TOLD THE GIRLS, WE NEED A REASON, OR WE'RE STARTING A WAR.
WE'VE *GOT* A REASON. SHE'S DRIVING PEOPLE *INSANE.*
YOU TAKE AWAY THEIR EMOTIONS, EVEN NEGATIVE ONES, YOU'RE SHUTTING OFF PART OF WHAT MAKES THEM HUMAN. IT'S NO WONDER SOME OF THEM SNAP.
DRUSILLA GETS OFF ON MESSING WITH PEOPLE'S HEADS. MAKING THEM CRAZY, THE WAY I DID TO HER. THE ABUSED KID GROWS UP TO BE AN ABUSER... AND IT'S *MY FAULT.*
YEAH, I KNOW THE SONG. *EVERYTHING'S* YOUR FAULT.
LOOK, IF THE GUYS SHE DOES THIS TO *CHOOSE* IT, I'M NOT SURE IT'S OUR CALL TO STOP 'EM.
THERE WERE PLENTY OF PEOPLE IN THERE WHO SEEMED FINE. Y'KNOW, IN AN EMO GROUPIE KINDA WAY. BUT THAT'S BETTER'N ADDICTS AND BASKET CASES.
ASK ME, THERE ARE SOME THINGS IT'S BETTER TO PUT OUT OF YOUR--
--HEAD...
DAD?
FAITH.

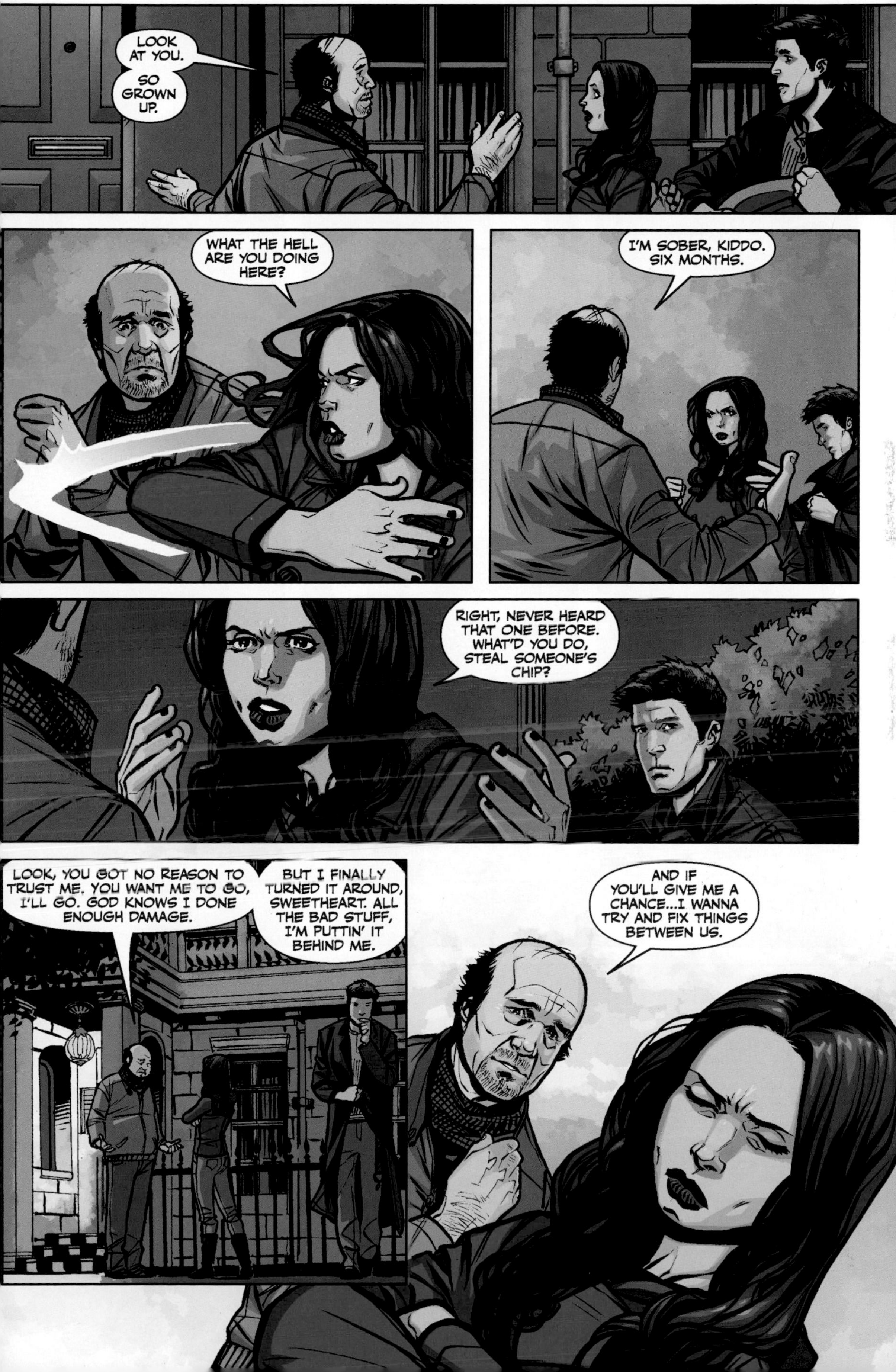
LOOK AT YOU.
SO GROWN UP.
WHAT THE HELL ARE YOU DOING HERE?
I'M SOBER, KIDDO. SIX MONTHS.
RIGHT, NEVER HEARD THAT ONE BEFORE. WHAT'D YOU DO, STEAL SOMEONE'S CHIP?
LOOK, YOU GOT NO REASON TO TRUST ME. YOU WANT ME TO GO, I'LL GO. GOD KNOWS I DONE ENOUGH DAMAGE.
BUT I FINALLY TURNED IT AROUND, SWEETHEART. ALL THE BAD STUFF, I'M PUTTIN' IT BEHIND ME.
AND IF YOU'LL GIVE ME A CHANCE...I WANNA TRY AND FIX THINGS BETWEEN US.

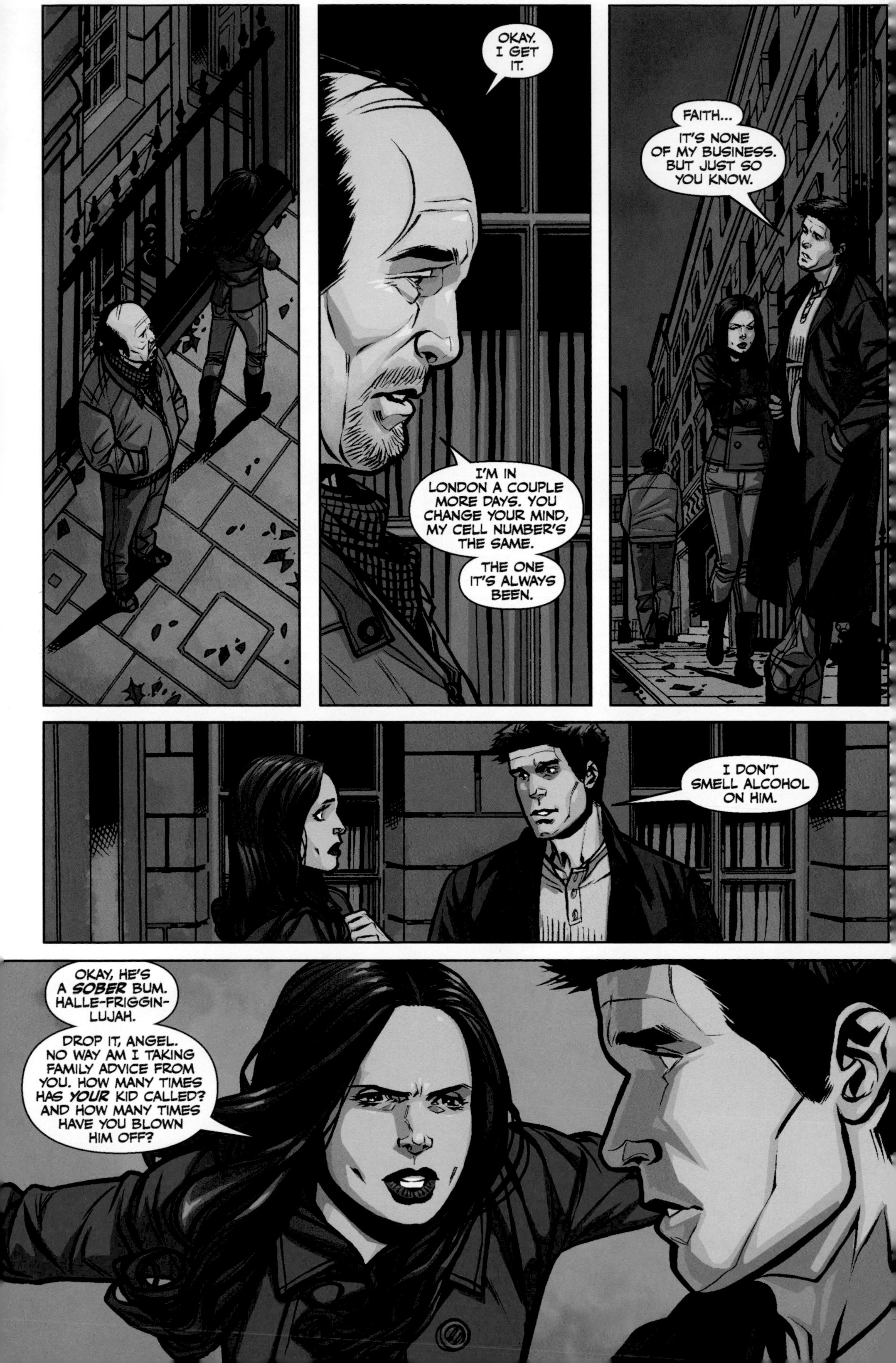
OKAY. I GET IT.
I'M IN LONDON A COUPLE MORE DAYS. YOU CHANGE YOUR MIND, MY CELL NUMBER'S THE SAME.
THE ONE IT'S ALWAYS BEEN.
FAITH...
IT'S NONE OF MY BUSINESS. BUT JUST SO YOU KNOW.
I DON'T SMELL ALCOHOL ON HIM.
OKAY, HE'S A SOBER BUM. HALLE-FRIGGIN-LUJAH.
DROP IT, ANGEL. NO WAY AM I TAKING FAMILY ADVICE FROM YOU. HOW MANY TIMES HAS YOUR KID CALLED? AND HOW MANY TIMES HAVE YOU BLOWN HIM OFF?

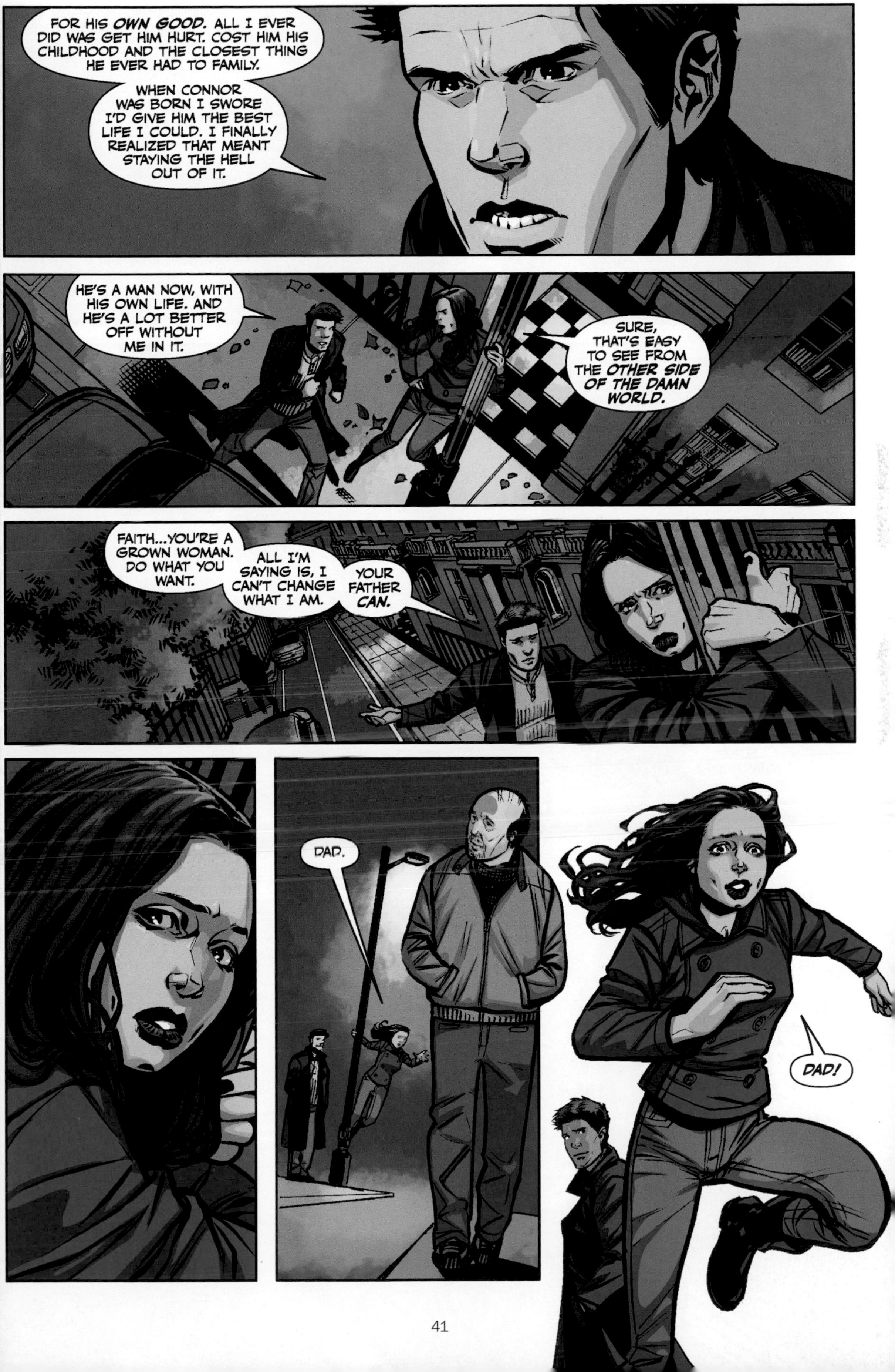
FOR HIS OWN GOOD. ALL I EVER DID WAS GET HIM HURT. COST HIM HIS CHILDHOOD AND THE CLOSEST THING HE EVER HAD TO FAMILY.
WHEN CONNOR WAS BORN I SWORE I'D GIVE HIM THE BEST LIFE I COULD. I FINALLY REALIZED THAT MEANT STAYING THE HELL OUT OF IT.
HE'S A MAN NOW, WITH HIS OWN LIFE. AND HE'S A LOT BETTER OFF WITHOUT ME IN IT.
SURE, THAT'S EASY TO SEE FROM THE OTHER SIDE OF THE DAMN WORLD.
FAITH...YOU'RE A GROWN WOMAN. DO WHAT YOU WANT.
ALL I'M SAYING IS, I CAN'T CHANGE WHAT I AM.
YOUR FATHER CAN.
DAD.
DAD!

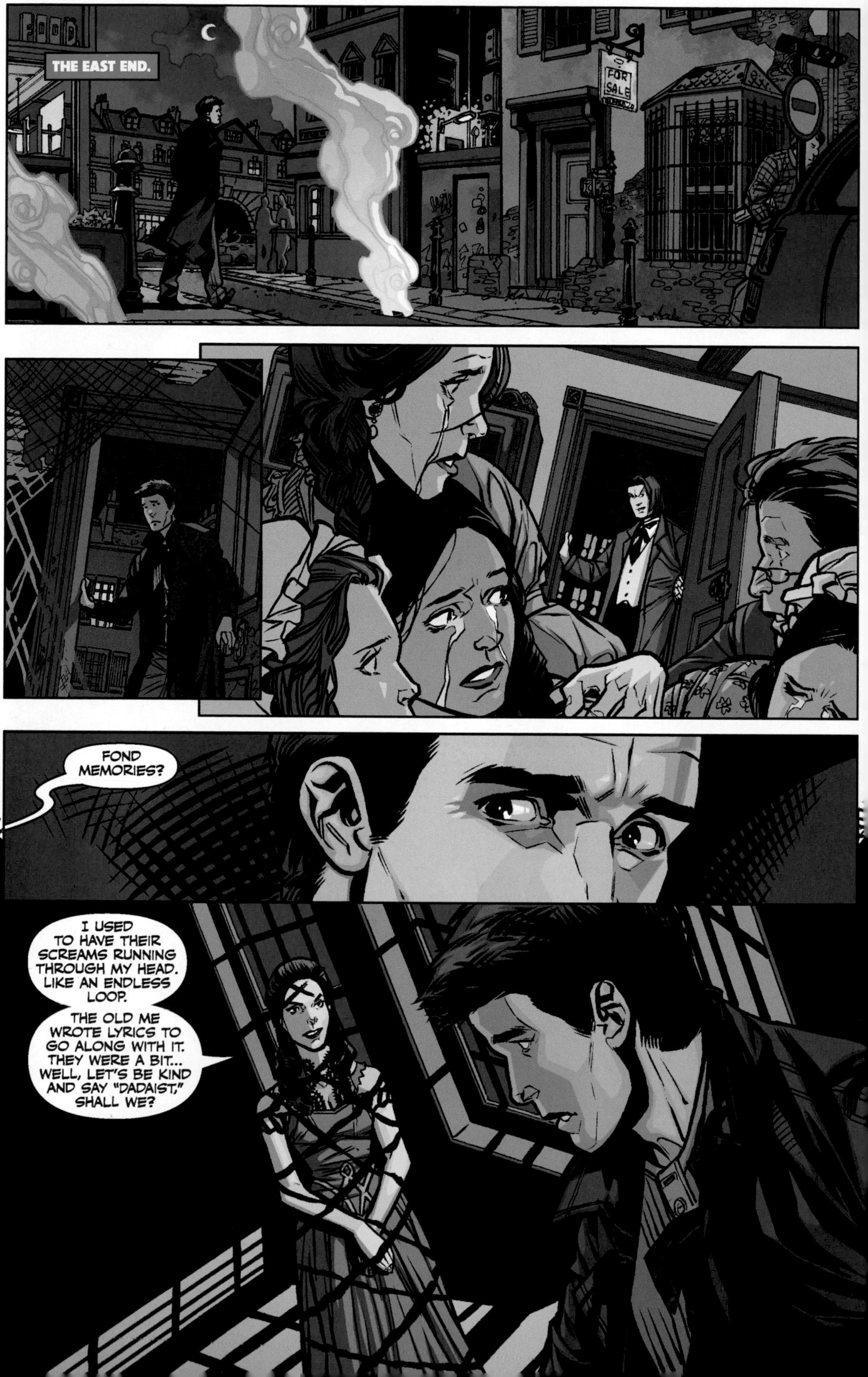
THE EAST END.
FOR SALE
FOND MEMORIES?
I USED TO HAVE THEIR SCREAMS RUNNING THROUGH MY HEAD. LIKE AN ENDLESS LOOP.
THE OLD ME WROTE LYRICS TO GO ALONG WITH IT. THEY WERE A BIT... WELL, LET'S BE KIND AND SAY "DADAIST," SHALL WE?

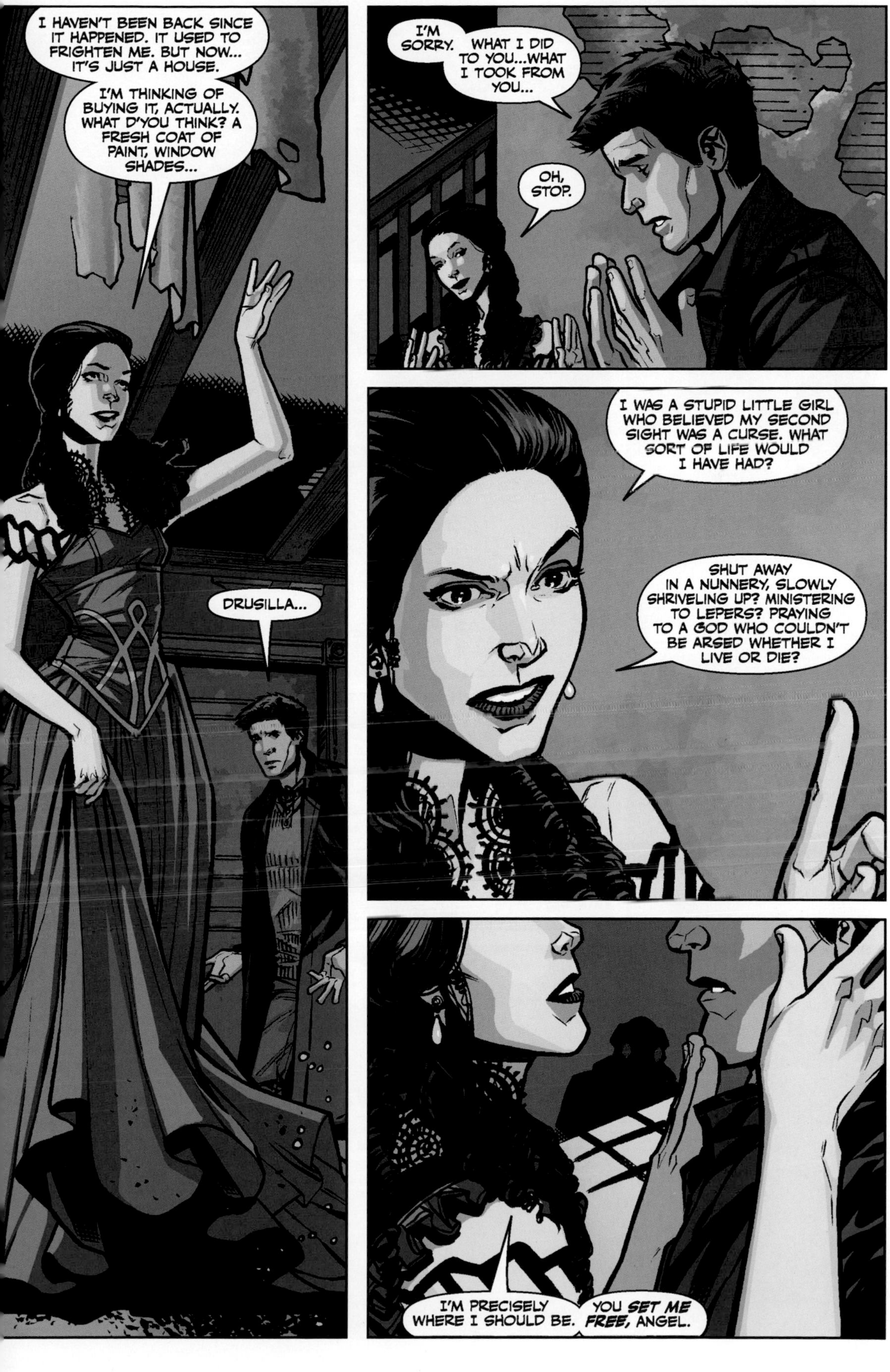
I HAVEN'T BEEN BACK SINCE IT HAPPENED. IT USED TO FRIGHTEN ME. BUT NOW... IT'S JUST A HOUSE.
I'M THINKING OF BUYING IT, ACTUALLY. WHAT D'YOU THINK? A FRESH COAT OF PAINT, WINDOW SHADES...
DRUSILLA...
I'M SORRY.
WHAT I DID TO YOU...WHAT I TOOK FROM YOU...
OH, STOP.
I WAS A STUPID LITTLE GIRL WHO BELIEVED MY SECOND SIGHT WAS A CURSE. WHAT SORT OF LIFE WOULD I HAVE HAD?
SHUT AWAY IN A NUNNERY, SLOWLY SHRIVELING UP? MINISTERING TO LEPERS? PRAYING TO A GOD WHO COULDN'T BE ARSED WHETHER I LIVE OR DIE?
I'M PRECISELY WHERE I SHOULD BE.
YOU *SET ME FREE*, ANGEL.

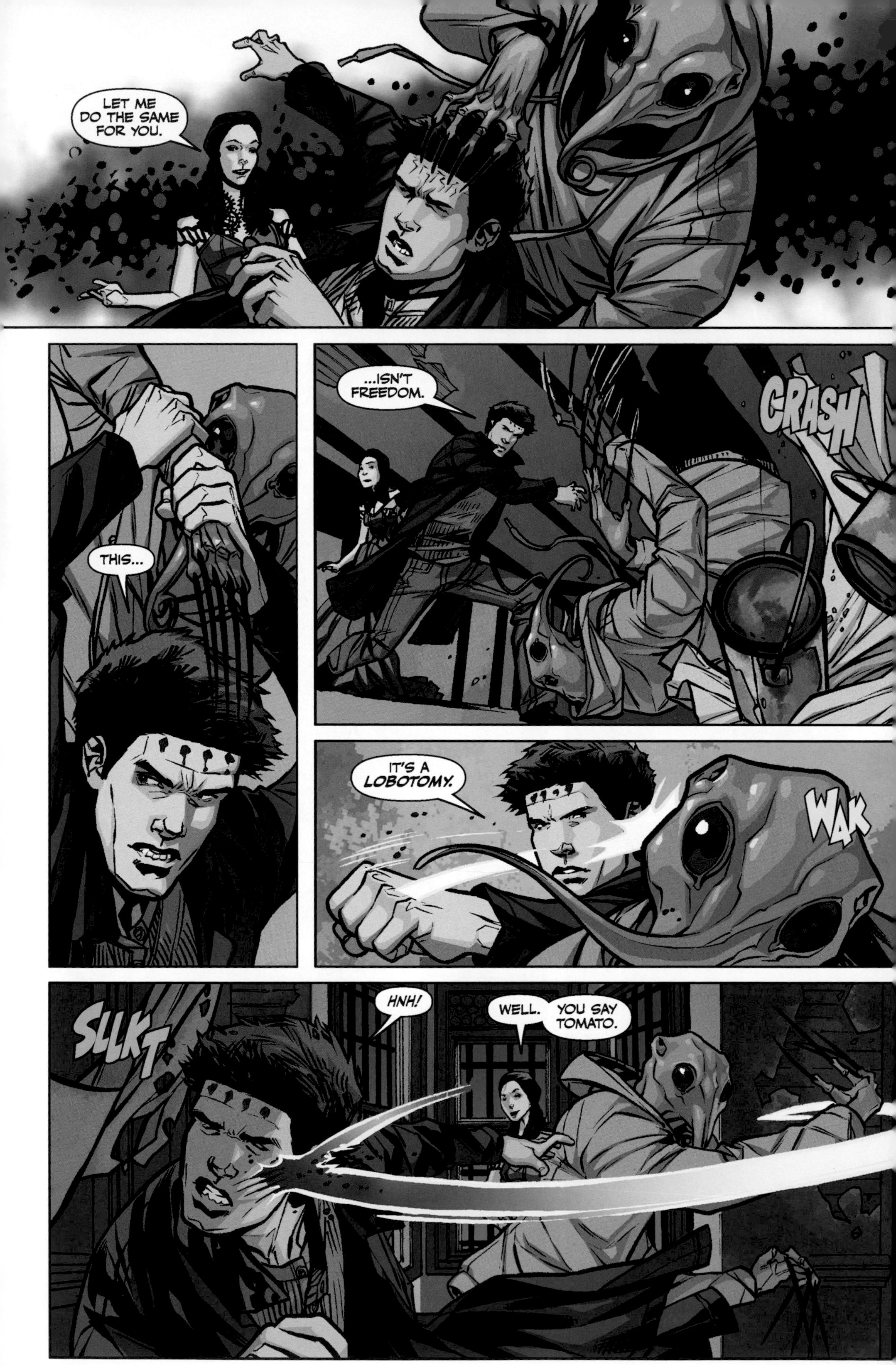
LET ME DO THE SAME FOR YOU.
THIS...
...ISN'T FREEDOM.
CRASH
IT'S A LOBOTOMY.
WAK
SLLKT
HNH!
WELL.
YOU SAY TOMATO.

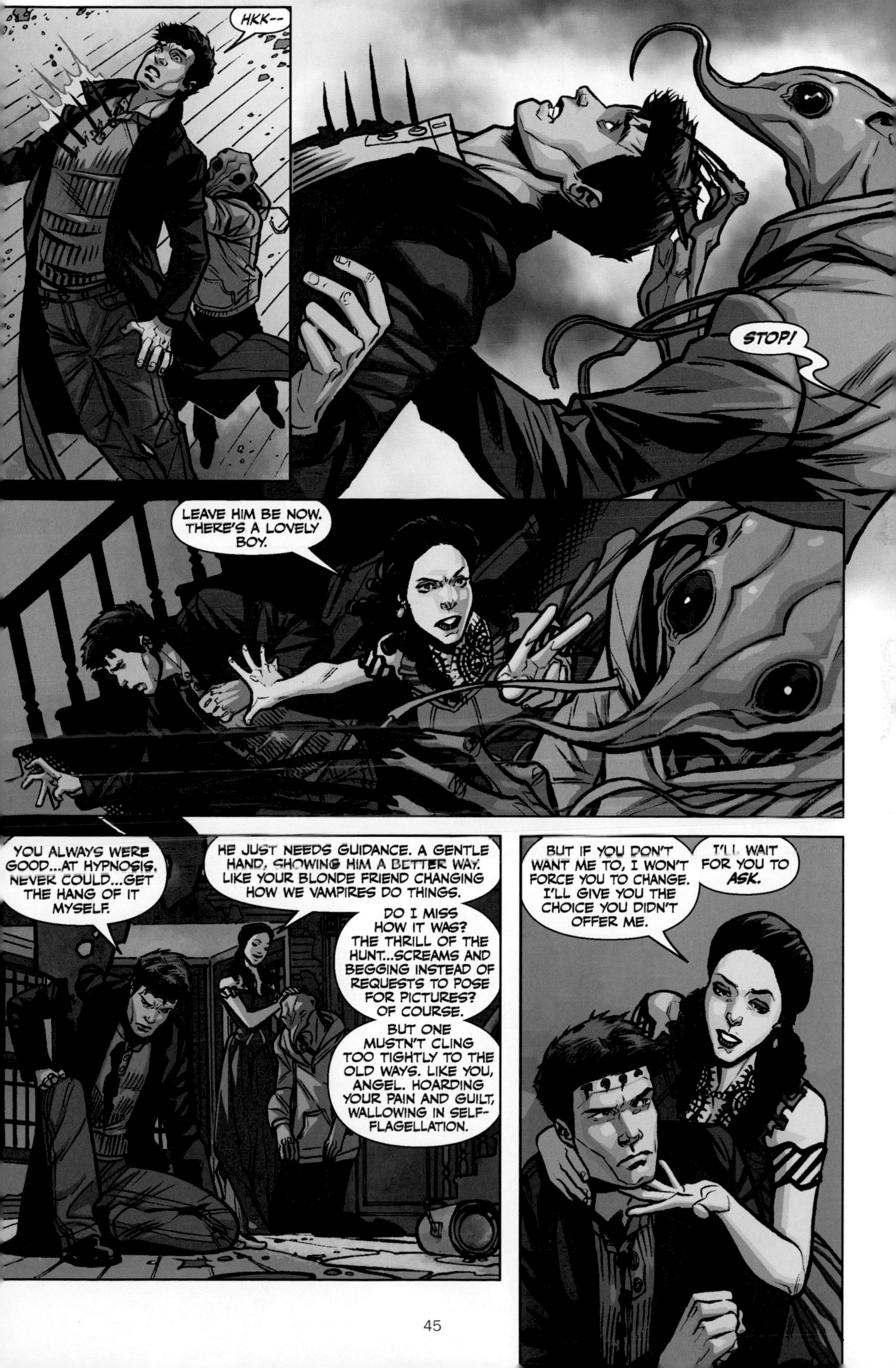
HKK--
STOP!
LEAVE HIM BE NOW. THERE'S A LOVELY BOY.
YOU ALWAYS WERE GOOD...AT HYPNOSIS. NEVER COULD...GET THE HANG OF IT MYSELF.
HE JUST NEEDS GUIDANCE. A GENTLE HAND, SHOWING HIM A BETTER WAY. LIKE YOUR BLONDE FRIEND CHANGING HOW WE VAMPIRES DO THINGS.
DO I MISS HOW IT WAS? THE THRILL OF THE HUNT...SCREAMS AND BEGGING INSTEAD OF REQUESTS TO POSE FOR PICTURES? OF COURSE.
BUT ONE MUSTN'T CLING TOO TIGHTLY TO THE OLD WAYS. LIKE YOU, ANGEL. HOARDING YOUR PAIN AND GUILT, WALLOWING IN SELF-FLAGELLATION.
BUT IF YOU DON'T WANT ME TO, I WON'T FORCE YOU TO CHANGE. I'LL GIVE YOU THE CHOICE YOU DIDN'T OFFER ME.
I'LL WAIT FOR YOU TO ASK.

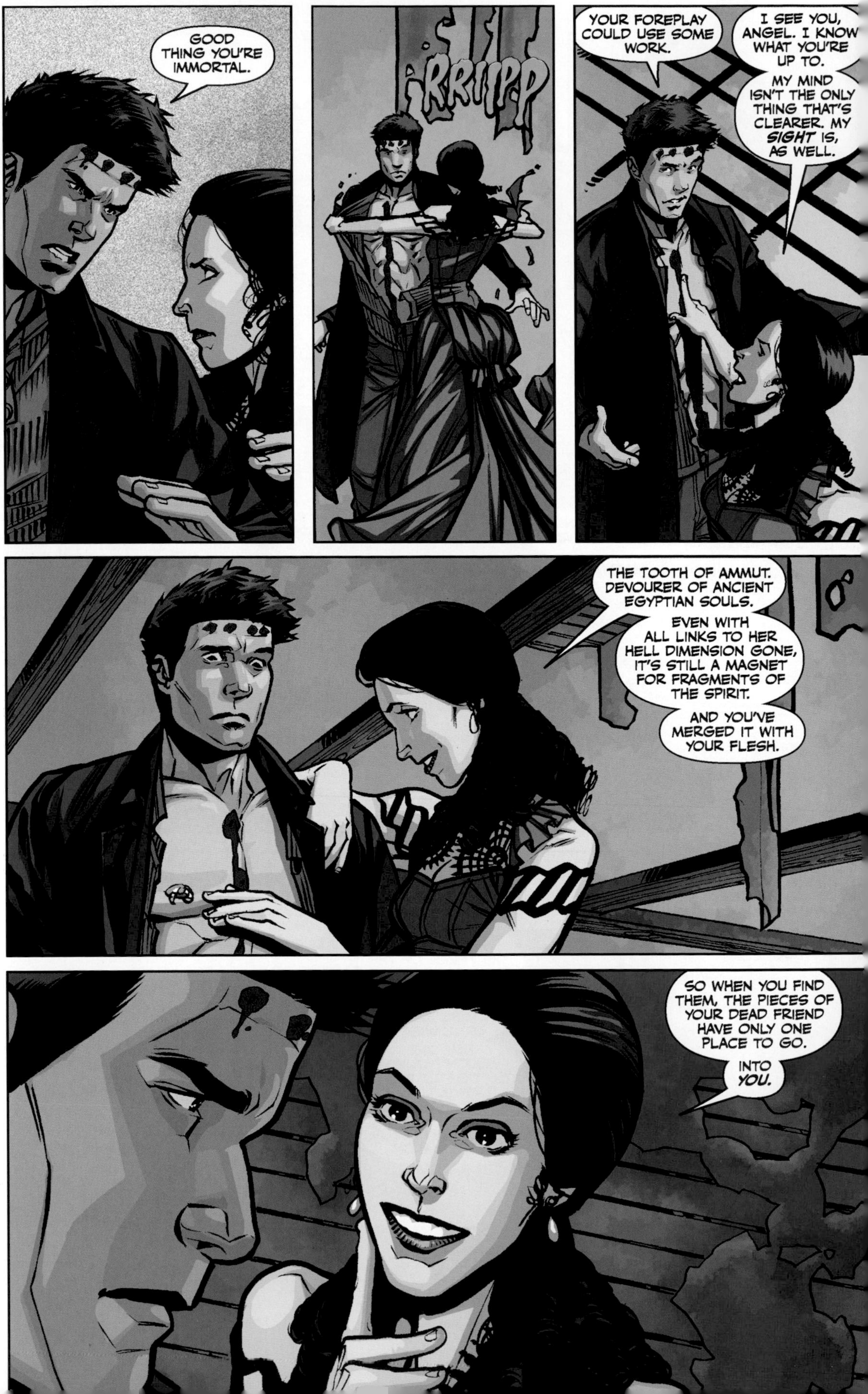
GOOD THING YOU'RE IMMORTAL.
RRIPP
YOUR FOREPLAY COULD USE SOME WORK.
I SEE YOU, ANGEL. I KNOW WHAT YOU'RE UP TO.
MY MIND ISN'T THE ONLY THING THAT'S CLEARER. MY SIGHT IS, AS WELL.
THE TOOTH OF AMMUT. DEVOURER OF ANCIENT EGYPTIAN SOULS.
EVEN WITH ALL LINKS TO HER HELL DIMENSION GONE, IT'S STILL A MAGNET FOR FRAGMENTS OF THE SPIRIT.
AND YOU'VE MERGED IT WITH YOUR FLESH.
SO WHEN YOU FIND THEM, THE PIECES OF YOUR DEAD FRIEND HAVE ONLY ONE PLACE TO GO.
INTO YOU.

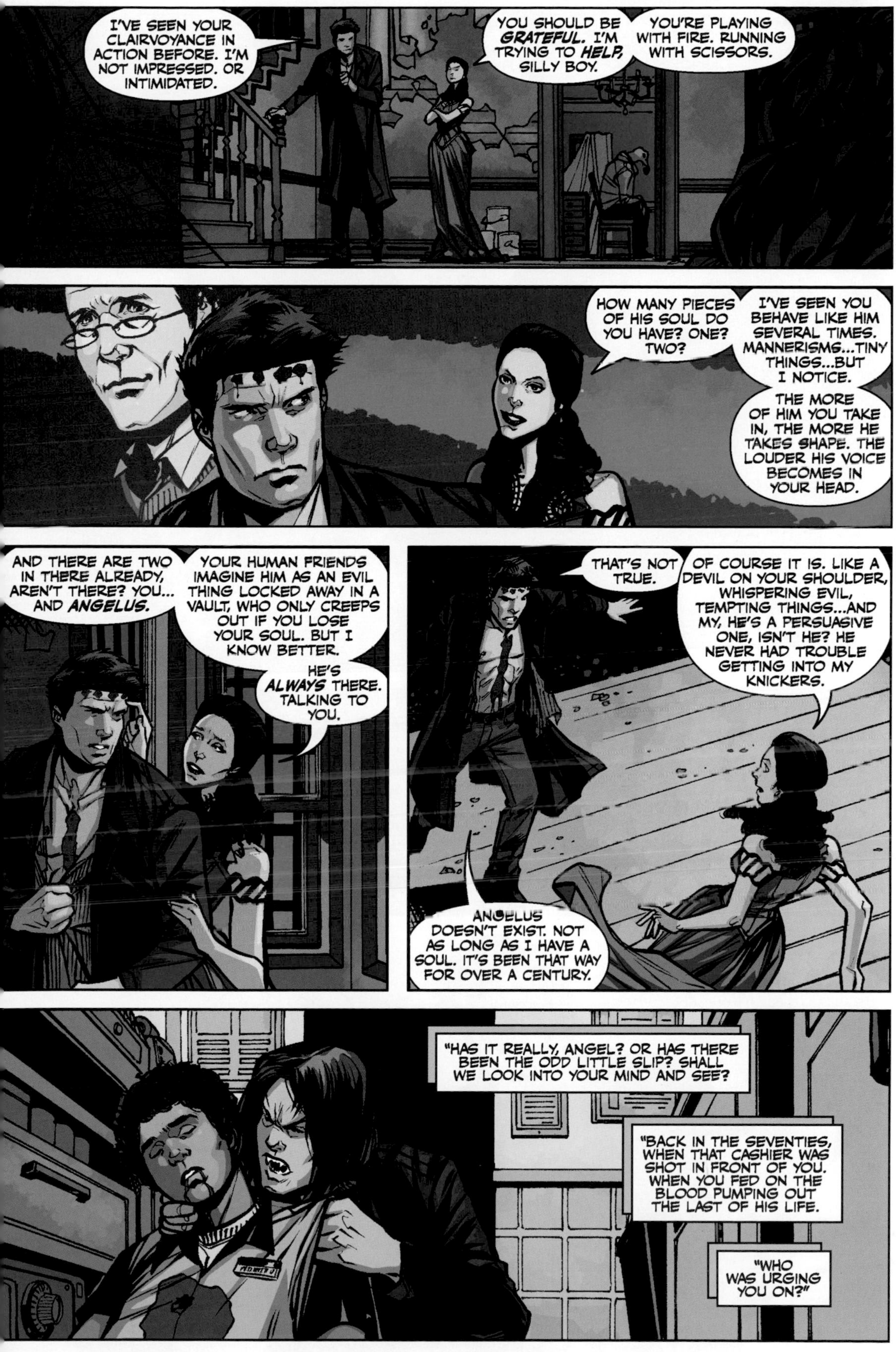
I'VE SEEN YOUR CLAIRVOYANCE IN ACTION BEFORE. I'M NOT IMPRESSED. OR INTIMIDATED.
YOU SHOULD BE GRATEFUL. I'M TRYING TO HELP, SILLY BOY.
YOU'RE PLAYING WITH FIRE. RUNNING WITH SCISSORS.
HOW MANY PIECES OF HIS SOUL DO YOU HAVE? ONE? TWO?
I'VE SEEN YOU BEHAVE LIKE HIM SEVERAL TIMES. MANNERISMS...TINY THINGS...BUT I NOTICE.
THE MORE OF HIM YOU TAKE IN, THE MORE HE TAKES SHAPE. THE LOUDER HIS VOICE BECOMES IN YOUR HEAD.
AND THERE ARE TWO IN THERE ALREADY, AREN'T THERE? YOU... AND ANGELUS.
YOUR HUMAN FRIENDS IMAGINE HIM AS AN EVIL THING LOCKED AWAY IN A VAULT, WHO ONLY CREEPS OUT IF YOU LOSE YOUR SOUL. BUT I KNOW BETTER.
HE'S ALWAYS THERE. TALKING TO YOU.
THAT'S NOT TRUE.
OF COURSE IT IS. LIKE A DEVIL ON YOUR SHOULDER, WHISPERING EVIL, TEMPTING THINGS...AND MY, HE'S A PERSUASIVE ONE, ISN'T HE? HE NEVER HAD TROUBLE GETTING INTO MY KNICKERS.
ANGELUS DOESN'T EXIST. NOT AS LONG AS I HAVE A SOUL. IT'S BEEN THAT WAY FOR OVER A CENTURY.
"HAS IT REALLY, ANGEL? OR HAS THERE BEEN THE ODD LITTLE SLIP? SHALL WE LOOK INTO YOUR MIND AND SEE?
"BACK IN THE SEVENTIES, WHEN THAT CASHIER WAS SHOT IN FRONT OF YOU. WHEN YOU FED ON THE BLOOD PUMPING OUT THE LAST OF HIS LIFE.
"WHO WAS URGING YOU ON?"

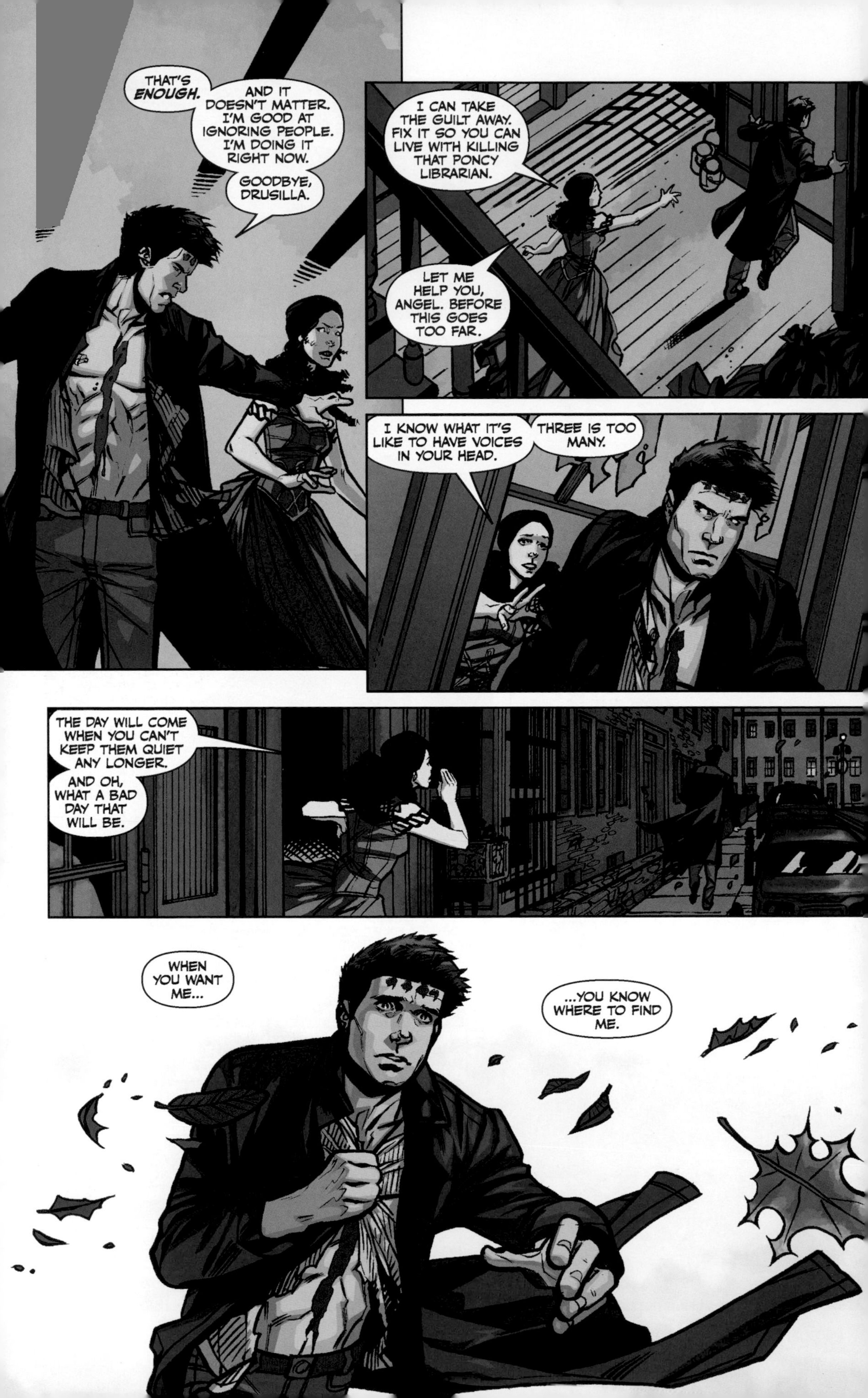
THAT'S *ENOUGH.*
AND IT DOESN'T MATTER. I'M GOOD AT IGNORING PEOPLE. I'M DOING IT RIGHT NOW.
GOODBYE, DRUSILLA.
I CAN TAKE THE GUILT AWAY. FIX IT SO YOU CAN LIVE WITH KILLING THAT PONCY LIBRARIAN.
LET ME HELP YOU, ANGEL. BEFORE THIS GOES TOO FAR.
I KNOW WHAT IT'S LIKE TO HAVE VOICES IN YOUR HEAD.
THREE IS TOO MANY.
THE DAY WILL COME WHEN YOU CAN'T KEEP THEM QUIET ANY LONGER.
AND OH, WHAT A BAD DAY THAT WILL BE.
WHEN YOU WANT ME...
...YOU KNOW WHERE TO FIND ME.

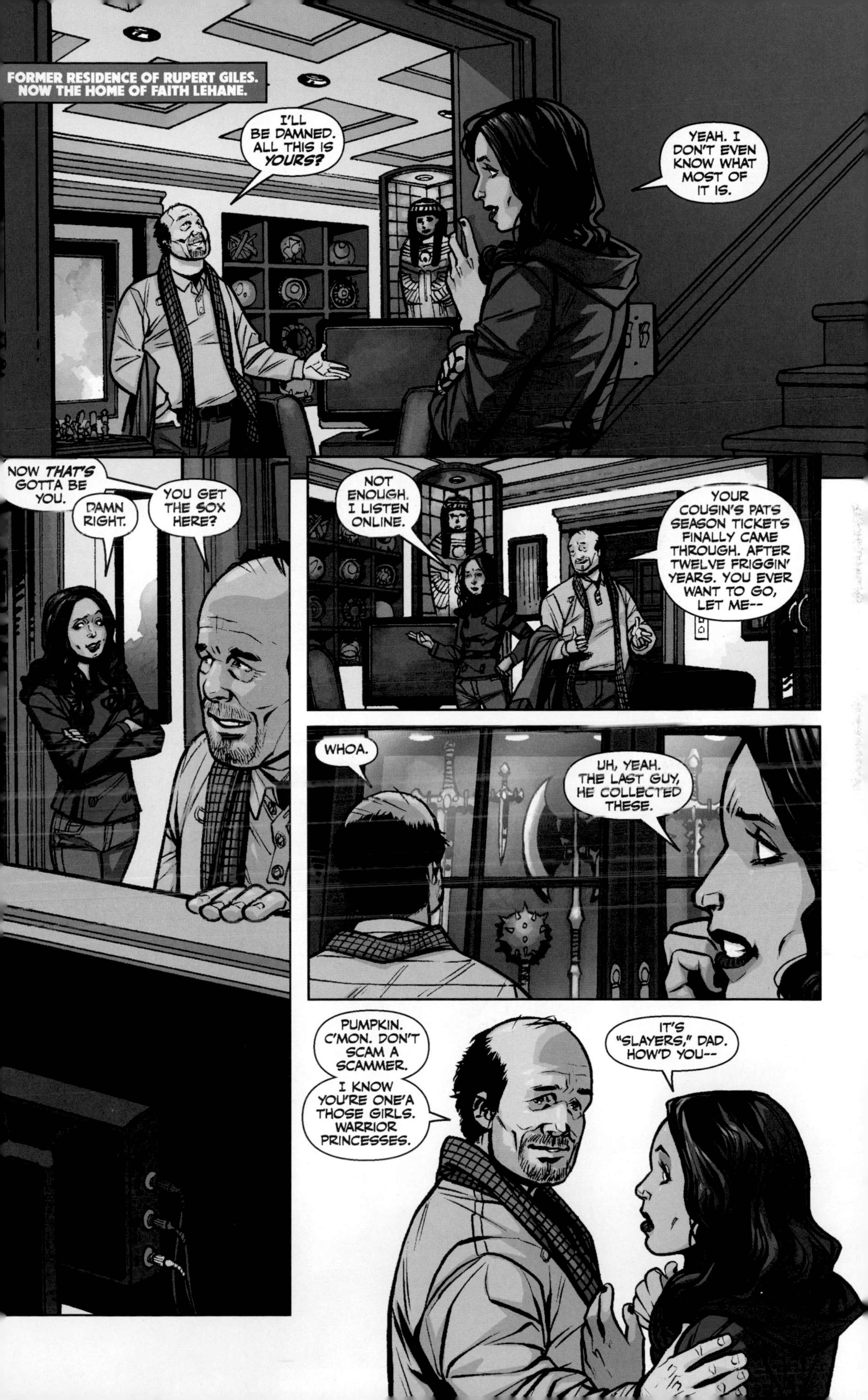
FORMER RESIDENCE OF RUPERT GILES. NOW THE HOME OF FAITH LEHANE.
I'LL BE DAMNED. ALL THIS IS YOURS?
YEAH. I DON'T EVEN KNOW WHAT MOST OF IT IS.
NOW THAT'S GOTTA BE YOU.
DAMN RIGHT.
YOU GET THE SOX HERE?
NOT ENOUGH. I LISTEN ONLINE.
YOUR COUSIN'S PATS SEASON TICKETS FINALLY CAME THROUGH. AFTER TWELVE FRIGGIN' YEARS. YOU EVER WANT TO GO, LET ME--
WHOA.
UH, YEAH. THE LAST GUY, HE COLLECTED THESE.
PUMPKIN. C'MON. DON'T SCAM A SCAMMER.
I KNOW YOU'RE ONE'A THOSE GIRLS. WARRIOR PRINCESSES.
IT'S "SLAYERS," DAD. HOW'D YOU--

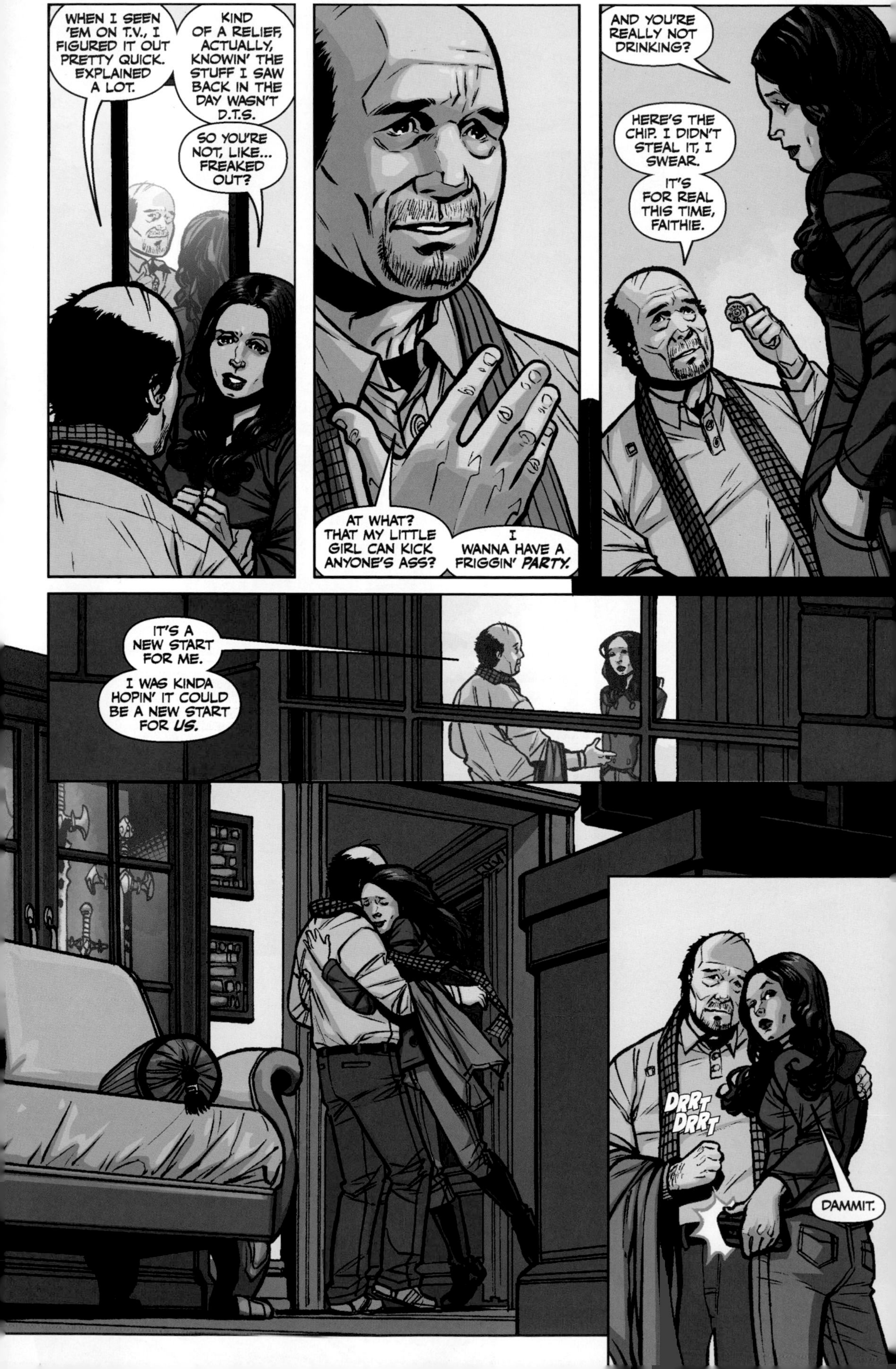
WHEN I SEEN 'EM ON T.V., I FIGURED IT OUT PRETTY QUICK. EXPLAINED A LOT.
KIND OF A RELIEF, ACTUALLY, KNOWIN' THE STUFF I SAW BACK IN THE DAY WASN'T D.T.S.
SO YOU'RE NOT, LIKE... FREAKED OUT?
AT WHAT? THAT MY LITTLE GIRL CAN KICK ANYONE'S ASS?
I WANNA HAVE A FRIGGIN' PARTY.
AND YOU'RE REALLY NOT DRINKING?
HERE'S THE CHIP. I DIDN'T STEAL IT, I SWEAR.
IT'S FOR REAL THIS TIME, FAITHIE.
IT'S A NEW START FOR ME.
I WAS KINDA HOPIN' IT COULD BE A NEW START FOR US.
DRRT DRRT
DAMMIT.

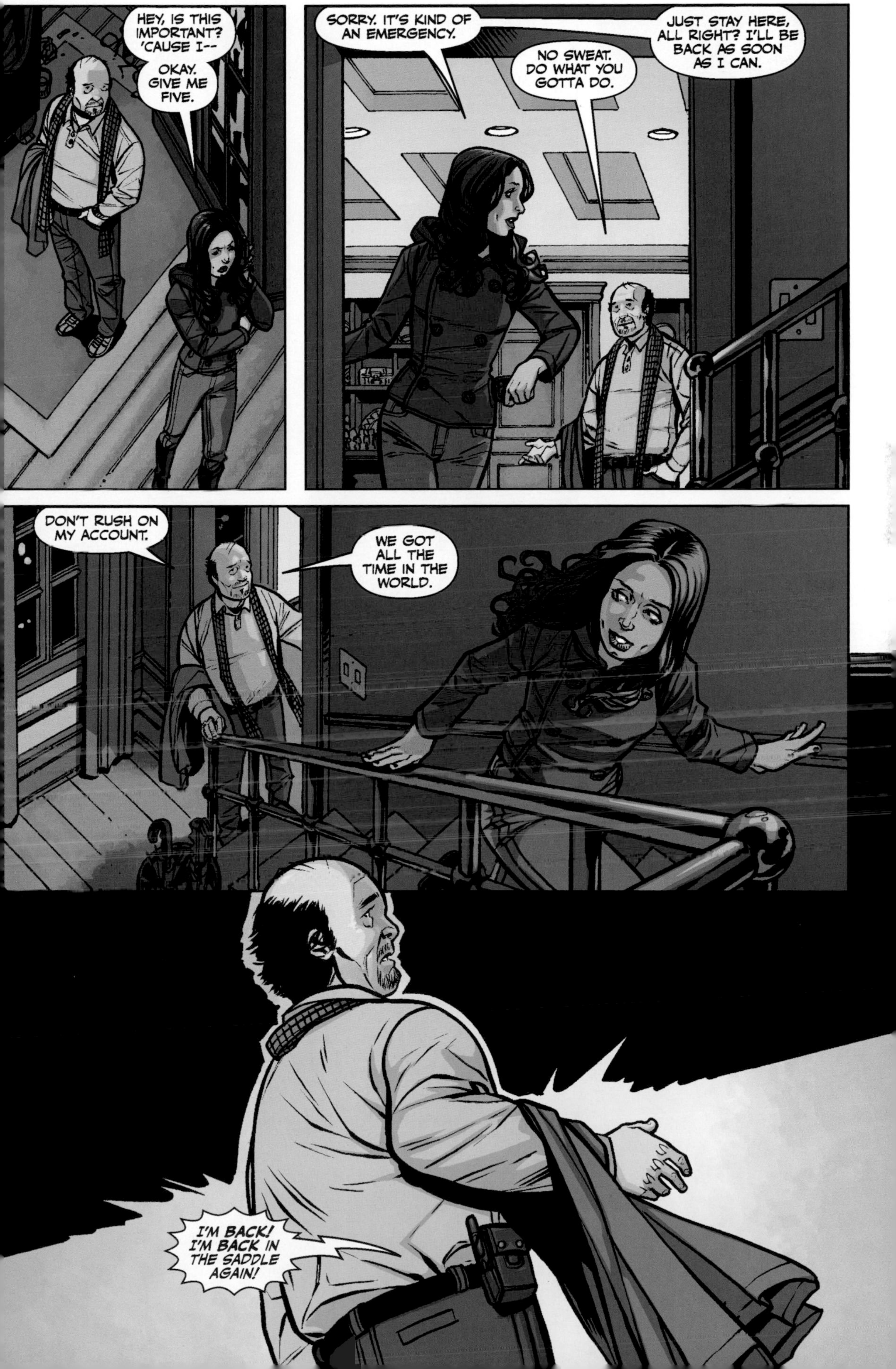
HEY, IS THIS IMPORTANT? 'CAUSE I--
OKAY. GIVE ME FIVE.
SORRY. IT'S KIND OF AN EMERGENCY.
JUST STAY HERE, ALL RIGHT? I'LL BE BACK AS SOON AS I CAN.
NO SWEAT. DO WHAT YOU GOTTA DO.
DON'T RUSH ON MY ACCOUNT.
WE GOT ALL THE TIME IN THE WORLD.
I'M BACK! I'M BACK IN THE SADDLE AGAIN!

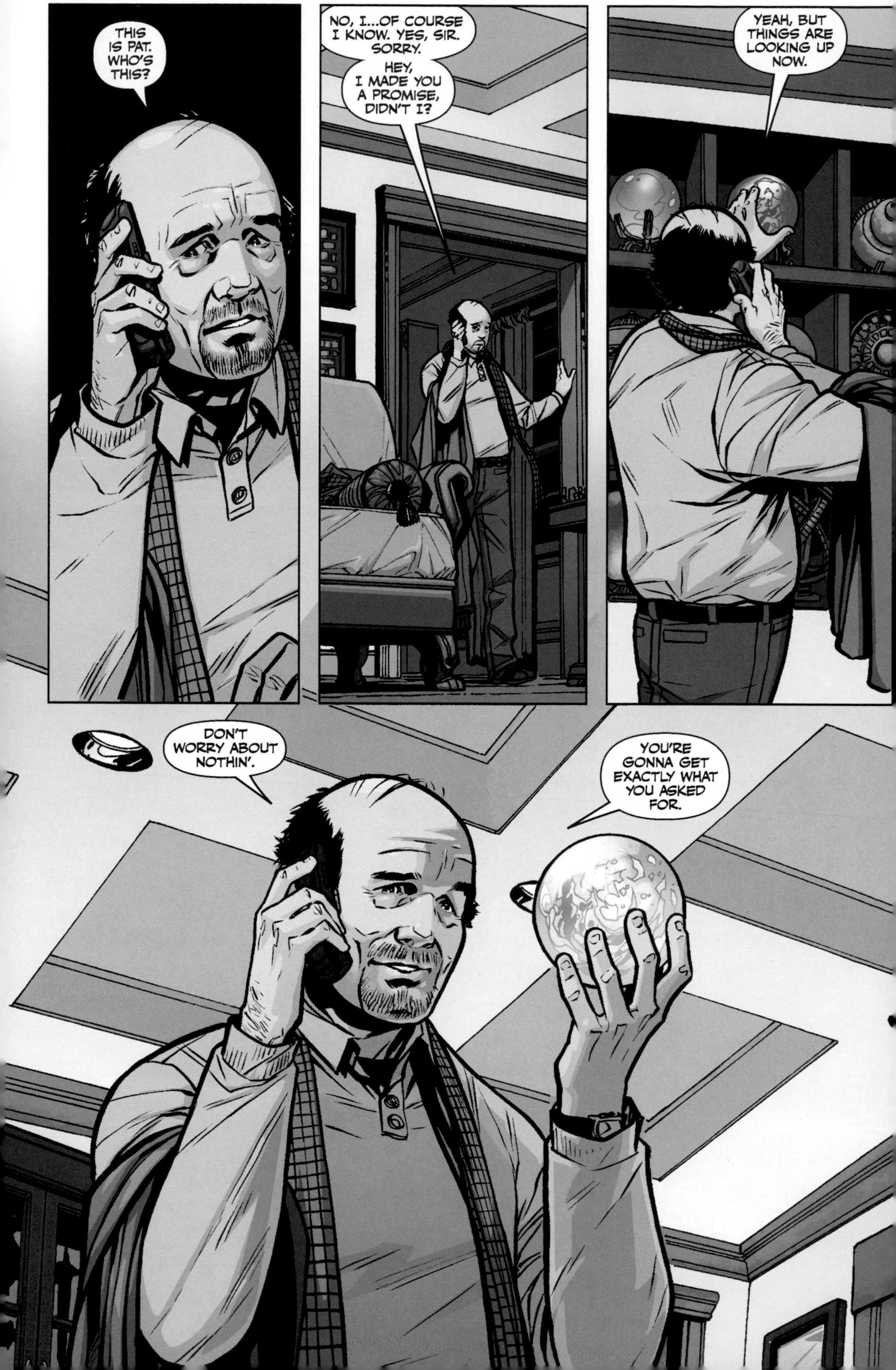
THIS IS PAT. WHO'S THIS?
NO, I...OF COURSE I KNOW. YES, SIR. SORRY.
HEY, I MADE YOU A PROMISE, DIDN'T I?
YEAH, BUT THINGS ARE LOOKING UP NOW.
DON'T WORRY ABOUT NOTHIN'.
YOU'RE GONNA GET EXACTLY WHAT YOU ASKED FOR.

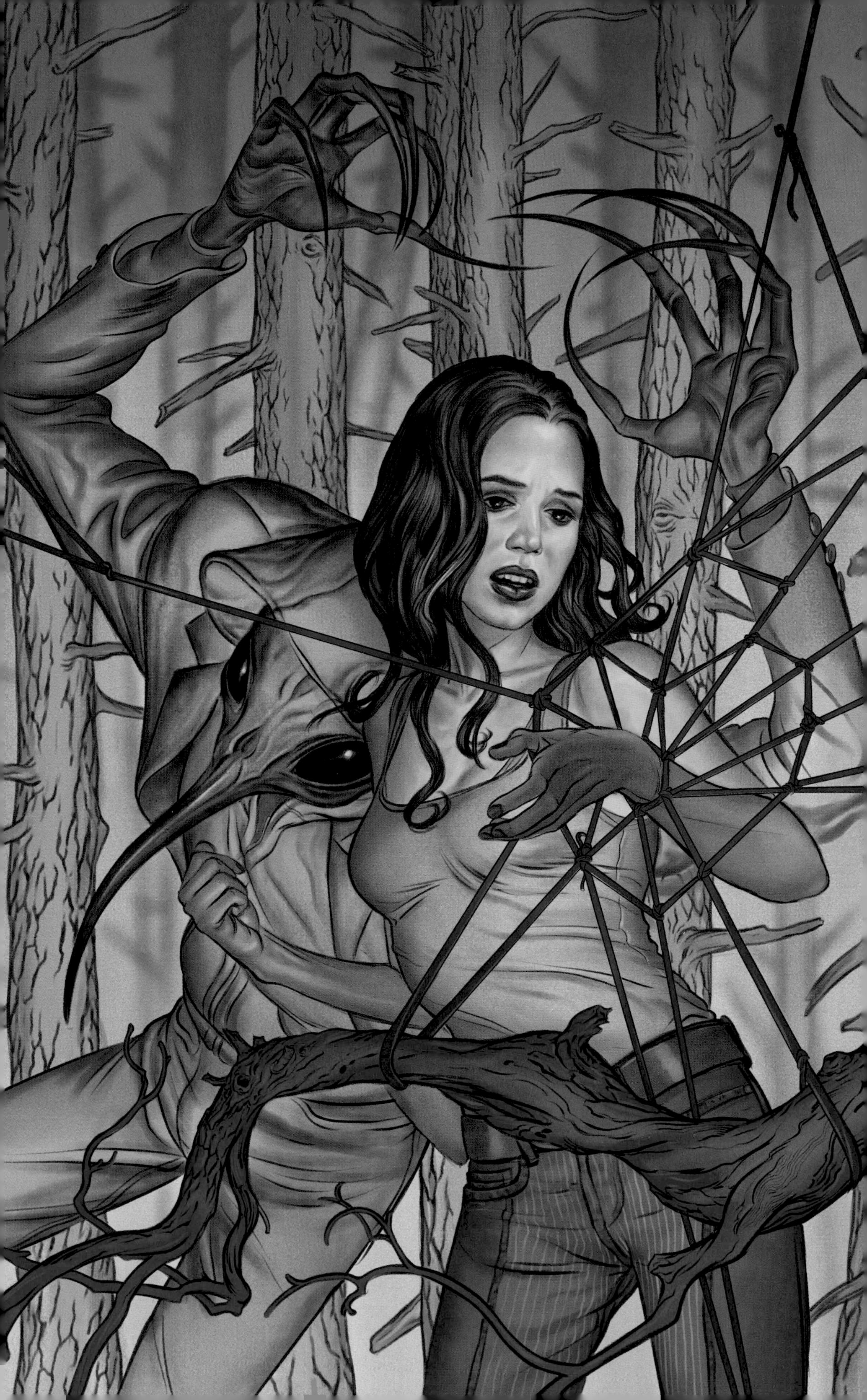

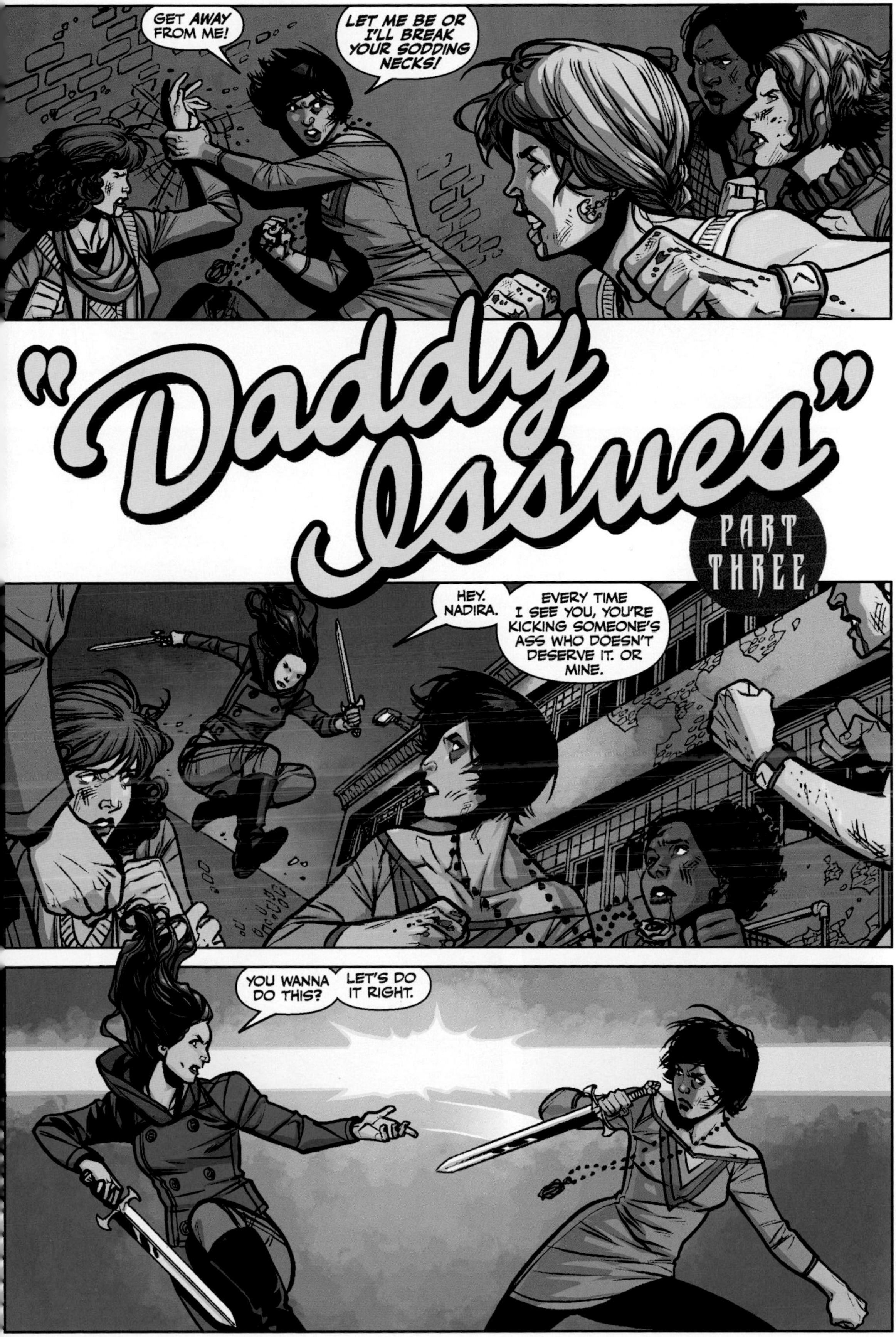
GET AWAY FROM ME!
LET ME BE OR I'LL BREAK YOUR SODDING NECKS!
"Daddy Issues"
PART THREE
HEY. NADIRA.
EVERY TIME I SEE YOU, YOU'RE KICKING SOMEONE'S ASS WHO DOESN'T DESERVE IT. OR MINE.
YOU WANNA DO THIS?
LET'S DO IT RIGHT.

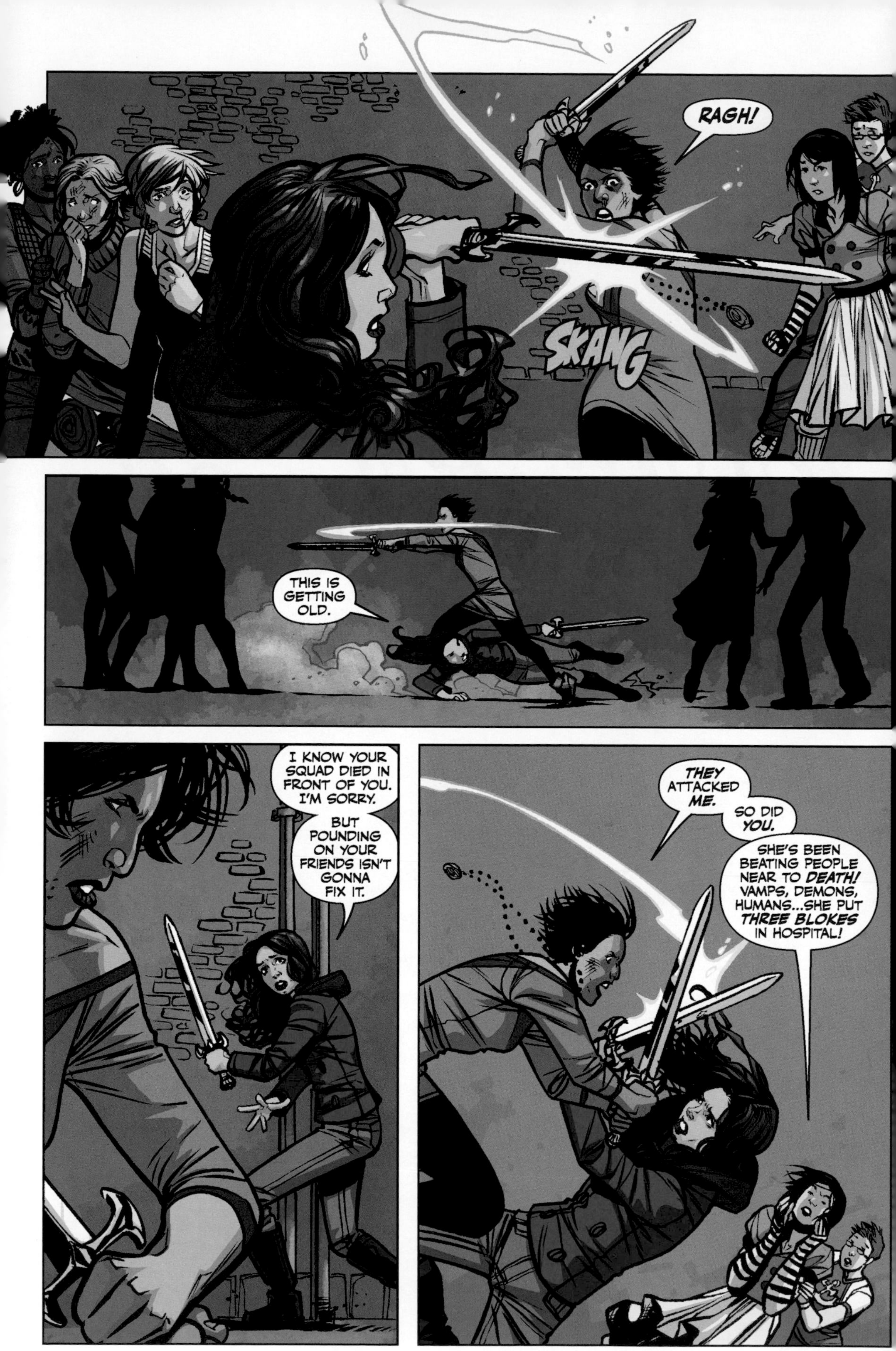
RAGH!
SKANG
THIS IS GETTING OLD.
I KNOW YOUR SQUAD DIED IN FRONT OF YOU. I'M SORRY.
BUT POUNDING ON YOUR FRIENDS ISN'T GONNA FIX IT.
THEY ATTACKED ME.
SO DID YOU.
SHE'S BEEN BEATING PEOPLE NEAR TO DEATH! VAMPS, DEMONS, HUMANS...SHE PUT THREE BLOKES IN HOSPITAL!

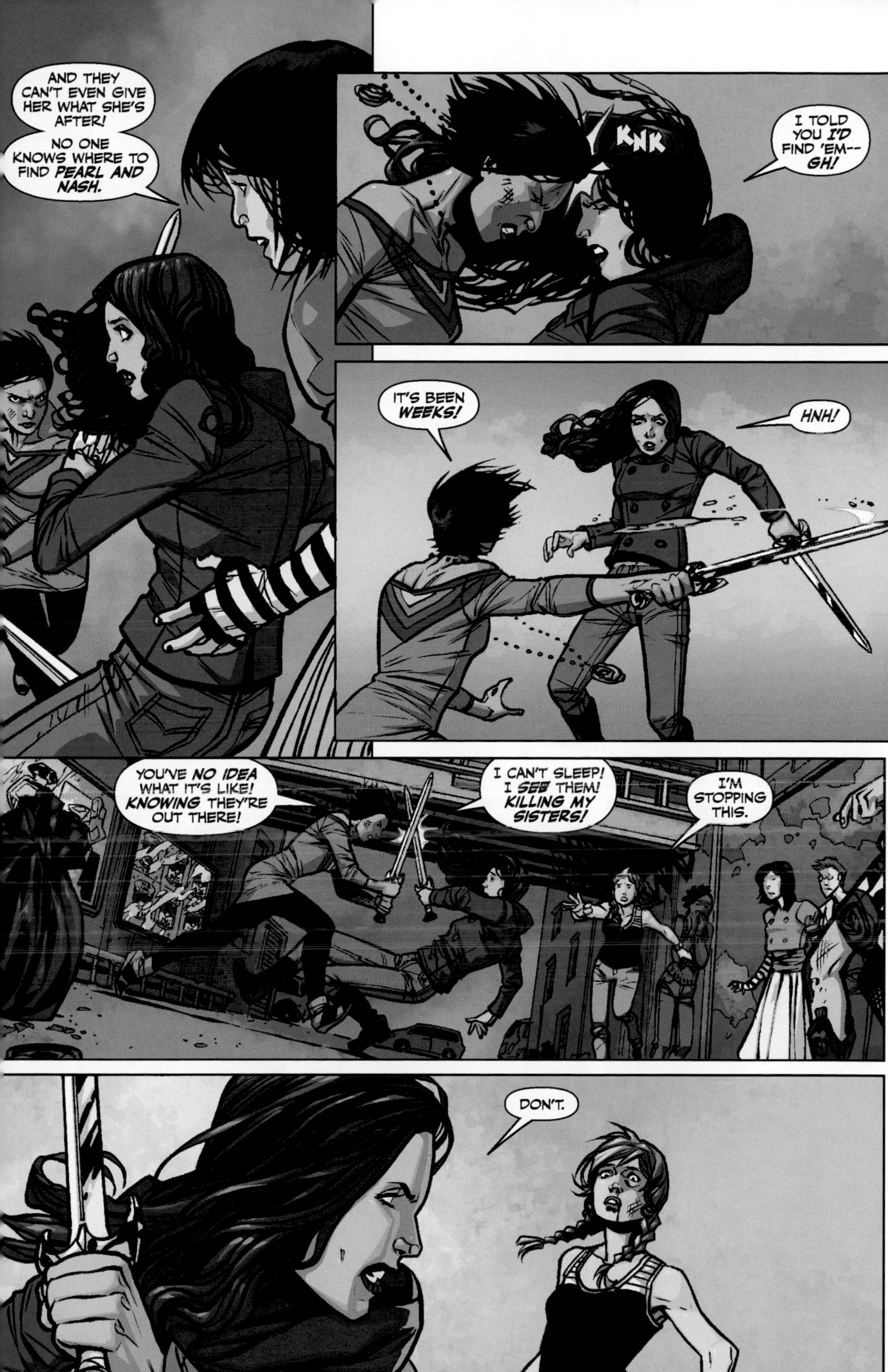
AND THEY CAN'T EVEN GIVE HER WHAT SHE'S AFTER!
NO ONE KNOWS WHERE TO FIND PEARL AND NASH.
KNK
I TOLD YOU I'D FIND 'EM-- GH!
IT'S BEEN WEEKS!
HNH!
YOU'VE NO IDEA WHAT IT'S LIKE! KNOWING THEY'RE OUT THERE!
I CAN'T SLEEP! I SEE THEM! KILLING MY SISTERS!
I'M STOPPING THIS.
DON'T.

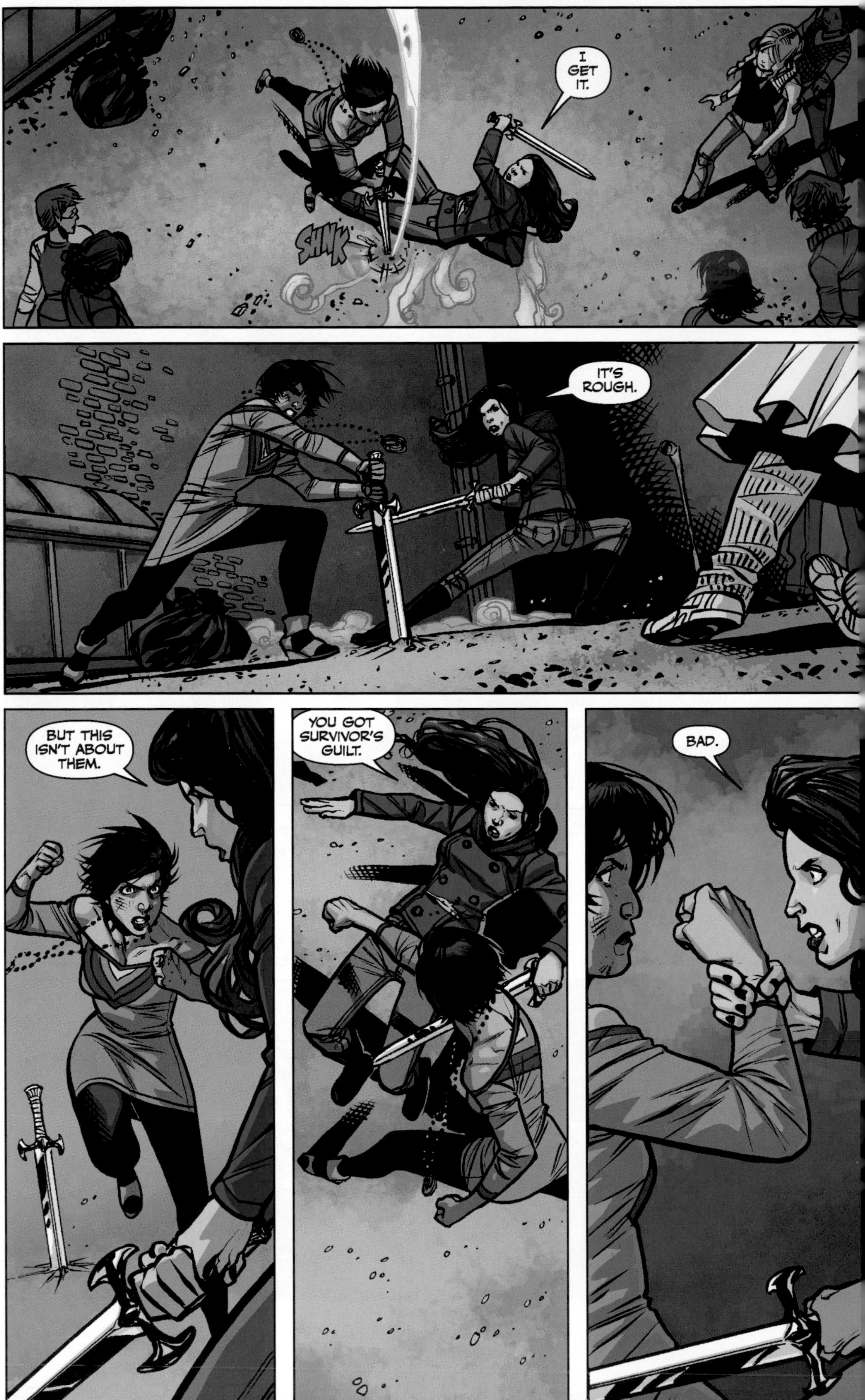
I GET IT.
SHNK
IT'S ROUGH.
BUT THIS ISN'T ABOUT THEM.
YOU GOT SURVIVOR'S GUILT.
BAD.

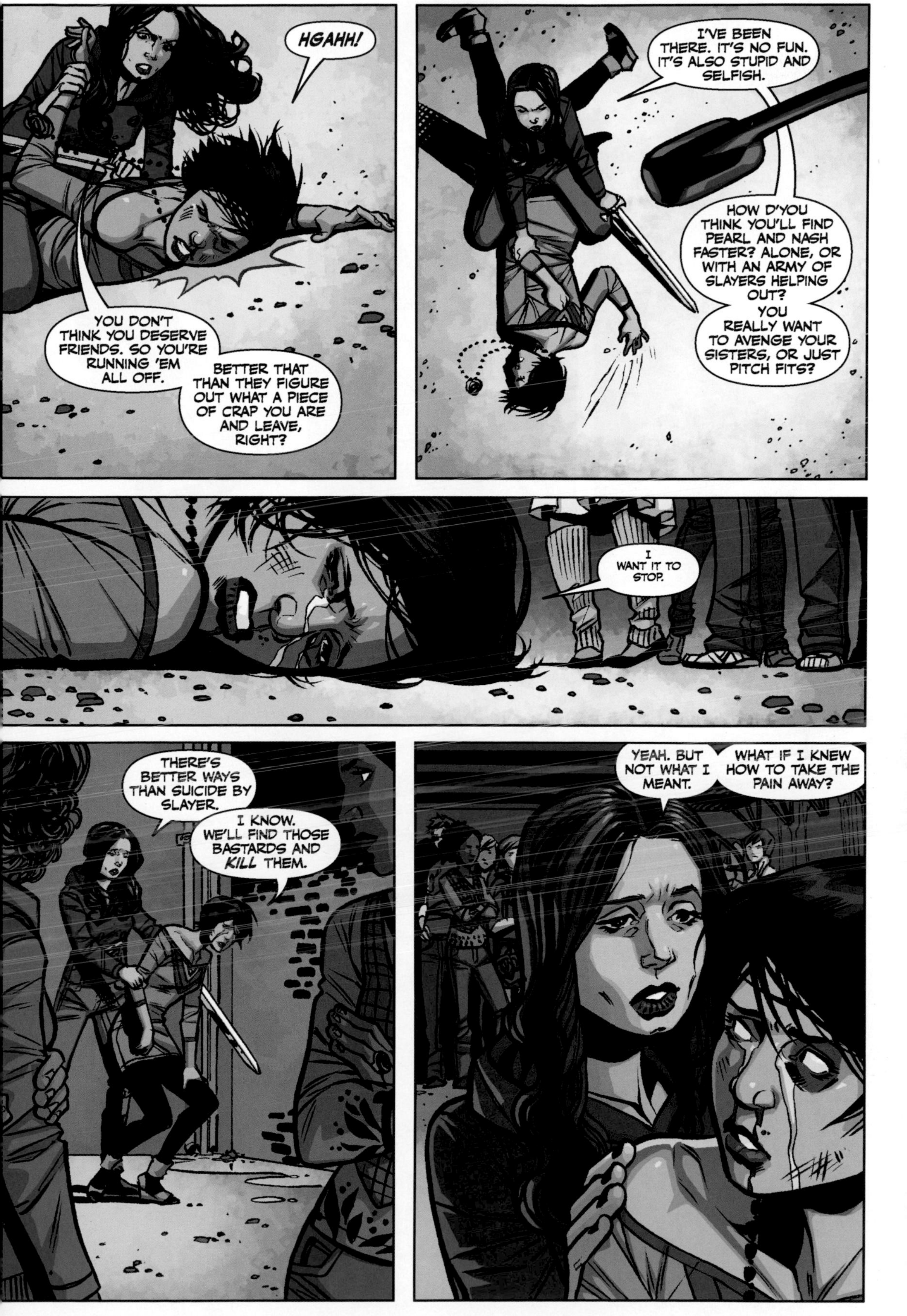
HGAHH!
YOU DON'T THINK YOU DESERVE FRIENDS. SO YOU'RE RUNNING 'EM ALL OFF.
BETTER THAT THAN THEY FIGURE OUT WHAT A PIECE OF CRAP YOU ARE AND LEAVE, RIGHT?
I'VE BEEN THERE. IT'S NO FUN. IT'S ALSO STUPID AND SELFISH.
HOW D'YOU THINK YOU'LL FIND PEARL AND NASH FASTER? ALONE, OR WITH AN ARMY OF SLAYERS HELPING OUT?
YOU REALLY WANT TO AVENGE YOUR SISTERS, OR JUST PITCH FITS?
I WANT IT TO STOP.
THERE'S BETTER WAYS THAN SUICIDE BY SLAYER.
I KNOW. WE'LL FIND THOSE BASTARDS AND KILL THEM.
YEAH. BUT NOT WHAT I MEANT.
WHAT IF I KNEW HOW TO TAKE THE PAIN AWAY?

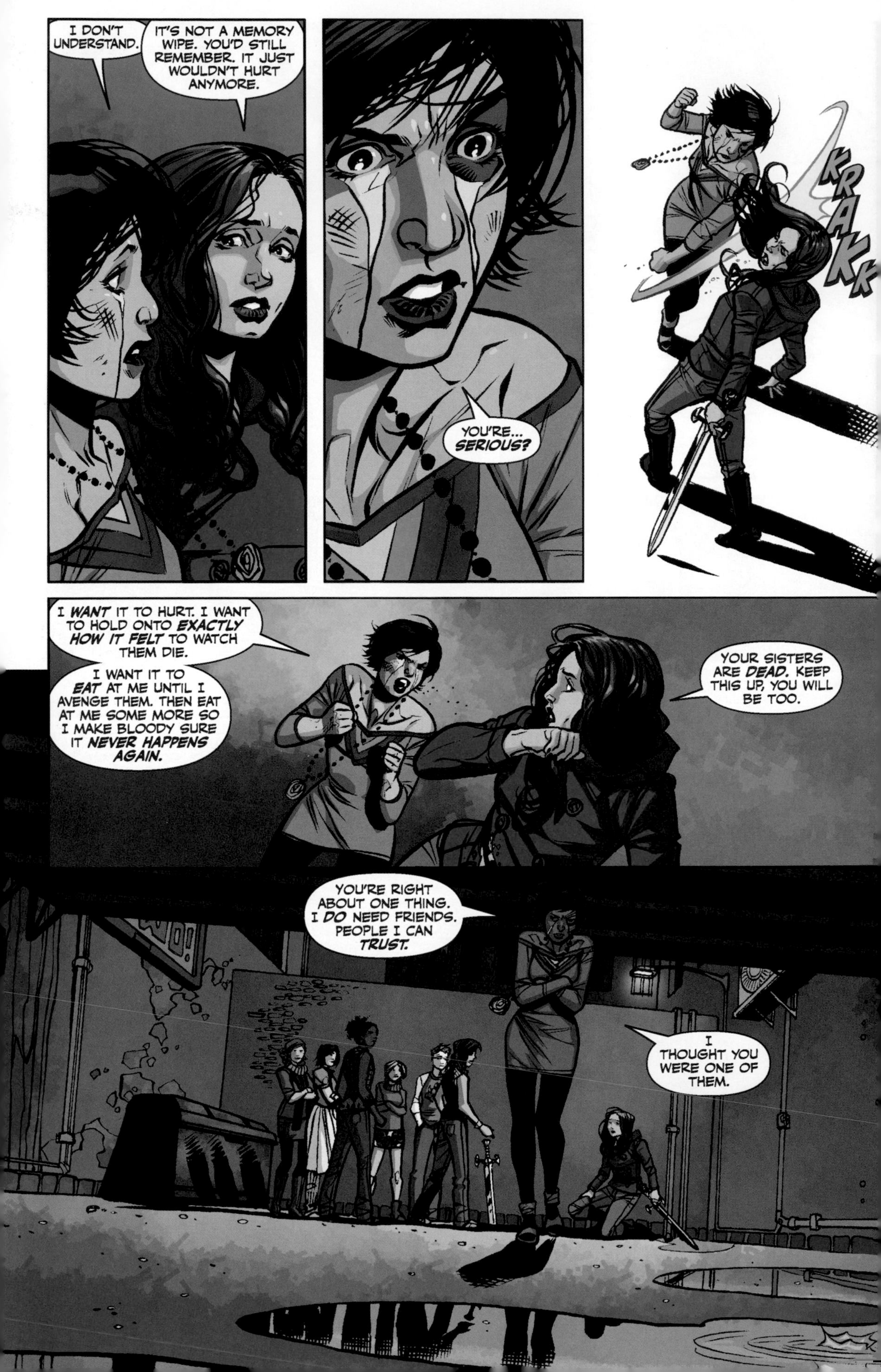
I DON'T UNDERSTAND.
IT'S NOT A MEMORY WIPE. YOU'D STILL REMEMBER. IT JUST WOULDN'T HURT ANYMORE.
YOU'RE... SERIOUS?
KRAKK
I WANT IT TO HURT. I WANT TO HOLD ONTO EXACTLY HOW IT FELT TO WATCH THEM DIE.
I WANT IT TO EAT AT ME UNTIL I AVENGE THEM. THEN EAT AT ME SOME MORE SO I MAKE BLOODY SURE IT NEVER HAPPENS AGAIN.
YOUR SISTERS ARE DEAD. KEEP THIS UP, YOU WILL BE TOO.
YOU'RE RIGHT ABOUT ONE THING. I DO NEED FRIENDS. PEOPLE I CAN TRUST.
I THOUGHT YOU WERE ONE OF THEM.

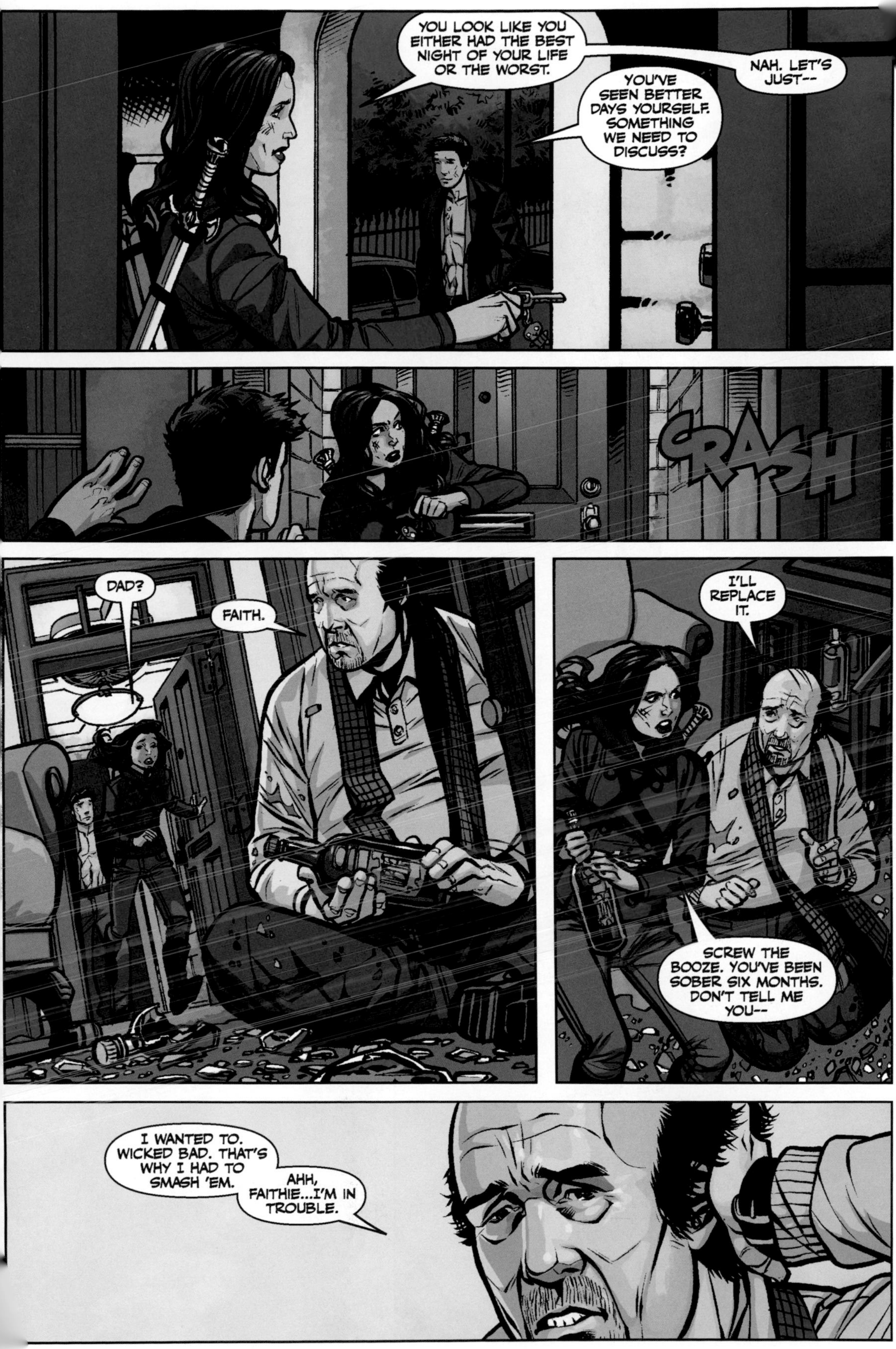
YOU LOOK LIKE YOU EITHER HAD THE BEST NIGHT OF YOUR LIFE OR THE WORST.
NAH. LET'S JUST--
YOU'VE SEEN BETTER DAYS YOURSELF. SOMETHING WE NEED TO DISCUSS?
CRASH
DAD?
FAITH.
I'LL REPLACE IT.
SCREW THE BOOZE. YOU'VE BEEN SOBER SIX MONTHS. DON'T TELL ME YOU--
I WANTED TO. WICKED BAD. THAT'S WHY I HAD TO SMASH 'EM.
AHH, FAITHIE...I'M IN TROUBLE.

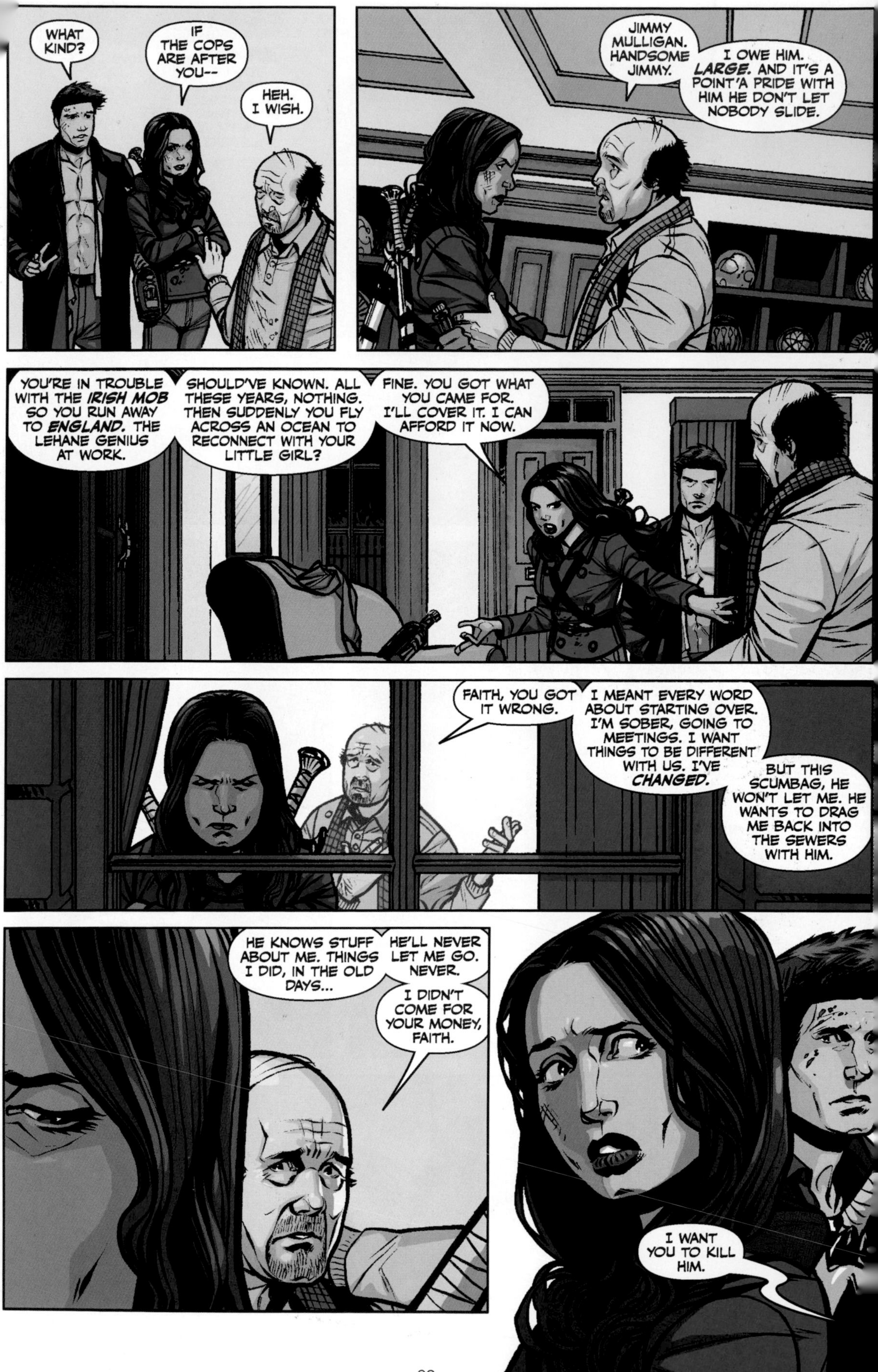
WHAT KIND?
IF THE COPS ARE AFTER YOU--
HEH. I WISH.
JIMMY MULLIGAN. HANDSOME JIMMY.
I OWE HIM. LARGE. AND IT'S A POINT'A PRIDE WITH HIM HE DON'T LET NOBODY SLIDE.
YOU'RE IN TROUBLE WITH THE IRISH MOB SO YOU RUN AWAY TO ENGLAND. THE LEHANE GENIUS AT WORK.
SHOULD'VE KNOWN. ALL THESE YEARS, NOTHING. THEN SUDDENLY YOU FLY ACROSS AN OCEAN TO RECONNECT WITH YOUR LITTLE GIRL?
FINE. YOU GOT WHAT YOU CAME FOR. I'LL COVER IT. I CAN AFFORD IT NOW.
FAITH, YOU GOT IT WRONG.
I MEANT EVERY WORD ABOUT STARTING OVER. I'M SOBER, GOING TO MEETINGS. I WANT THINGS TO BE DIFFERENT WITH US. I'VE CHANGED.
BUT THIS SCUMBAG, HE WON'T LET ME. HE WANTS TO DRAG ME BACK INTO THE SEWERS WITH HIM.
HE KNOWS STUFF ABOUT ME. THINGS I DID, IN THE OLD DAYS...
HE'LL NEVER LET ME GO. NEVER.
I DIDN'T COME FOR YOUR MONEY, FAITH.
I WANT YOU TO KILL HIM.

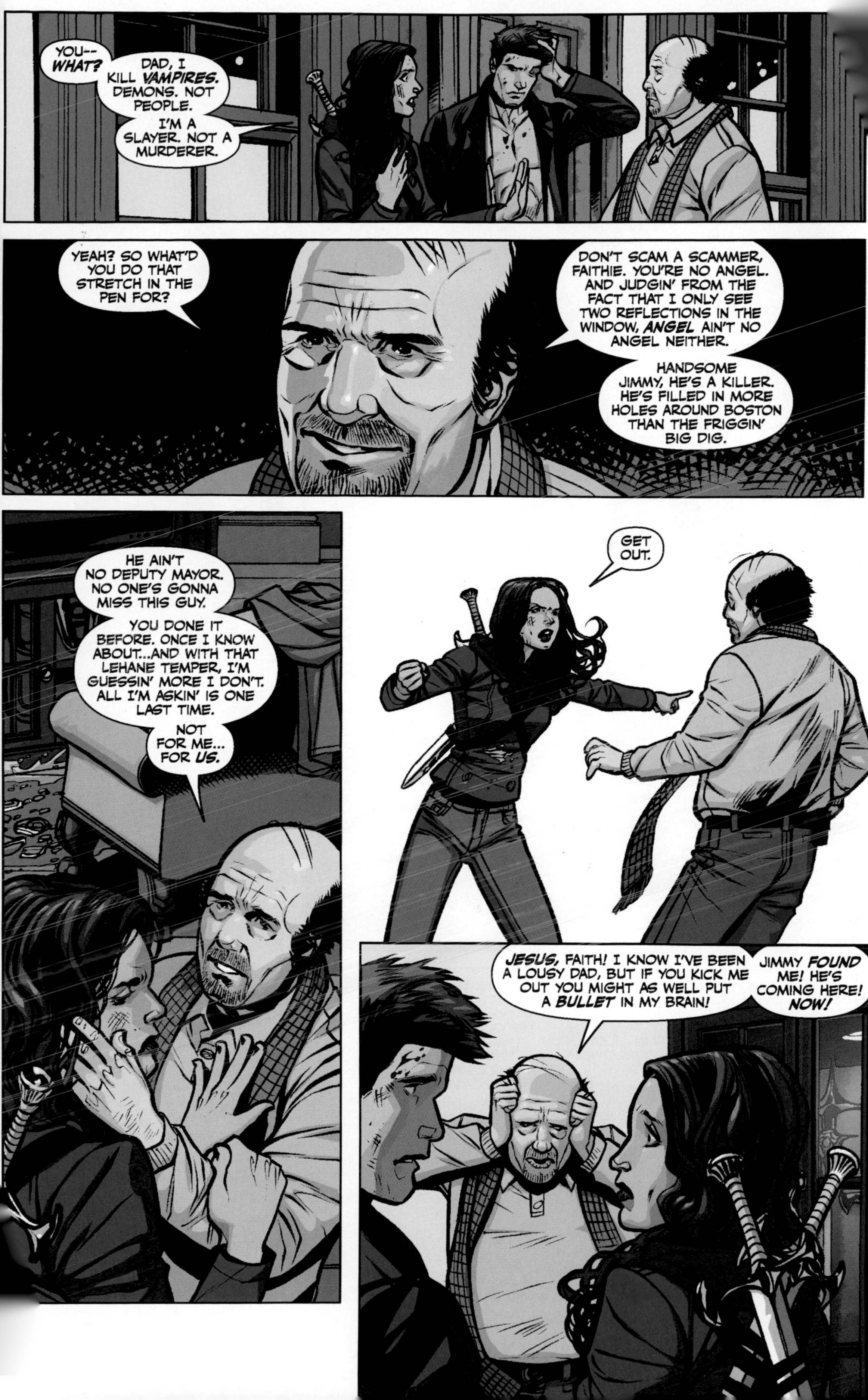
YOU-- WHAT?
DAD, I KILL VAMPIRES. DEMONS. NOT PEOPLE.
I'M A SLAYER. NOT A MURDERER.
YEAH? SO WHAT'D YOU DO THAT STRETCH IN THE PEN FOR?
DON'T SCAM A SCAMMER, FAITHIE. YOU'RE NO ANGEL. AND JUDGIN' FROM THE FACT THAT I ONLY SEE TWO REFLECTIONS IN THE WINDOW, ANGEL AIN'T NO ANGEL NEITHER.
HANDSOME JIMMY, HE'S A KILLER. HE'S FILLED IN MORE HOLES AROUND BOSTON THAN THE FRIGGIN' BIG DIG.
HE AIN'T NO DEPUTY MAYOR. NO ONE'S GONNA MISS THIS GUY.
YOU DONE IT BEFORE. ONCE I KNOW ABOUT...AND WITH THAT LEHANE TEMPER, I'M GUESSIN' MORE I DON'T. ALL I'M ASKIN' IS ONE LAST TIME.
NOT FOR ME... FOR US.
GET OUT.
JESUS, FAITH! I KNOW I'VE BEEN A LOUSY DAD, BUT IF YOU KICK ME OUT YOU MIGHT AS WELL PUT A BULLET IN MY BRAIN!
JIMMY FOUND ME! HE'S COMING HERE! NOW!

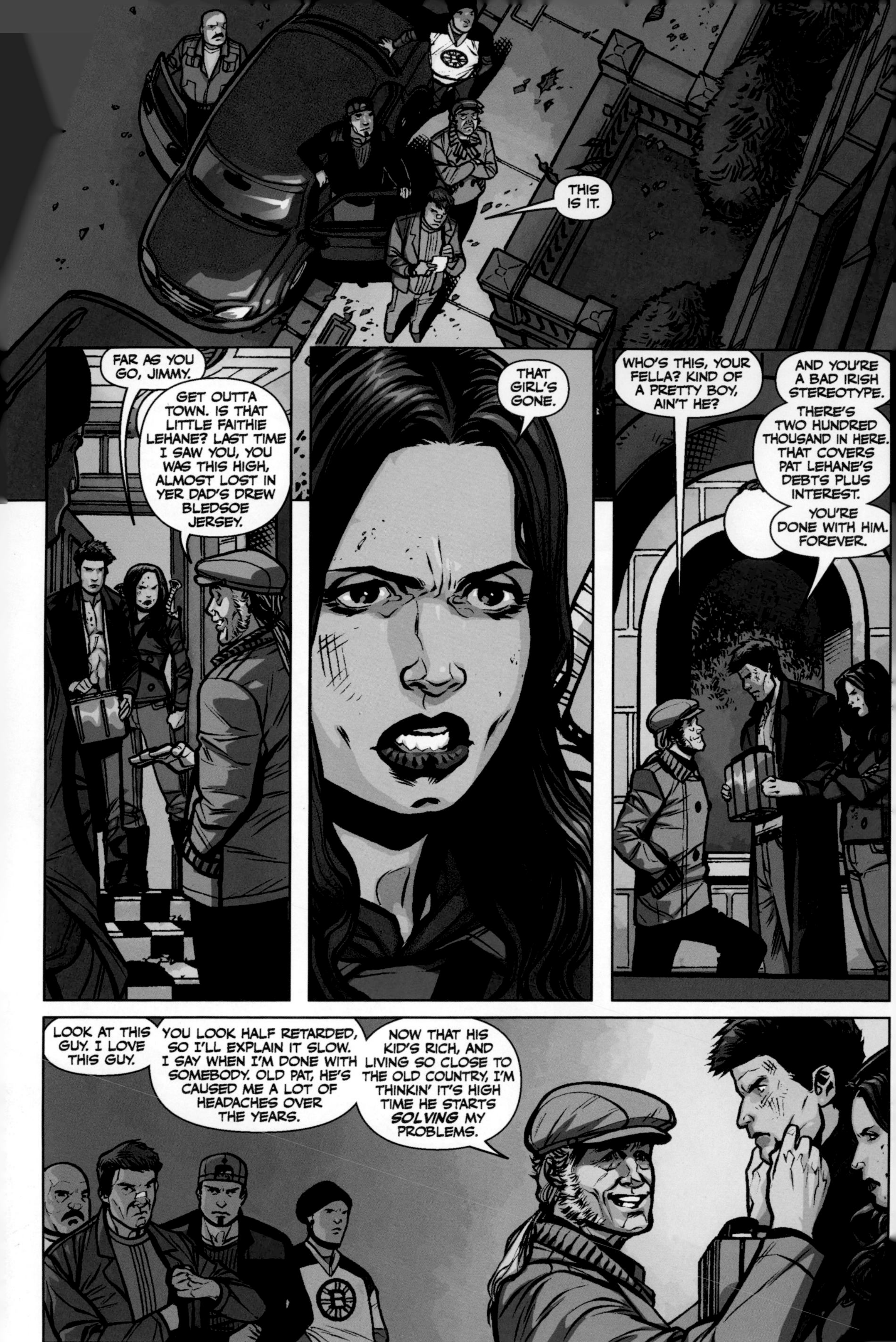
THIS IS IT.
FAR AS YOU GO, JIMMY.
GET OUTTA TOWN. IS THAT LITTLE FAITHIE LEHANE? LAST TIME I SAW YOU, YOU WAS THIS HIGH, ALMOST LOST IN YER DAD'S DREW BLEDSOE JERSEY.
THAT GIRL'S GONE.
WHO'S THIS, YOUR FELLA? KIND OF A PRETTY BOY, AIN'T HE?
AND YOU'RE A BAD IRISH STEREOTYPE.
THERE'S TWO HUNDRED THOUSAND IN HERE. THAT COVERS PAT LEHANE'S DEBTS PLUS INTEREST.
YOU'RE DONE WITH HIM. FOREVER.
LOOK AT THIS GUY. I LOVE THIS GUY.
YOU LOOK HALF RETARDED, SO I'LL EXPLAIN IT SLOW. I SAY WHEN I'M DONE WITH SOMEBODY. OLD PAT, HE'S CAUSED ME A LOT OF HEADACHES OVER THE YEARS.
NOW THAT HIS KID'S RICH, AND LIVING SO CLOSE TO THE OLD COUNTRY, I'M THINKIN' IT'S HIGH TIME HE STARTS *SOLVING* MY PROBLEMS.

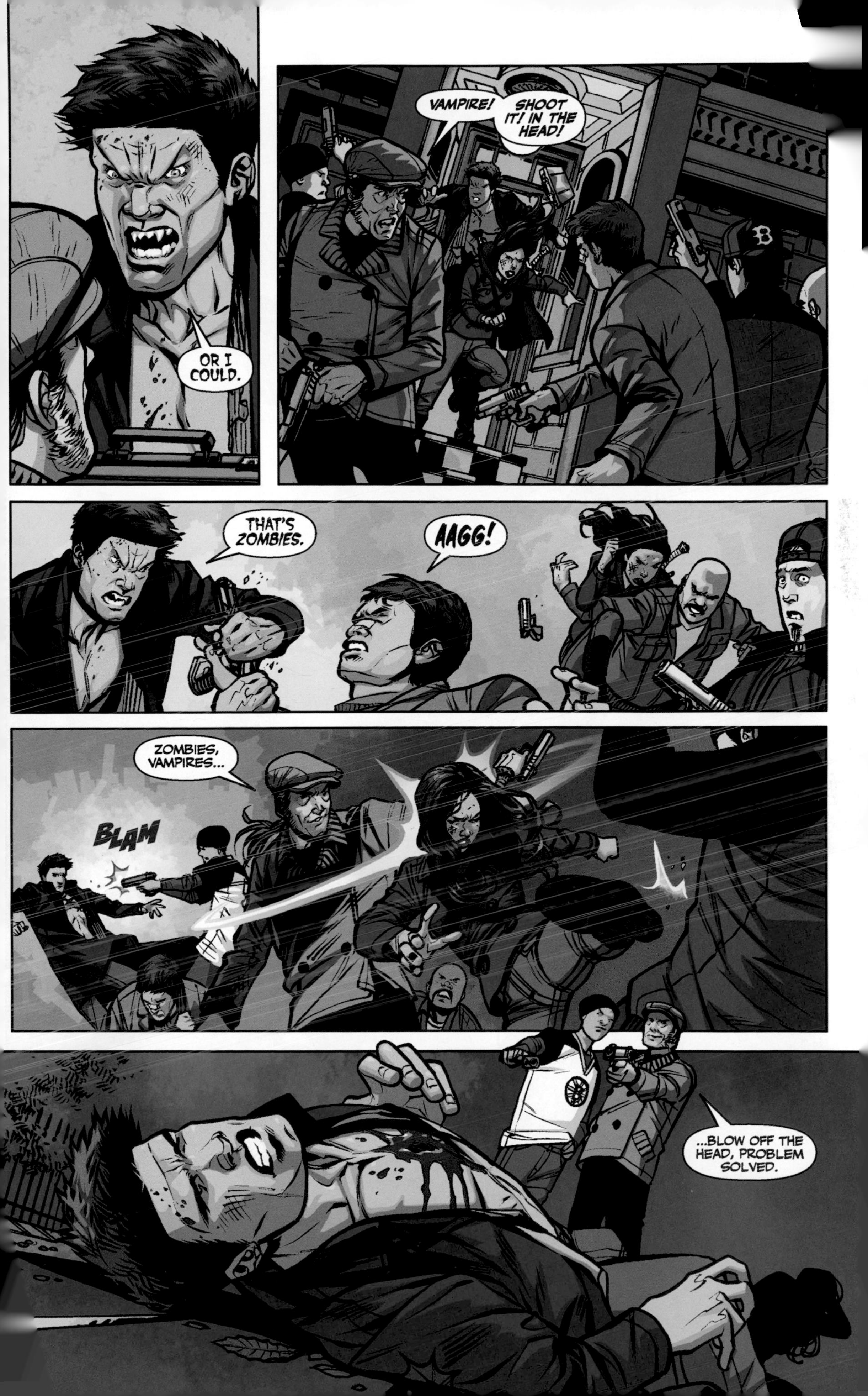
OR I COULD.
VAMPIRE!
SHOOT IT! IN THE HEAD!
THAT'S ZOMBIES.
AAGG!
ZOMBIES, VAMPIRES...
BLAM
...BLOW OFF THE HEAD, PROBLEM SOLVED.

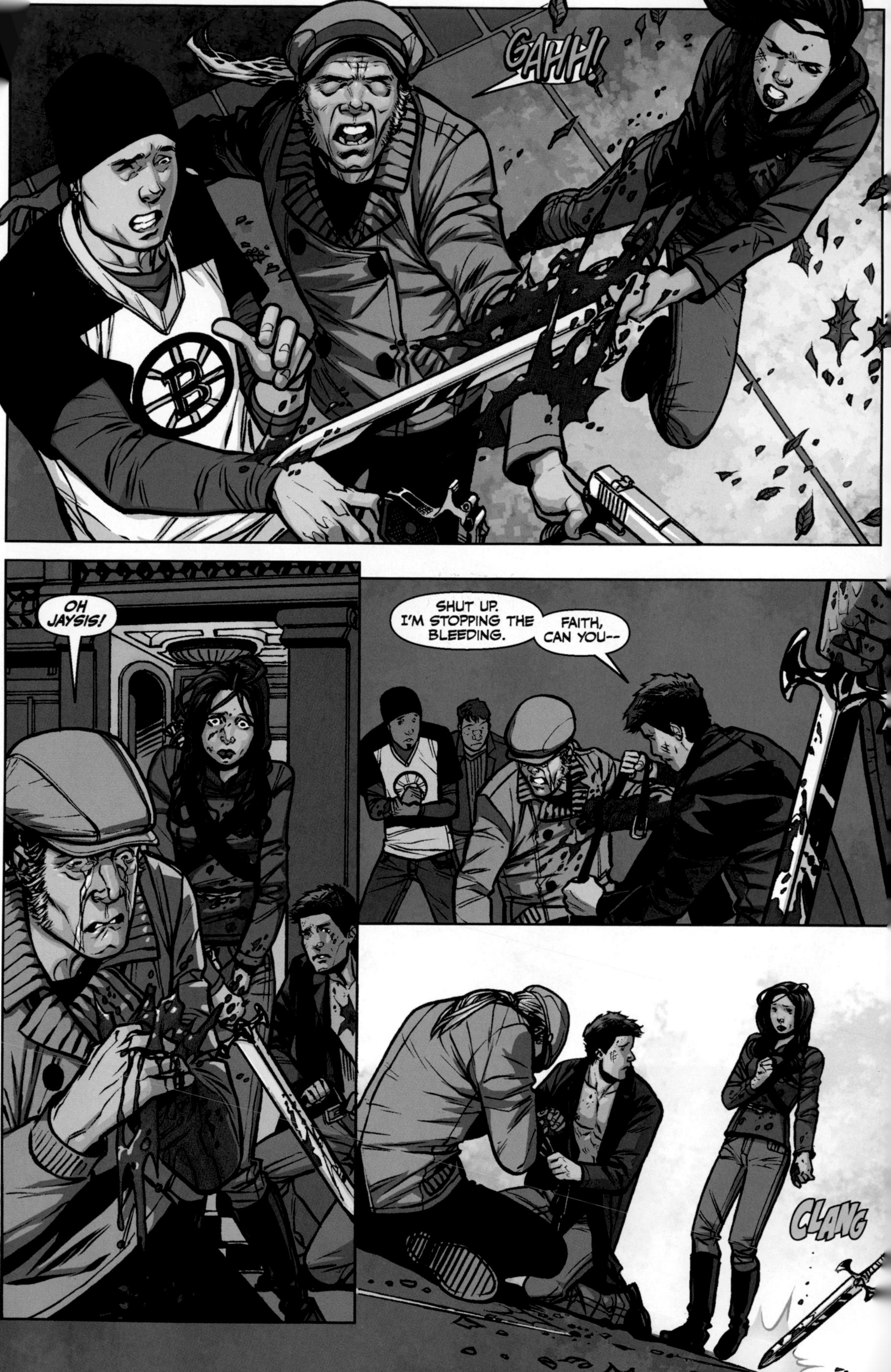
GAHH!
OH JAYSIS!
SHUT UP. I'M STOPPING THE BLEEDING.
FAITH, CAN YOU--
CLANG

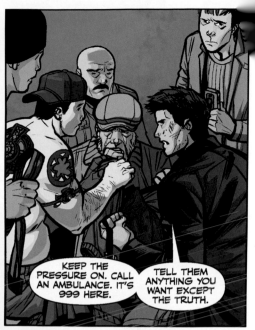

OKAY--YOU. SEE WHAT I'M DOING? TAKE OFF YOUR BELT AND DO IT TO YOURSELF. AND *YOU*--GIVE ME YOUR SHIRT.

KEEP THE PRESSURE ON. CALL AN AMBULANCE. IT'S 999 HERE.

TELL THEM ANYTHING YOU WANT EXCEPT THE TRUTH.

TAKE YOUR MONEY. GO BACK TO BOSTON. NEVER BOTHER US AGAIN.

'CAUSE WHAT I'D REALLY LIKE TO DO WITH THIS ARM IS DRINK FROM IT LIKE A HOSE.

AND IF YOU *REALLY* SCREW UP, YOU'LL DEAL WITH *HER*. WE CLEAR?

YES SIR.

GOOD.

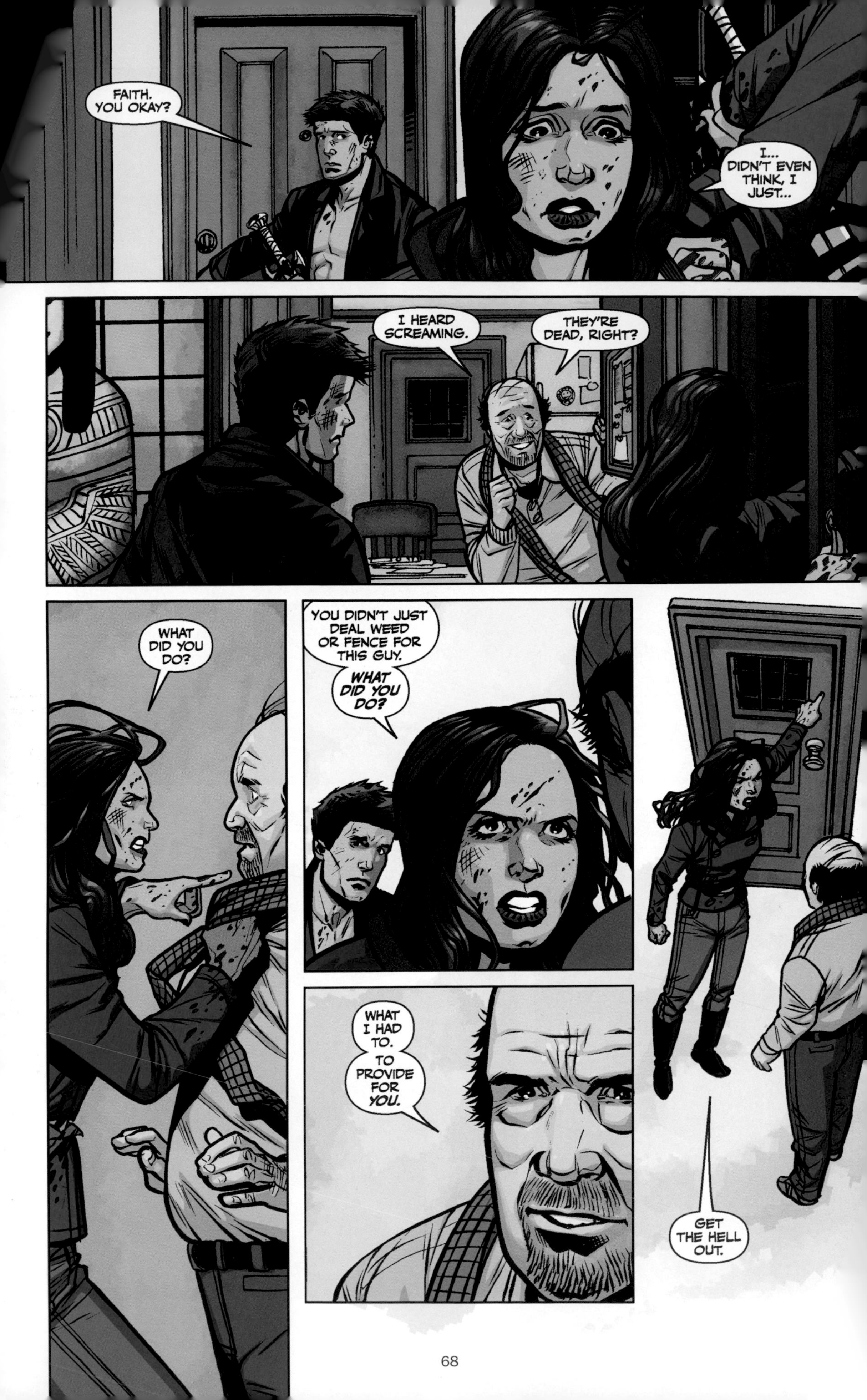
FAITH. YOU OKAY?
I... DIDN'T EVEN THINK, I JUST...
I HEARD SCREAMING.
THEY'RE DEAD, RIGHT?
WHAT DID YOU DO?
YOU DIDN'T JUST DEAL WEED OR FENCE FOR THIS GUY.
WHAT DID YOU DO?
WHAT I HAD TO.
TO PROVIDE FOR *YOU.*
GET THE HELL OUT.

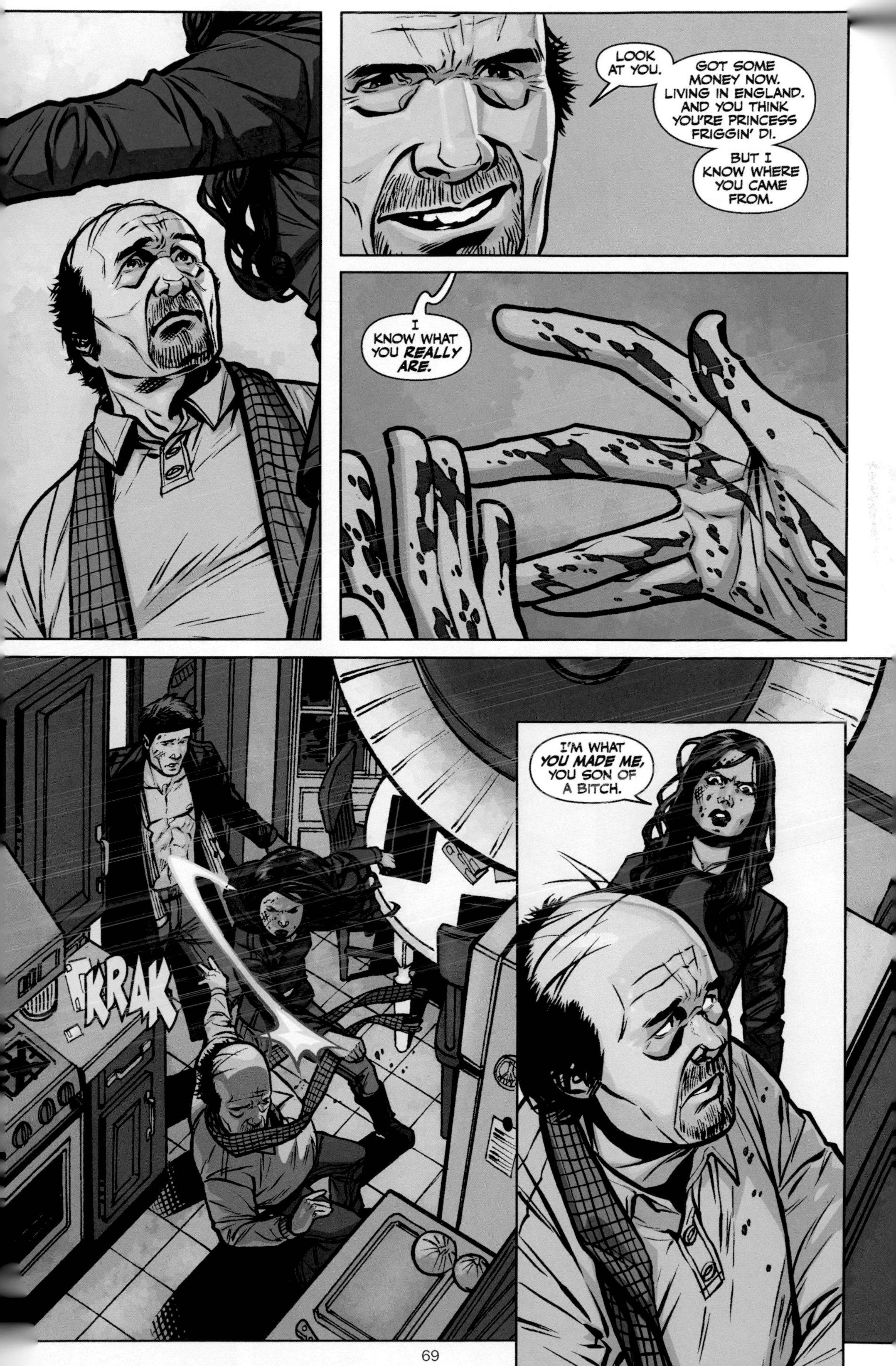
LOOK AT YOU.
GOT SOME MONEY NOW. LIVING IN ENGLAND. AND YOU THINK YOU'RE PRINCESS FRIGGIN' DI.
BUT I KNOW WHERE YOU CAME FROM.
I KNOW WHAT YOU REALLY ARE.
KRAK
I'M WHAT YOU MADE ME, YOU SON OF A BITCH.

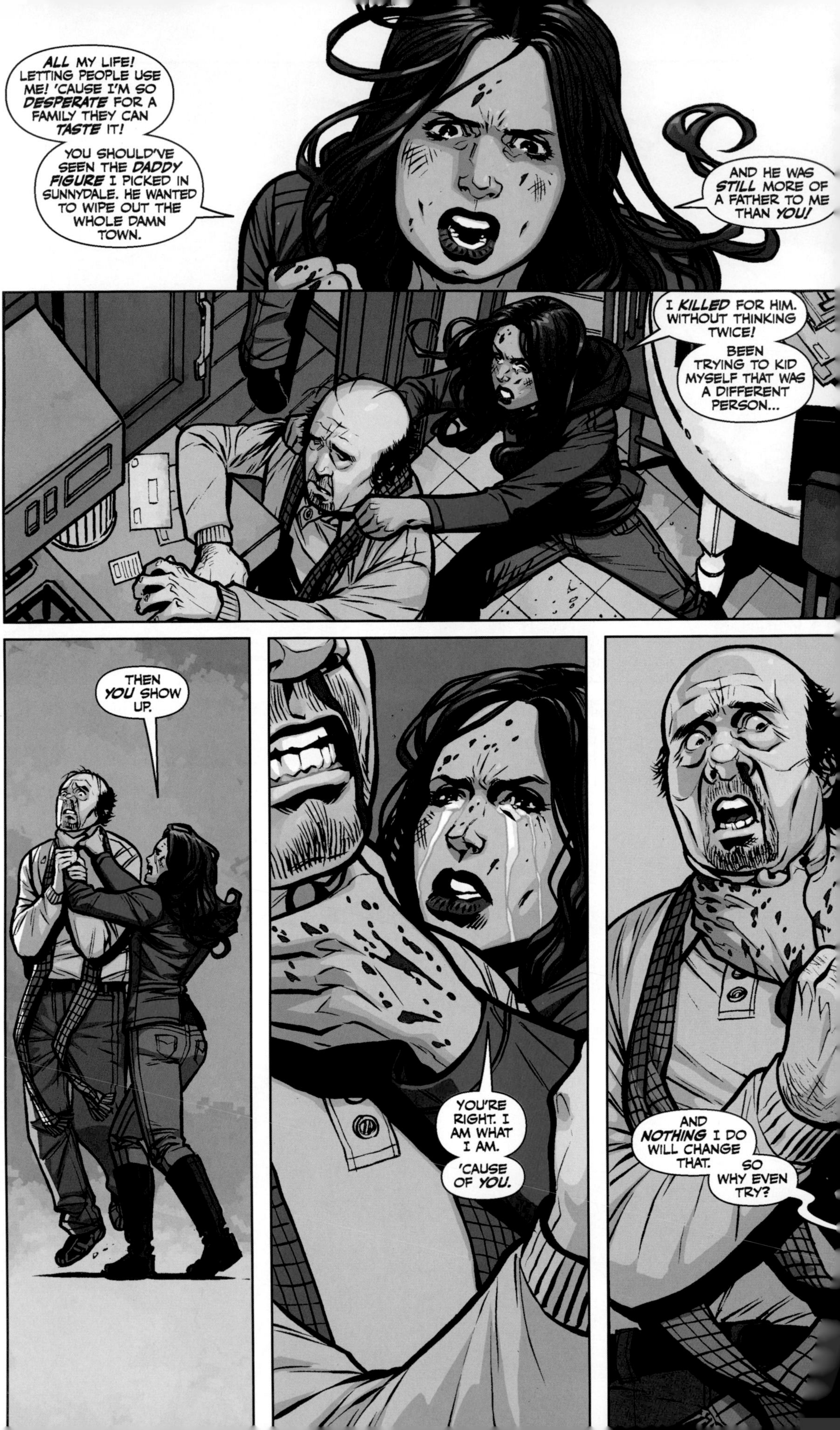
ALL MY LIFE! LETTING PEOPLE USE ME! 'CAUSE I'M SO DESPERATE FOR A FAMILY THEY CAN TASTE IT!
YOU SHOULD'VE SEEN THE DADDY FIGURE I PICKED IN SUNNYDALE. HE WANTED TO WIPE OUT THE WHOLE DAMN TOWN.
AND HE WAS STILL MORE OF A FATHER TO ME THAN YOU!
I KILLED FOR HIM. WITHOUT THINKING TWICE!
BEEN TRYING TO KID MYSELF THAT WAS A DIFFERENT PERSON...
THEN YOU SHOW UP.
YOU'RE RIGHT. I AM WHAT I AM.
'CAUSE OF YOU.
AND NOTHING I DO WILL CHANGE THAT.
SO WHY EVEN TRY?

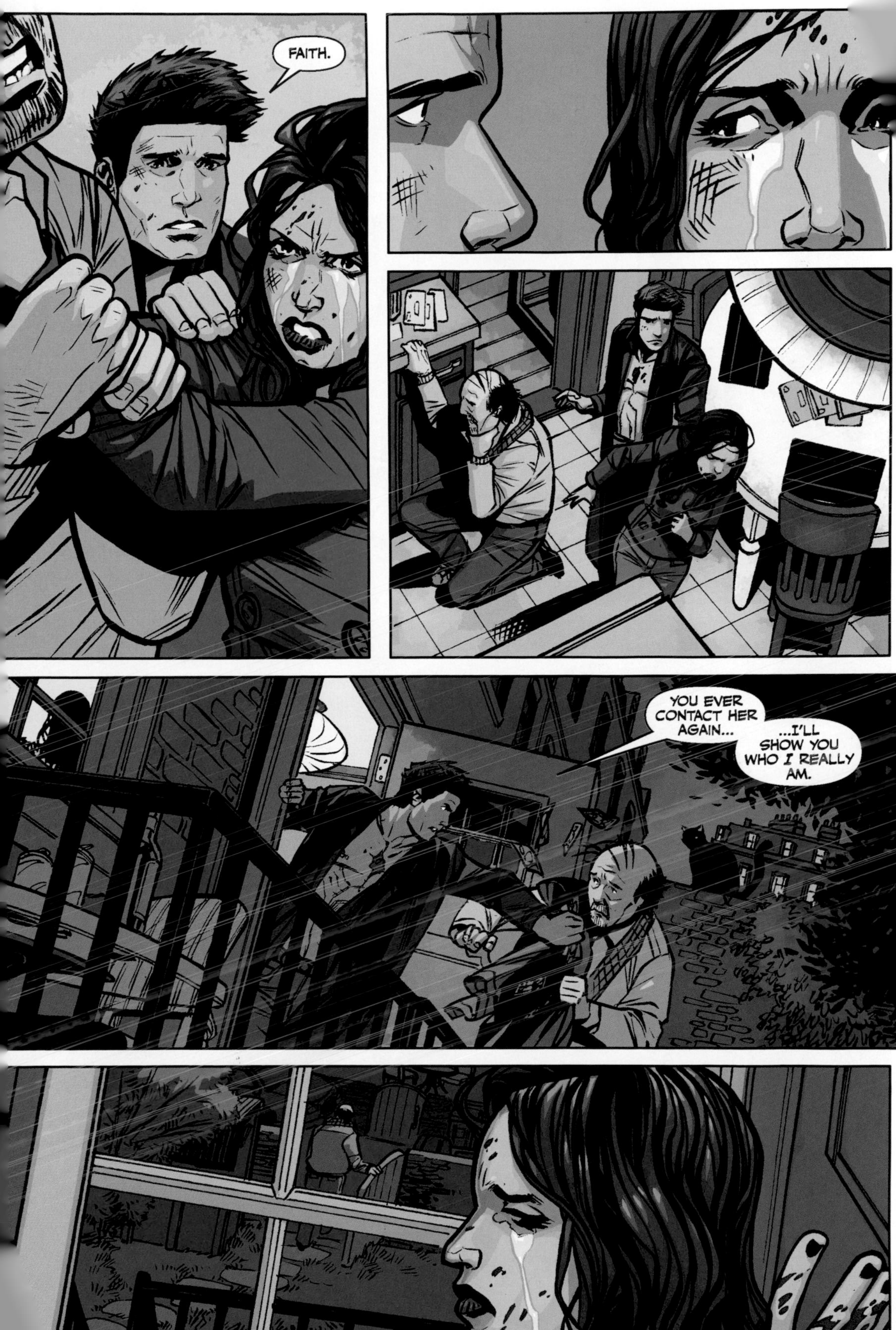
FAITH.
YOU EVER CONTACT HER AGAIN...
...I'LL SHOW YOU WHO I REALLY AM.

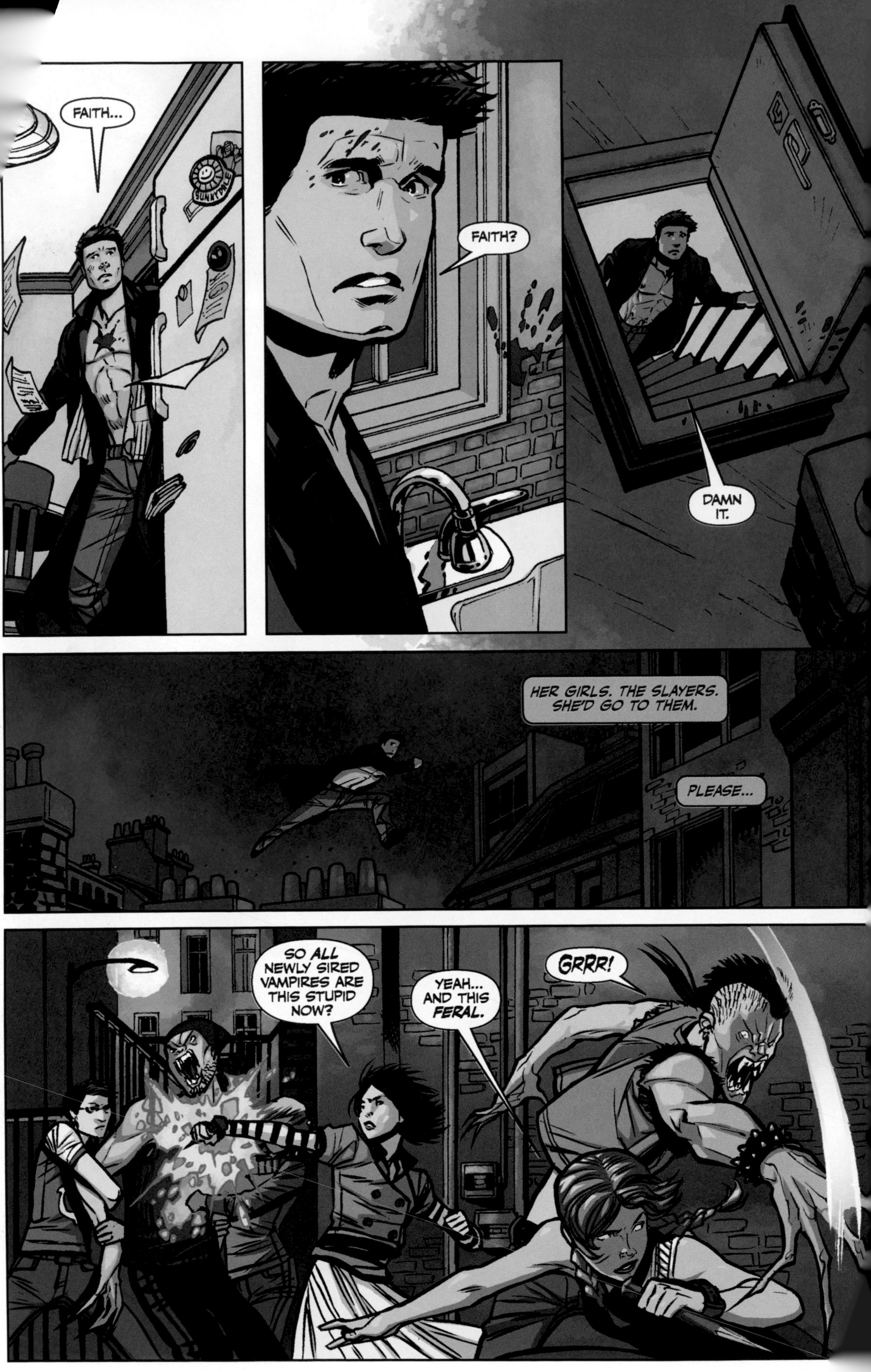
FAITH...
FAITH?
DAMN IT.
HER GIRLS. THE SLAYERS. SHE'D GO TO THEM.
PLEASE...
SO ALL NEWLY SIRED VAMPIRES ARE THIS STUPID NOW?
YEAH... AND THIS FERAL.
GRRR!

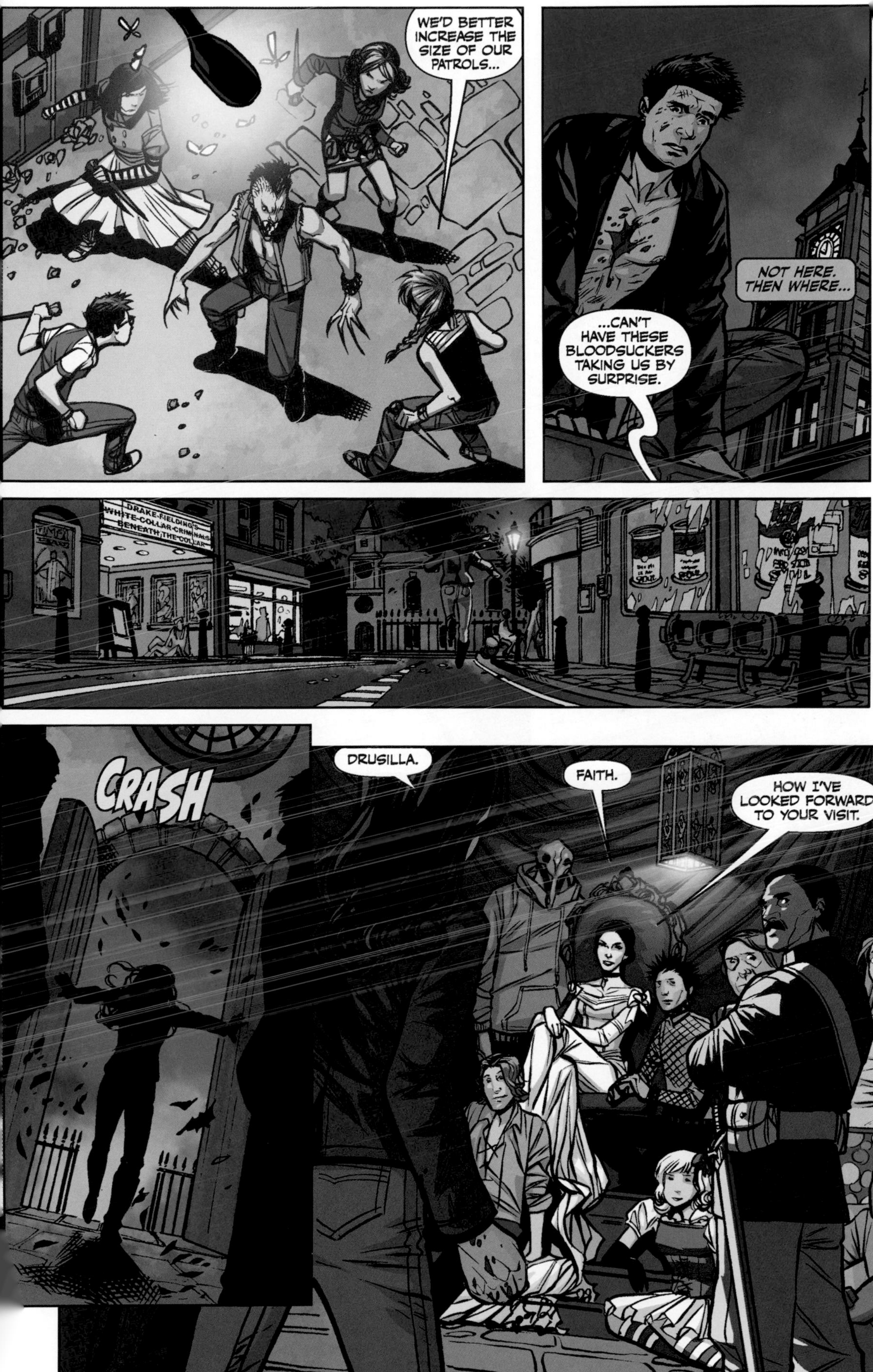
WE'D BETTER INCREASE THE SIZE OF OUR PATROLS...
NOT HERE. THEN WHERE...
...CAN'T HAVE THESE BLOODSUCKERS TAKING US BY SURPRISE.
DRAKE FIELDING'S
WHITE-COLLAR CRIMINALS
BENEATH THE COLLAR
CRASH
DRUSILLA.
FAITH.
HOW I'VE LOOKED FORWARD TO YOUR VISIT.

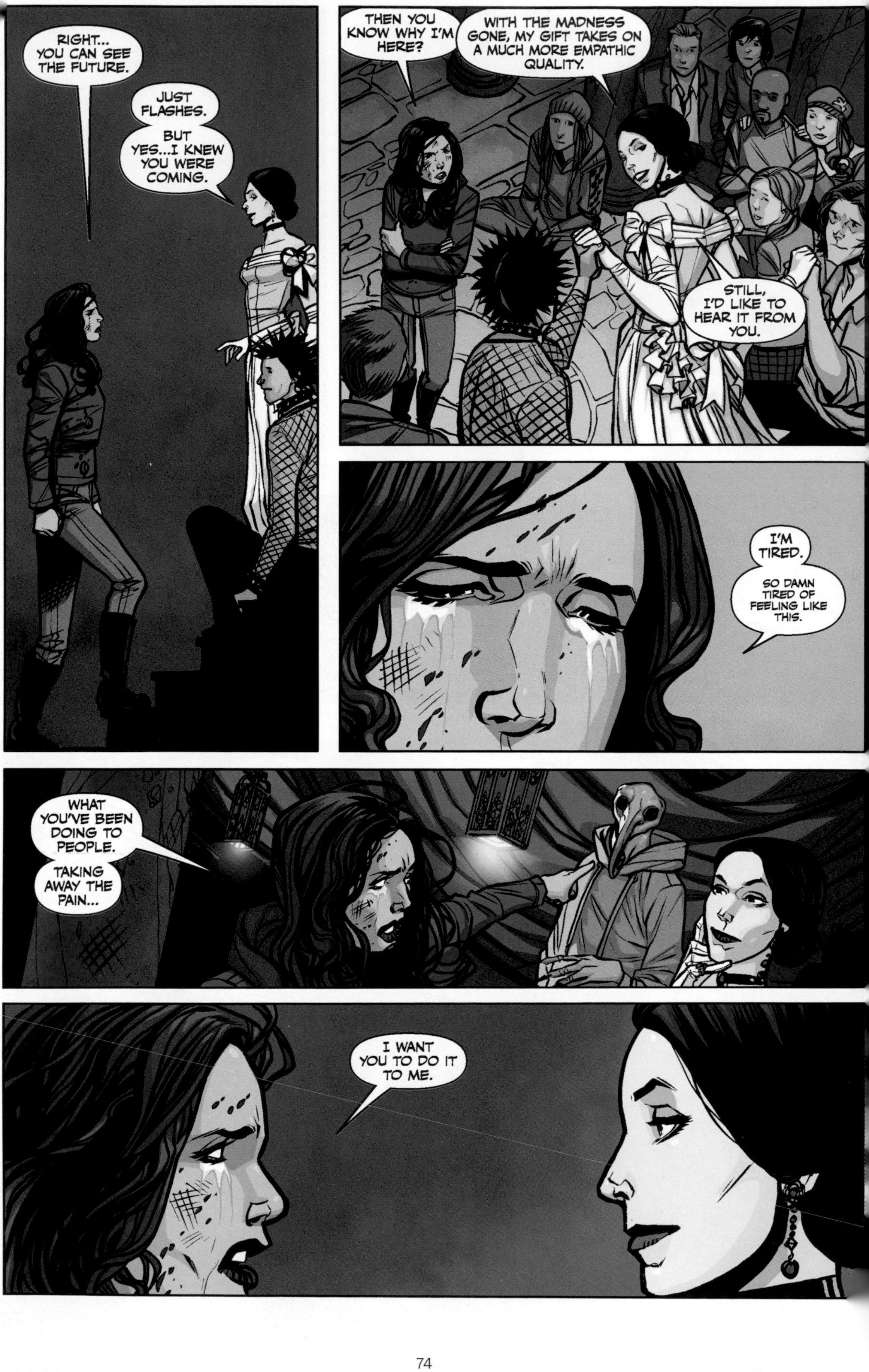

RIGHT... YOU CAN SEE THE FUTURE.
JUST FLASHES.
BUT YES...I KNEW YOU WERE COMING.
THEN YOU KNOW WHY I'M HERE?
WITH THE MADNESS GONE, MY GIFT TAKES ON A MUCH MORE EMPATHIC QUALITY.
STILL, I'D LIKE TO HEAR IT FROM YOU.
I'M TIRED.
SO DAMN TIRED OF FEELING LIKE THIS.
WHAT YOU'VE BEEN DOING TO PEOPLE.
TAKING AWAY THE PAIN...
I WANT YOU TO DO IT TO ME.

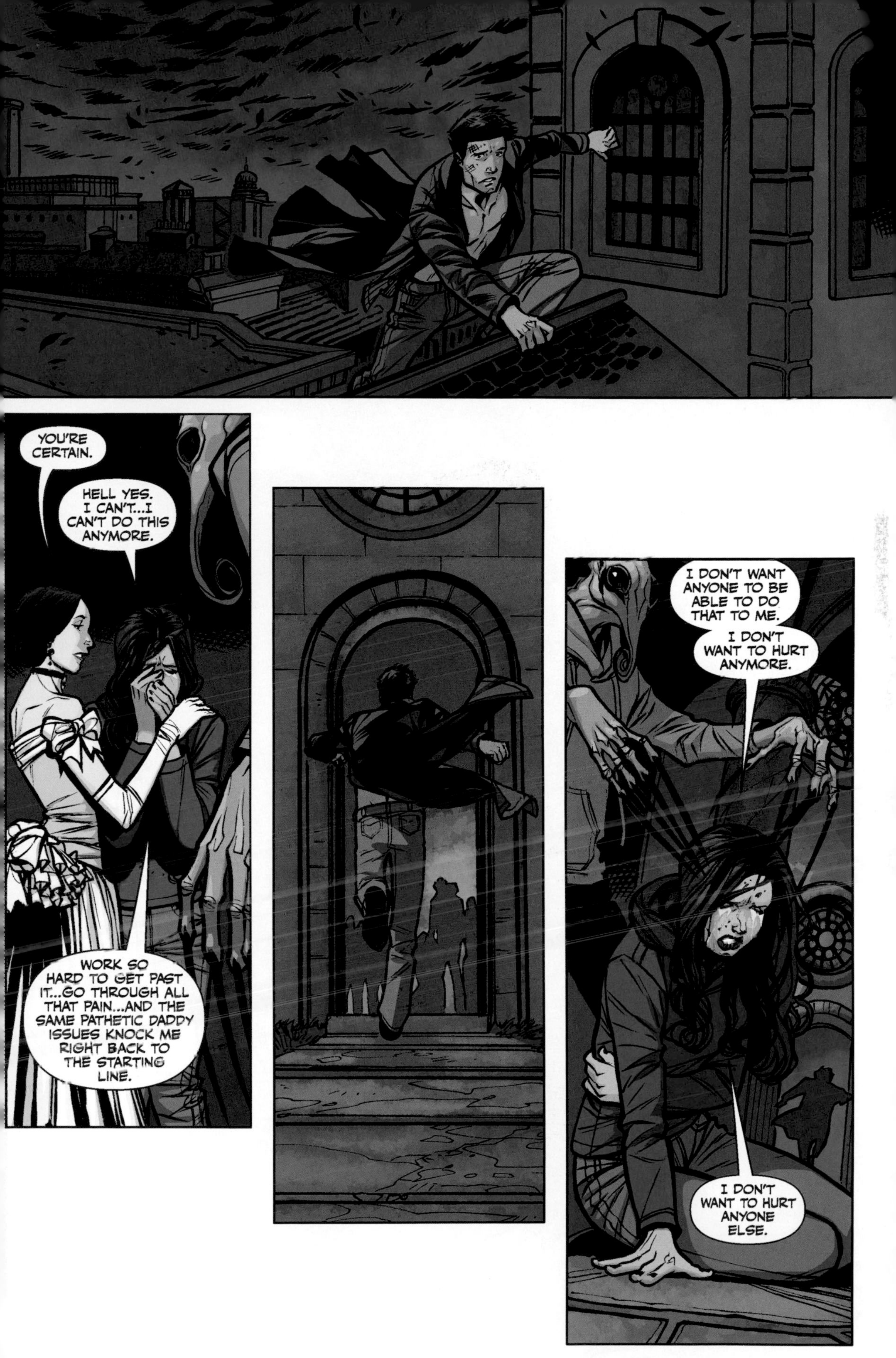
YOU'RE CERTAIN.
HELL YES. I CAN'T...I CAN'T DO THIS ANYMORE.
WORK SO HARD TO GET PAST IT...GO THROUGH ALL THAT PAIN...AND THE SAME PATHETIC DADDY ISSUES KNOCK ME RIGHT BACK TO THE STARTING LINE.
I DON'T WANT ANYONE TO BE ABLE TO DO THAT TO ME.
I DON'T WANT TO HURT ANYMORE.
I DON'T WANT TO HURT ANYONE ELSE.

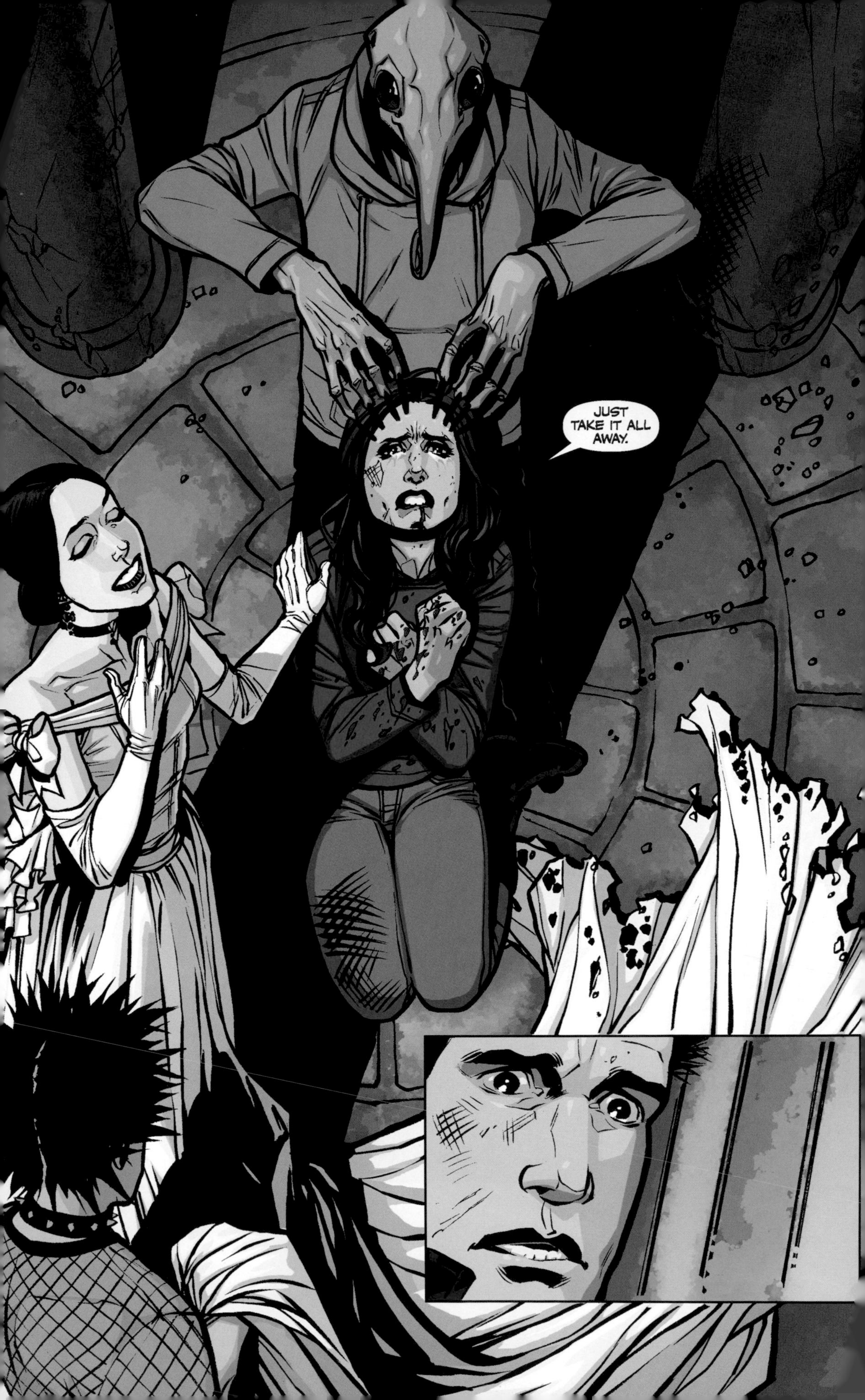
JUST TAKE IT ALL AWAY.

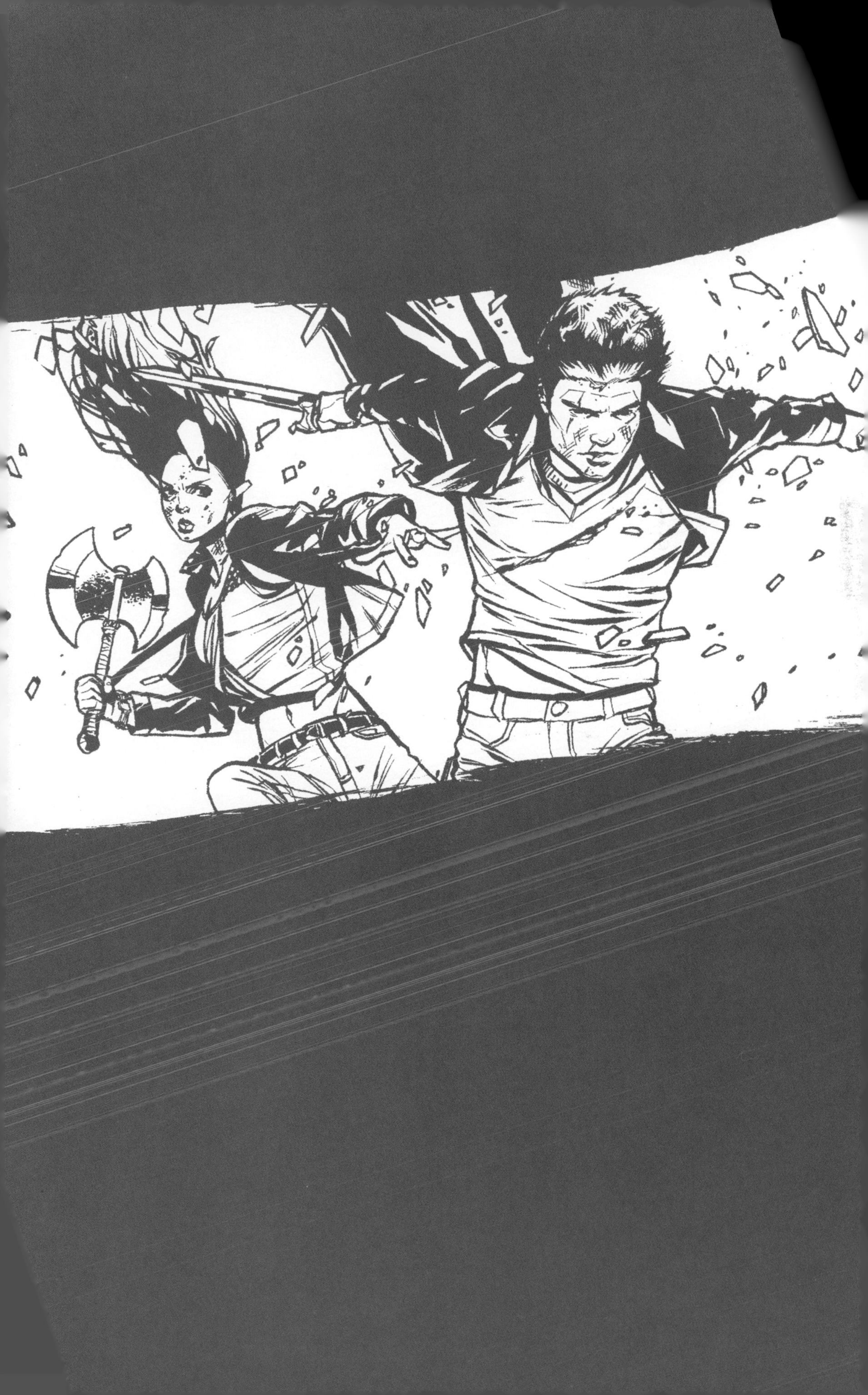

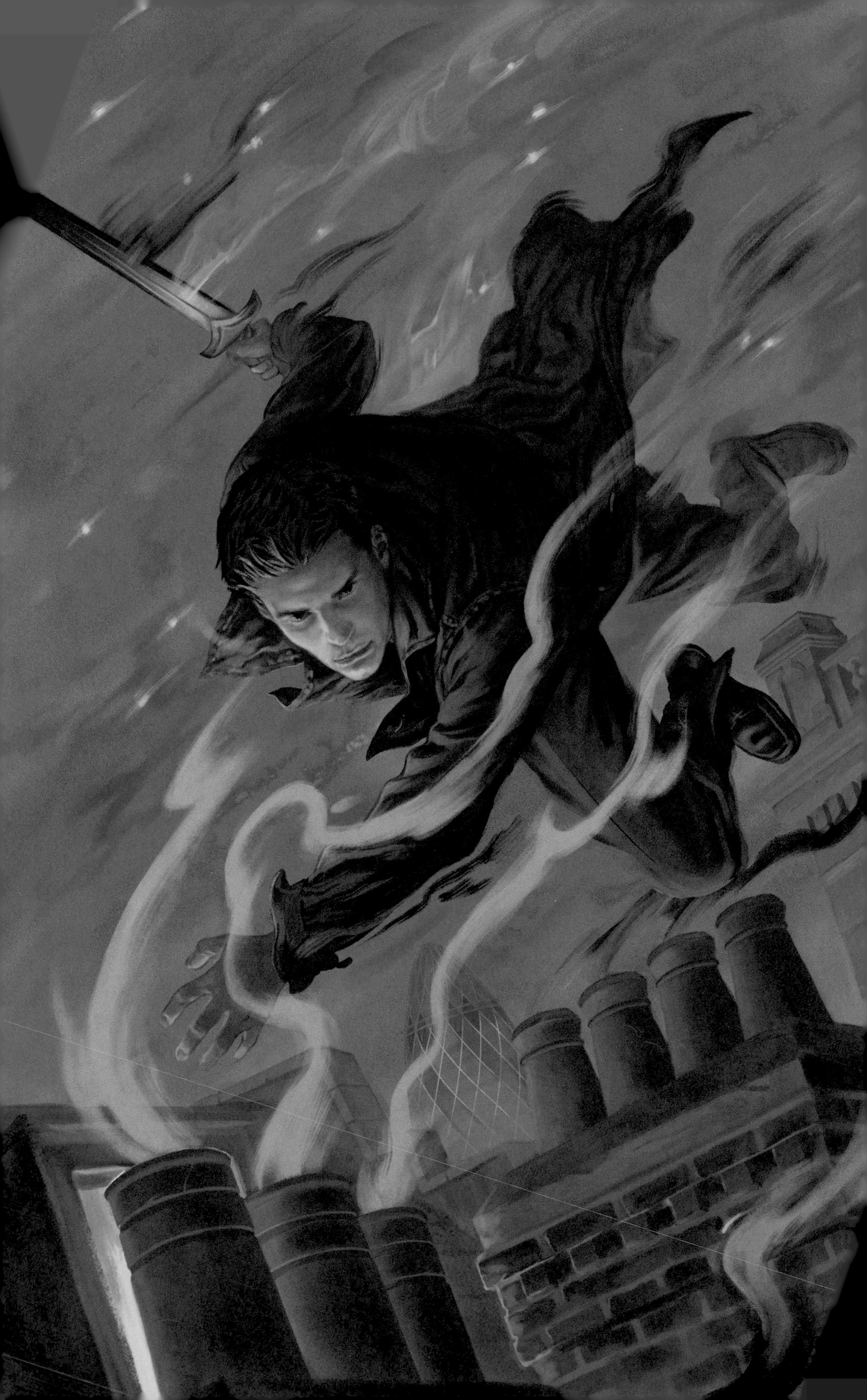

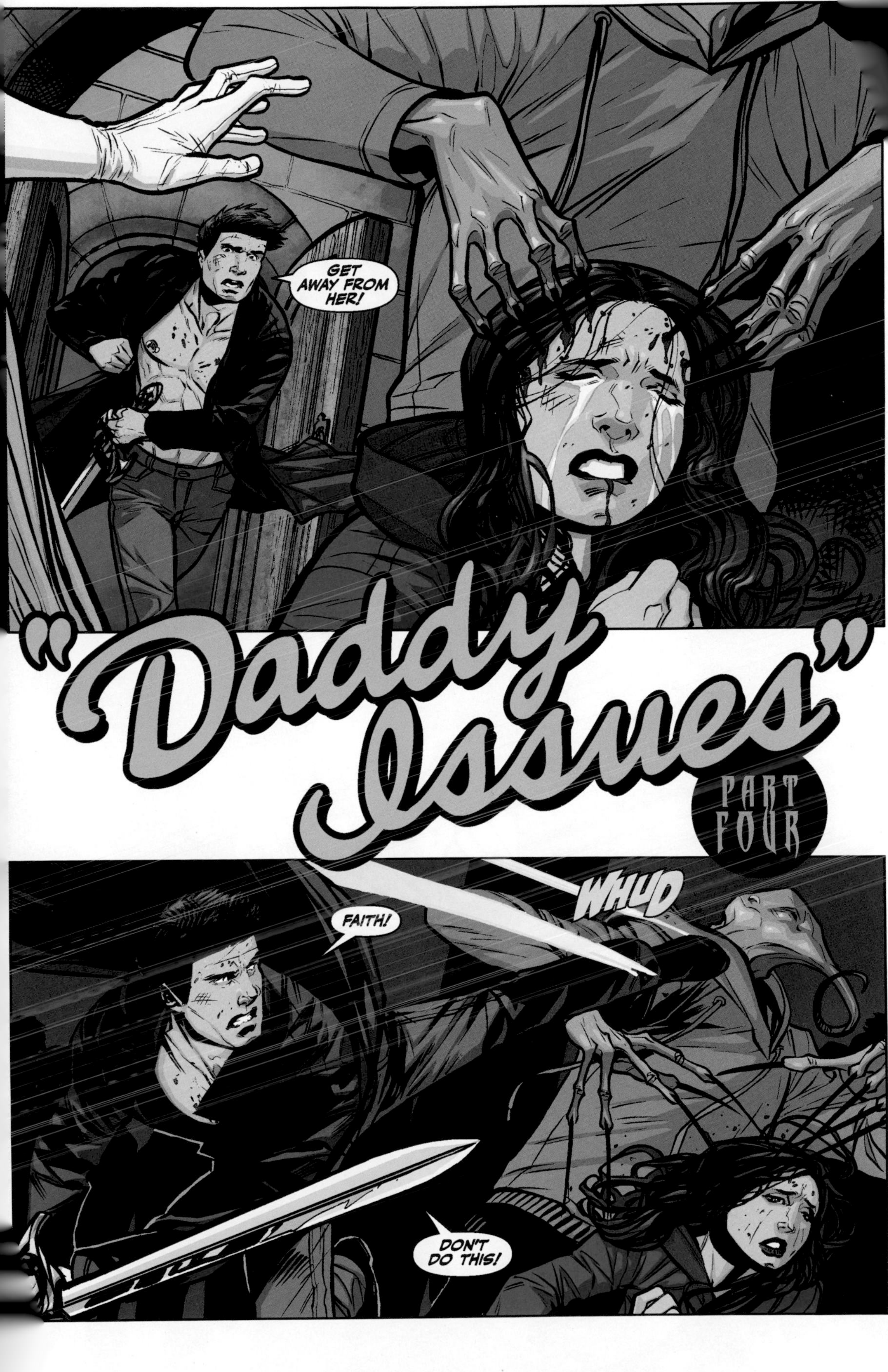
GET AWAY FROM HER!
"Daddy Issues"
PART FOUR
FAITH!
WHUD
DON'T DO THIS!

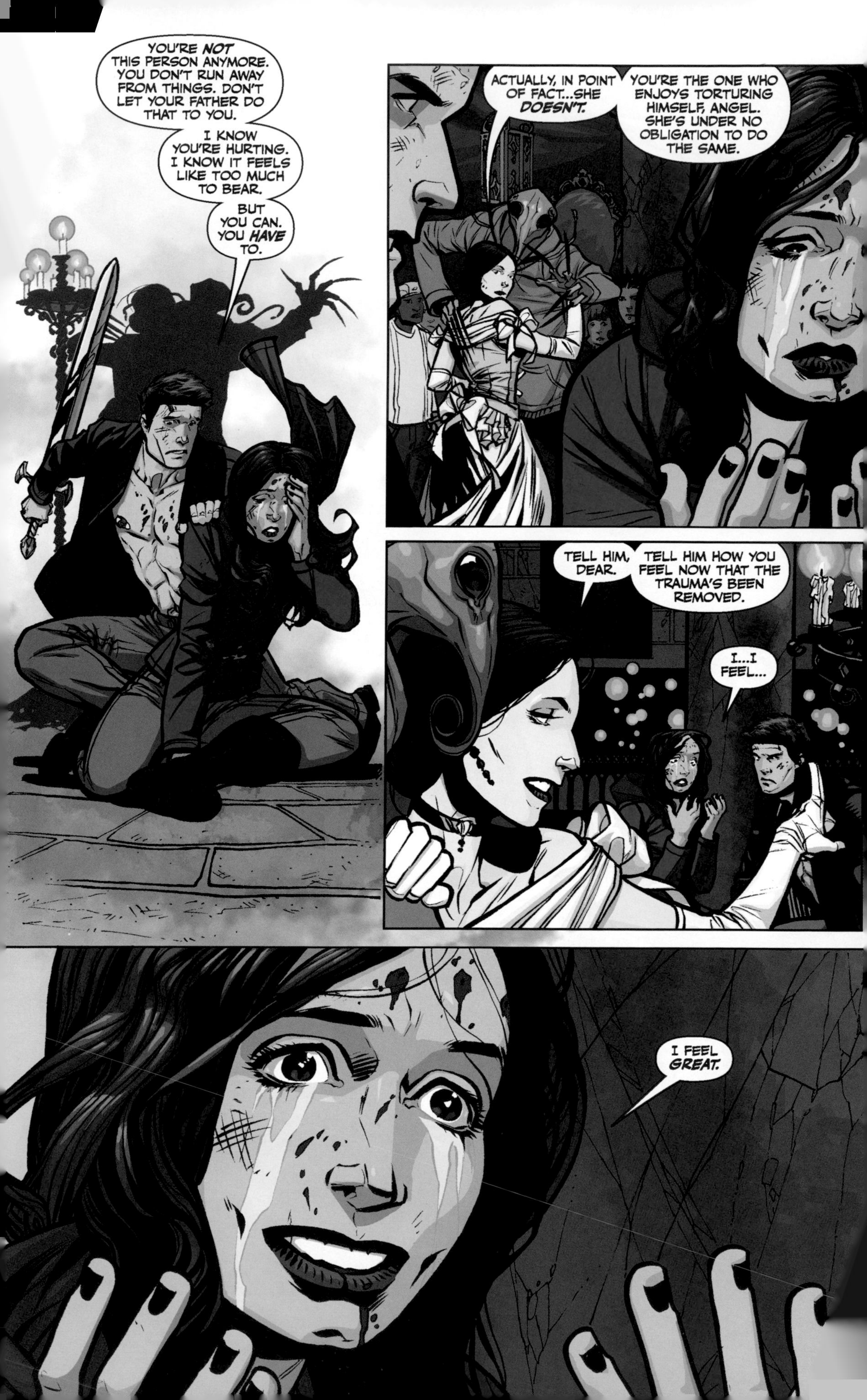
YOU'RE NOT THIS PERSON ANYMORE. YOU DON'T RUN AWAY FROM THINGS. DON'T LET YOUR FATHER DO THAT TO YOU.
I KNOW YOU'RE HURTING. I KNOW IT FEELS LIKE TOO MUCH TO BEAR.
BUT YOU CAN. YOU HAVE TO.
ACTUALLY, IN POINT OF FACT...SHE DOESN'T.
YOU'RE THE ONE WHO ENJOYS TORTURING HIMSELF, ANGEL. SHE'S UNDER NO OBLIGATION TO DO THE SAME.
TELL HIM, DEAR.
TELL HIM HOW YOU FEEL NOW THAT THE TRAUMA'S BEEN REMOVED.
I...I FEEL...
I FEEL GREAT.

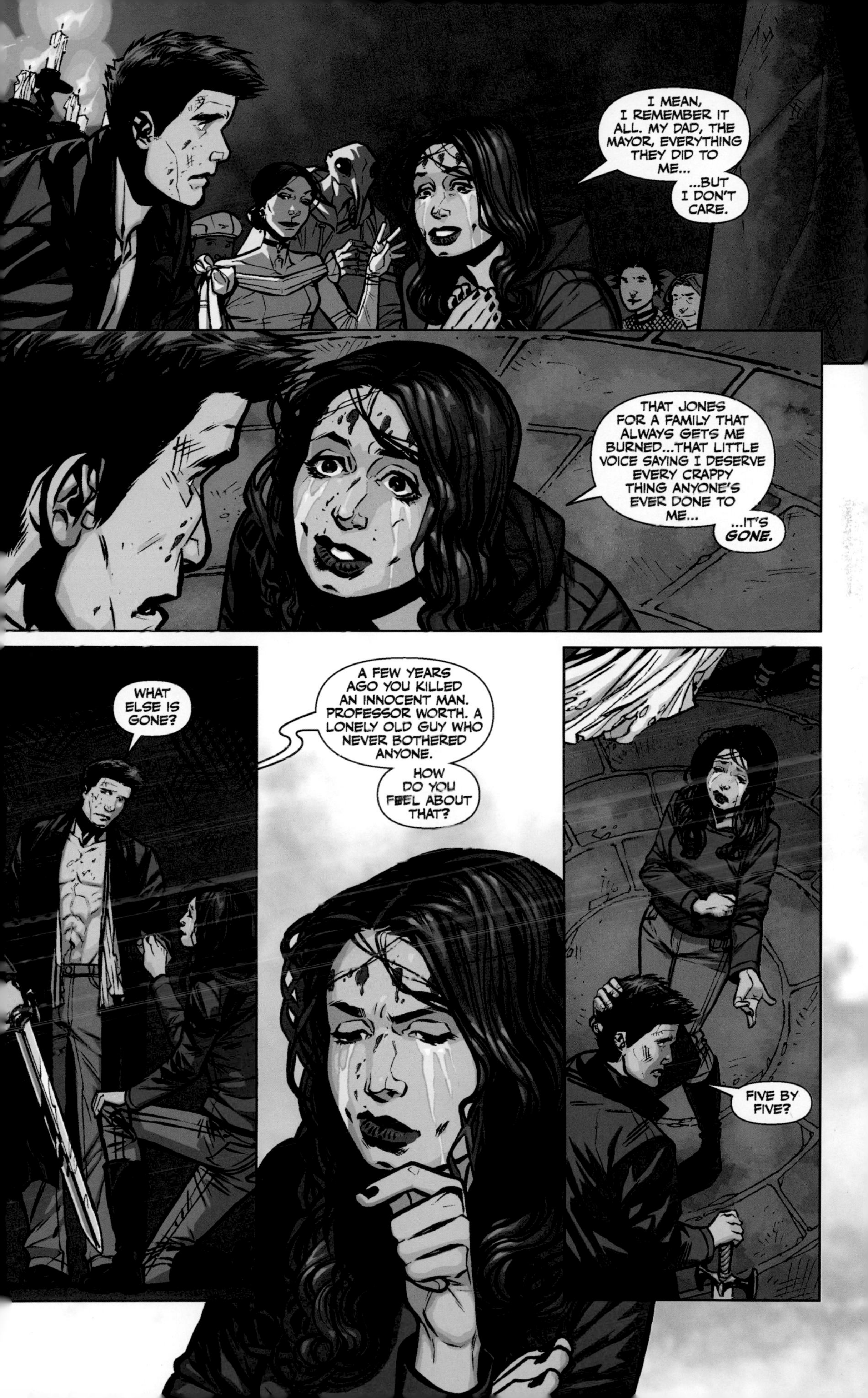
I MEAN, I REMEMBER IT ALL. MY DAD, THE MAYOR, EVERYTHING THEY DID TO ME...
...BUT I DON'T CARE.
THAT JONES FOR A FAMILY THAT ALWAYS GETS ME BURNED...THAT LITTLE VOICE SAYING I DESERVE EVERY CRAPPY THING ANYONE'S EVER DONE TO ME...
...IT'S *GONE.*
WHAT ELSE IS GONE?
A FEW YEARS AGO YOU KILLED AN INNOCENT MAN. PROFESSOR WORTH. A LONELY OLD GUY WHO NEVER BOTHERED ANYONE.
HOW DO YOU FEEL ABOUT THAT?
FIVE BY FIVE?

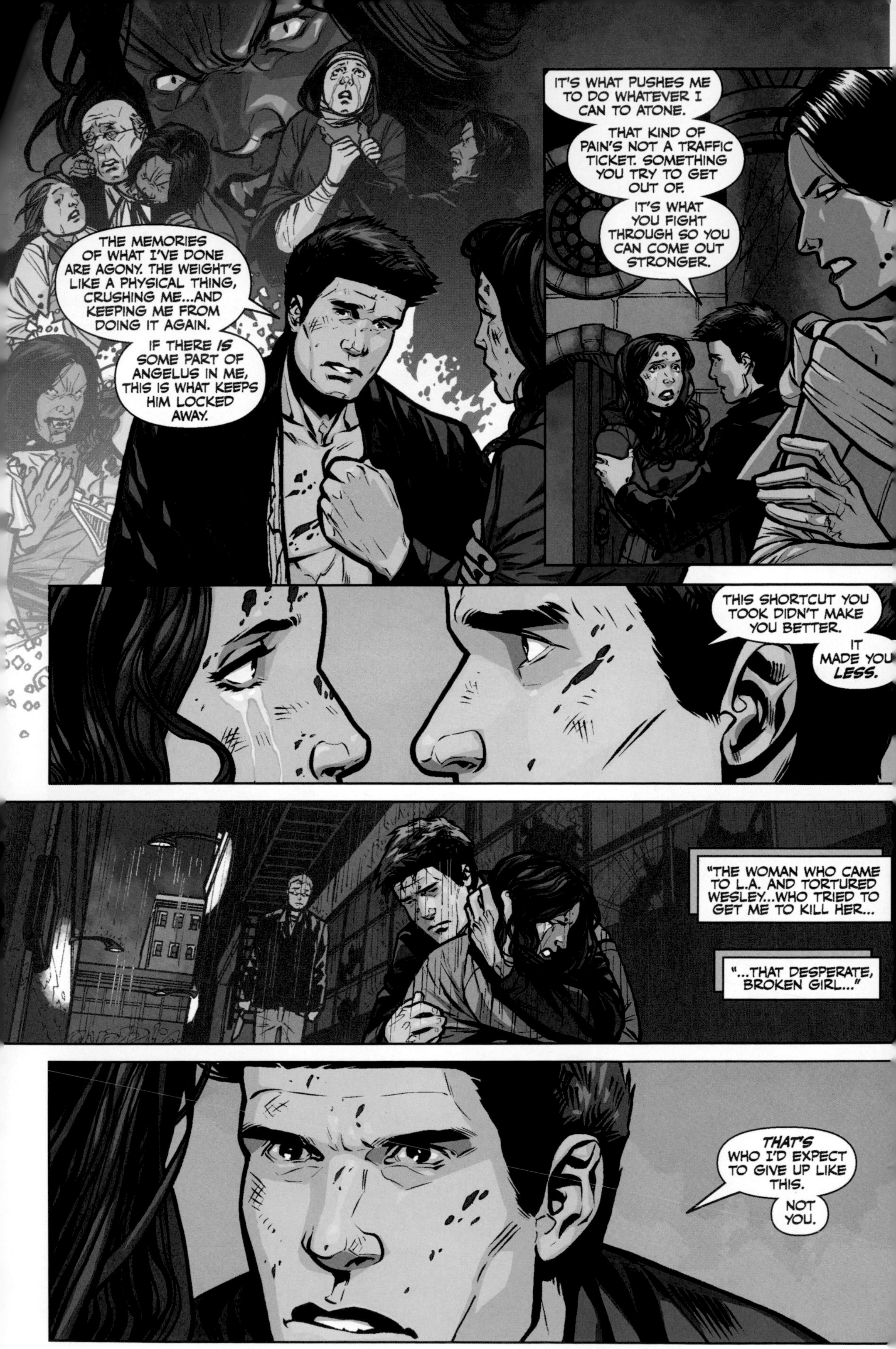
THE MEMORIES OF WHAT I'VE DONE ARE AGONY. THE WEIGHT'S LIKE A PHYSICAL THING, CRUSHING ME...AND KEEPING ME FROM DOING IT AGAIN.
IF THERE *IS* SOME PART OF ANGELUS IN ME, THIS IS WHAT KEEPS HIM LOCKED AWAY.
IT'S WHAT PUSHES ME TO DO WHATEVER I CAN TO ATONE.
THAT KIND OF PAIN'S NOT A TRAFFIC TICKET. SOMETHING YOU TRY TO GET OUT OF.
IT'S WHAT YOU FIGHT THROUGH SO YOU CAN COME OUT STRONGER.
THIS SHORTCUT YOU TOOK DIDN'T MAKE YOU BETTER.
IT MADE YOU *LESS.*
"THE WOMAN WHO CAME TO L.A. AND TORTURED WESLEY...WHO TRIED TO GET ME TO KILL HER...
"...THAT DESPERATE, BROKEN GIRL..."
THAT'S WHO I'D EXPECT TO GIVE UP LIKE THIS.
NOT YOU.

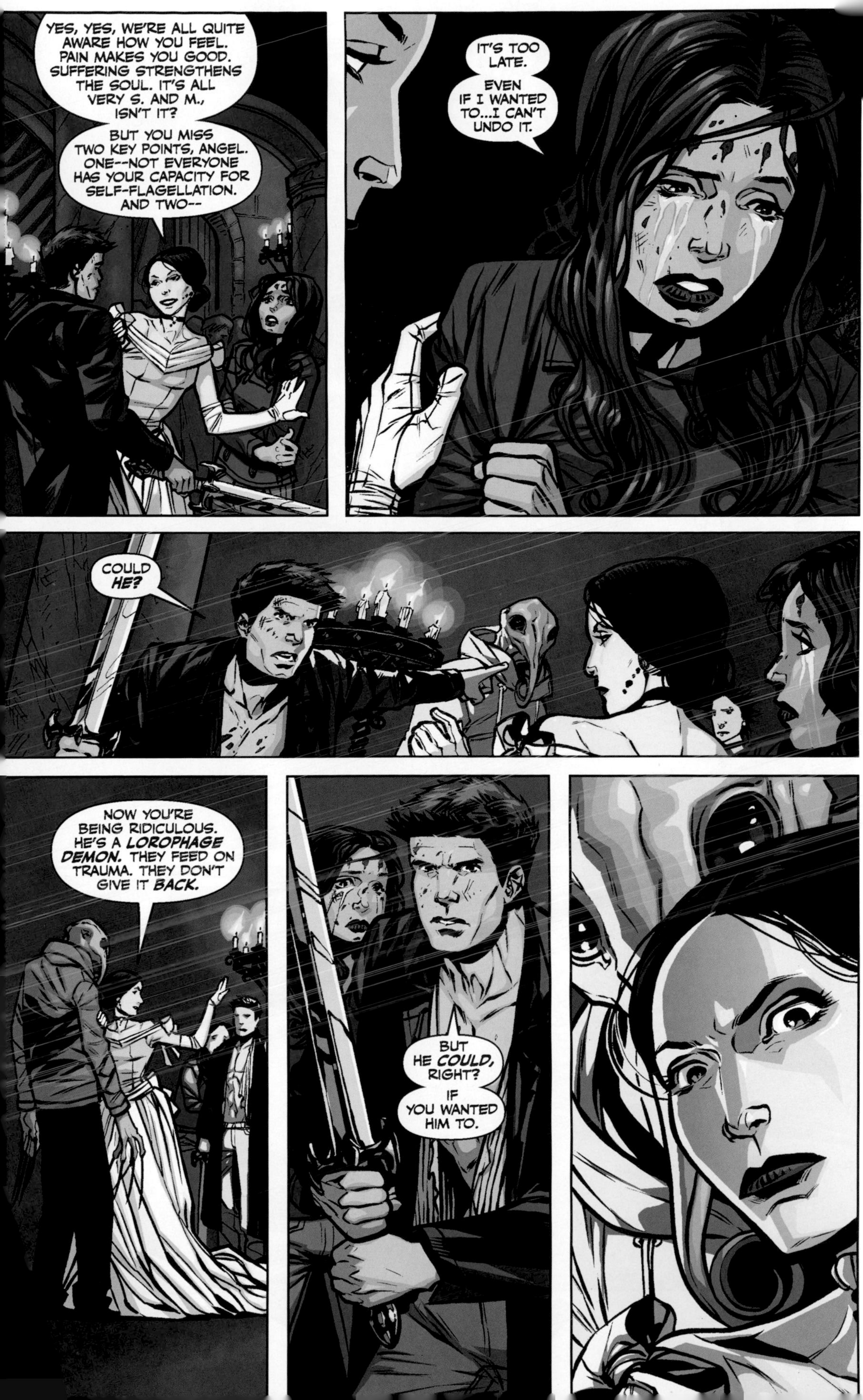
YES, YES, WE'RE ALL QUITE AWARE HOW YOU FEEL. PAIN MAKES YOU GOOD. SUFFERING STRENGTHENS THE SOUL. IT'S ALL VERY S. AND M., ISN'T IT?
BUT YOU MISS TWO KEY POINTS, ANGEL. ONE--NOT EVERYONE HAS YOUR CAPACITY FOR SELF-FLAGELLATION. AND TWO--
IT'S TOO LATE.
EVEN IF I WANTED TO...I CAN'T UNDO IT.
COULD *HE?*
NOW YOU'RE BEING RIDICULOUS. HE'S A ***LOROPHAGE DEMON.*** THEY FEED ON TRAUMA. THEY DON'T GIVE IT ***BACK.***
BUT HE *COULD,* RIGHT?
IF YOU WANTED HIM TO.

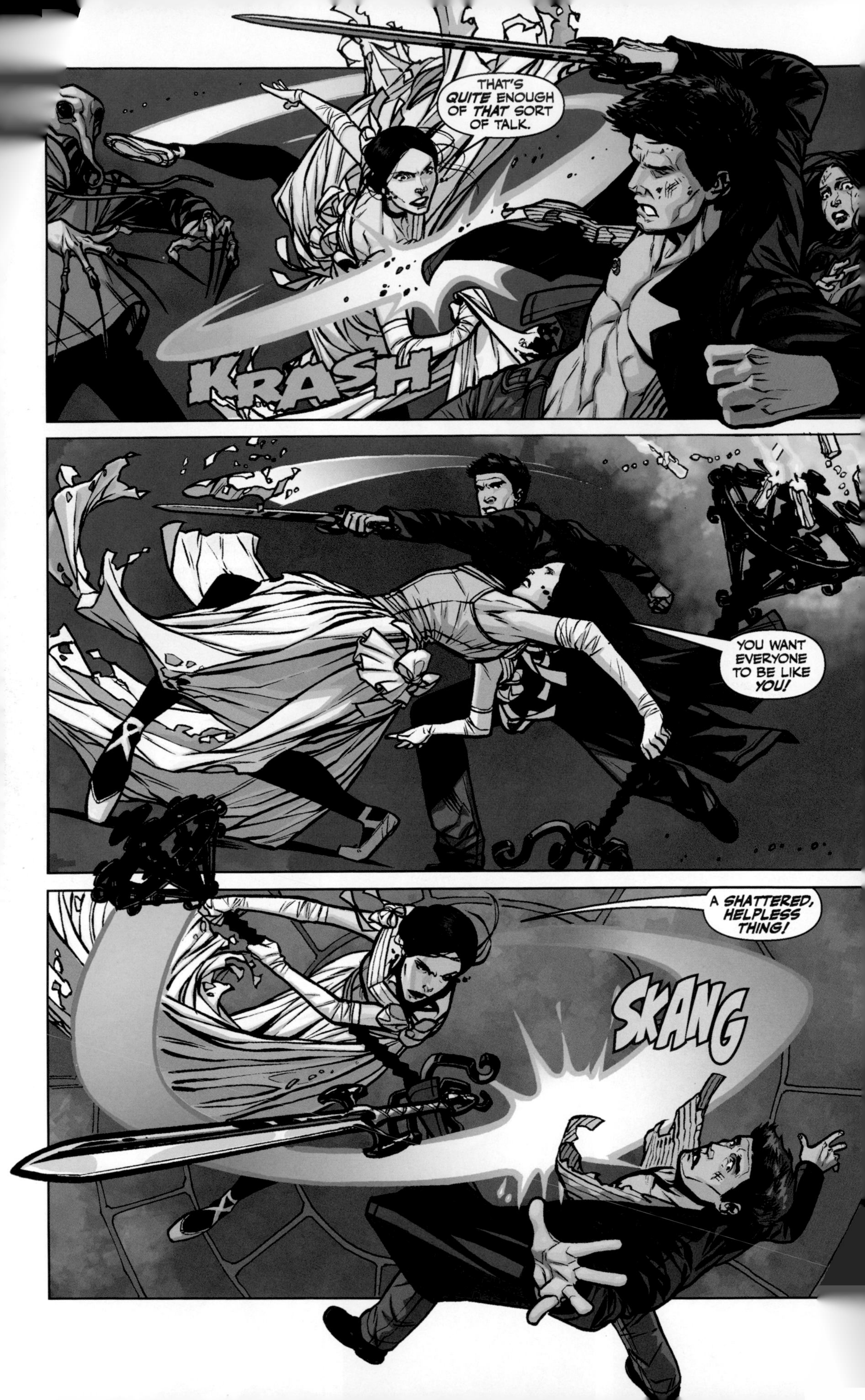
THAT'S QUITE ENOUGH OF THAT SORT OF TALK.
KRASH
YOU WANT EVERYONE TO BE LIKE YOU!
A SHATTERED, HELPLESS THING!
SKANG

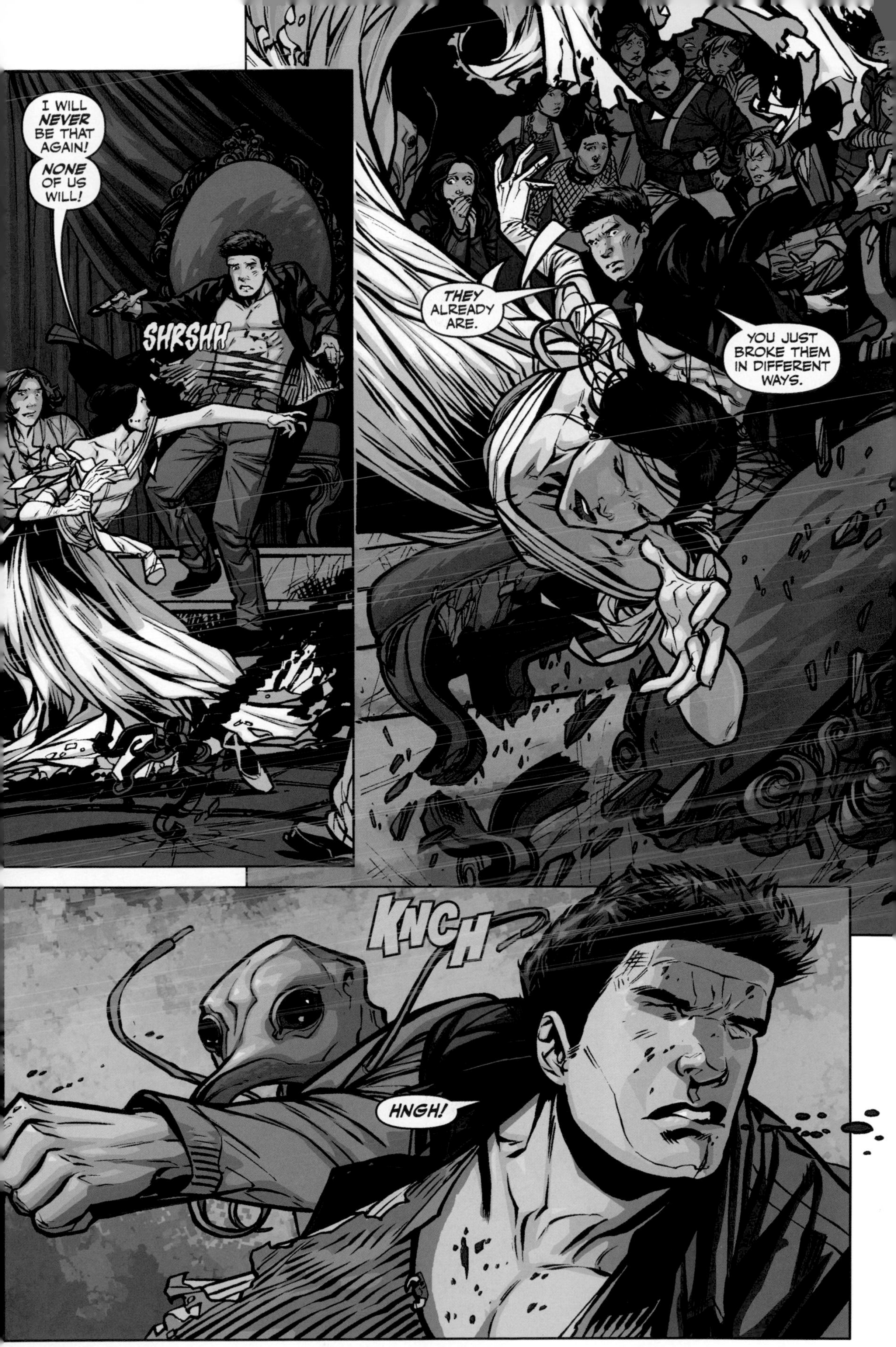
I WILL NEVER BE THAT AGAIN!
NONE OF US WILL!
SHRSHH
THEY ALREADY ARE.
YOU JUST BROKE THEM IN DIFFERENT WAYS.
KNCH
HNGH!

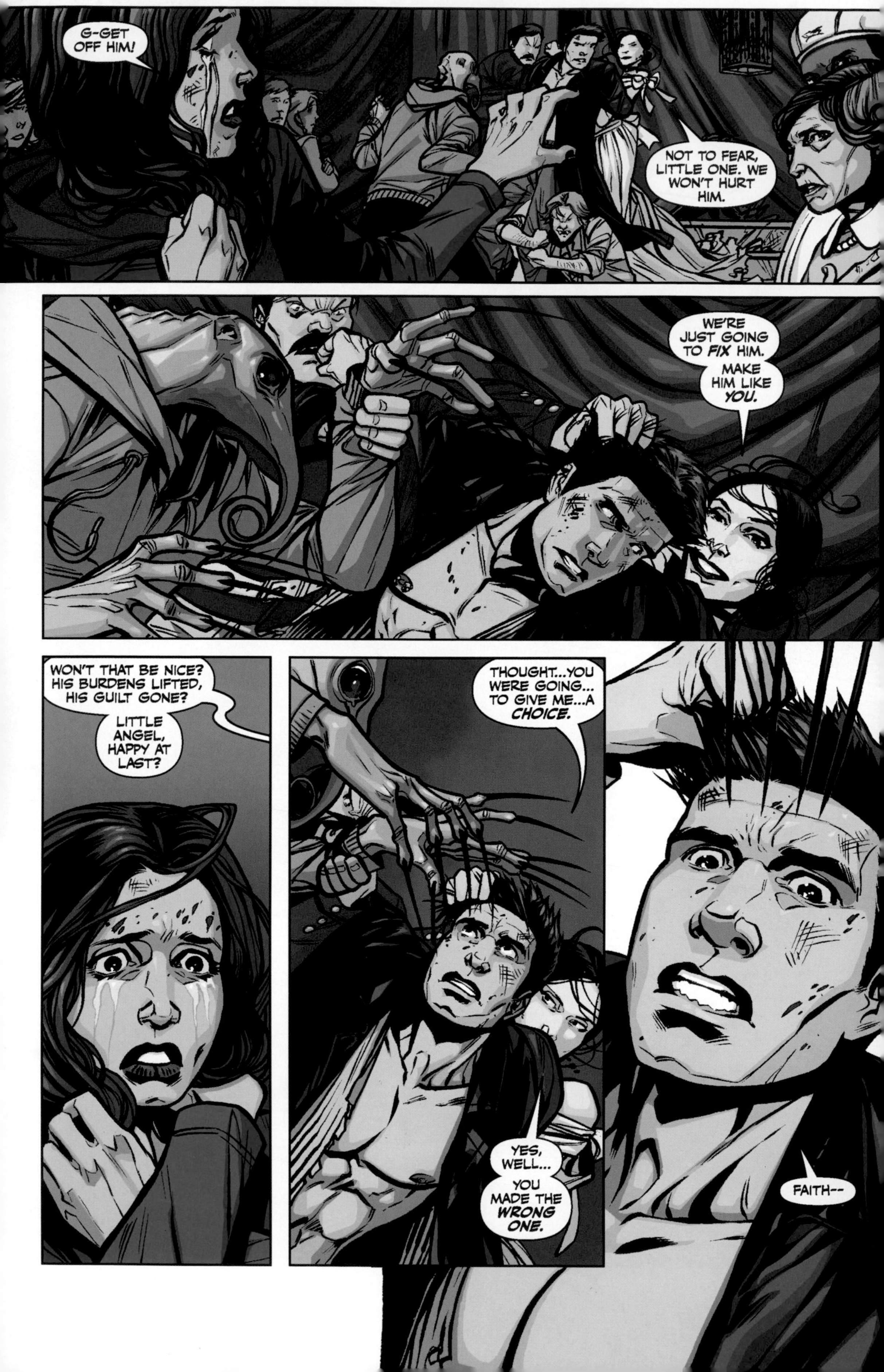
G-GET OFF HIM!
NOT TO FEAR, LITTLE ONE. WE WON'T HURT HIM.
WE'RE JUST GOING TO FIX HIM.
MAKE HIM LIKE YOU.
WON'T THAT BE NICE? HIS BURDENS LIFTED, HIS GUILT GONE?
LITTLE ANGEL, HAPPY AT LAST?
THOUGHT...YOU WERE GOING... TO GIVE ME...A CHOICE.
YES, WELL...
YOU MADE THE WRONG ONE.
FAITH--

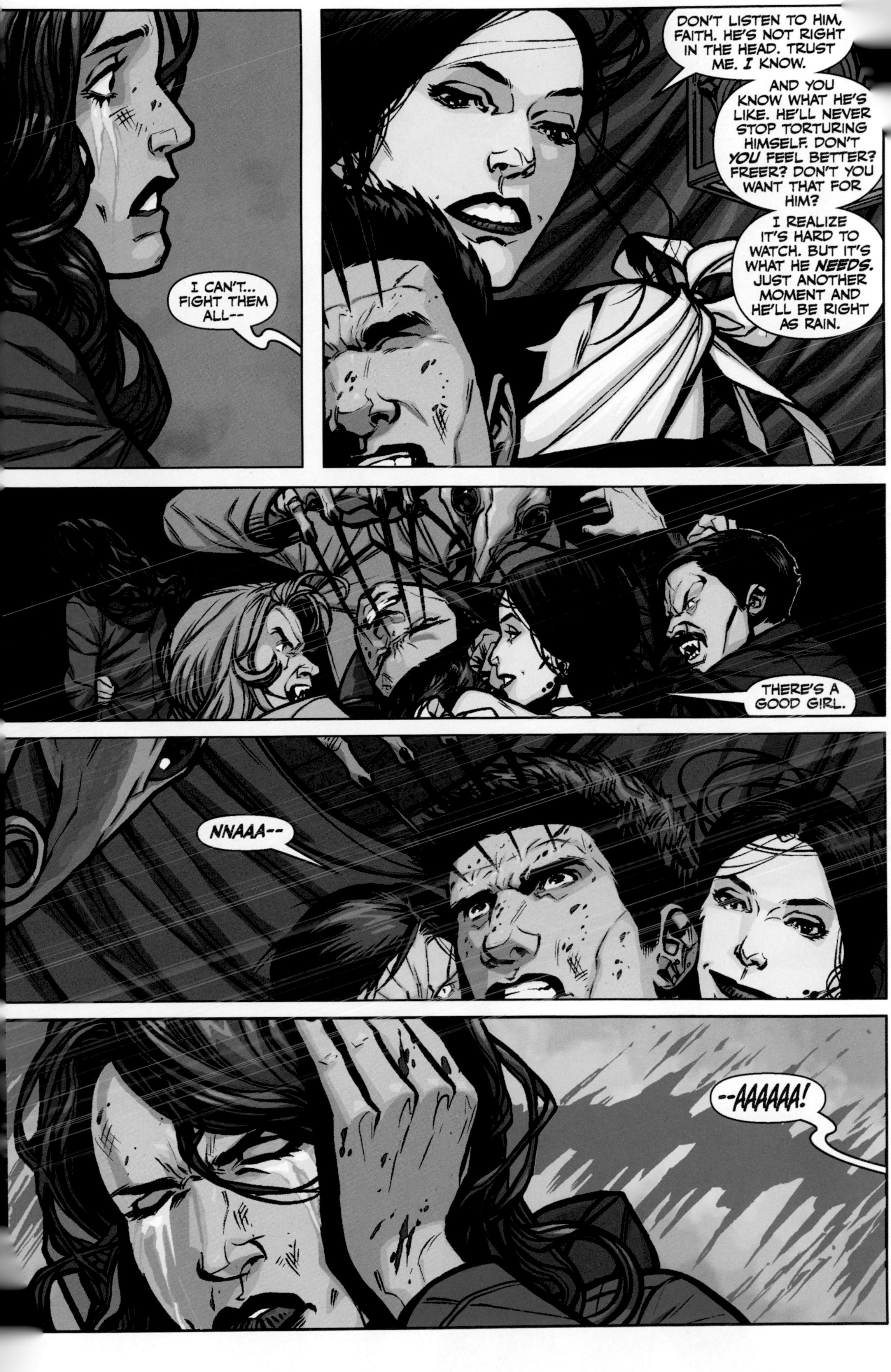
I CAN'T... FIGHT THEM ALL--
DON'T LISTEN TO HIM, FAITH. HE'S NOT RIGHT IN THE HEAD. TRUST ME. I KNOW.
AND YOU KNOW WHAT HE'S LIKE. HE'LL NEVER STOP TORTURING HIMSELF. DON'T YOU FEEL BETTER? FREER? DON'T YOU WANT THAT FOR HIM?
I REALIZE IT'S HARD TO WATCH. BUT IT'S WHAT HE NEEDS. JUST ANOTHER MOMENT AND HE'LL BE RIGHT AS RAIN.
THERE'S A GOOD GIRL.
NNAAA--
--AAAAAA!

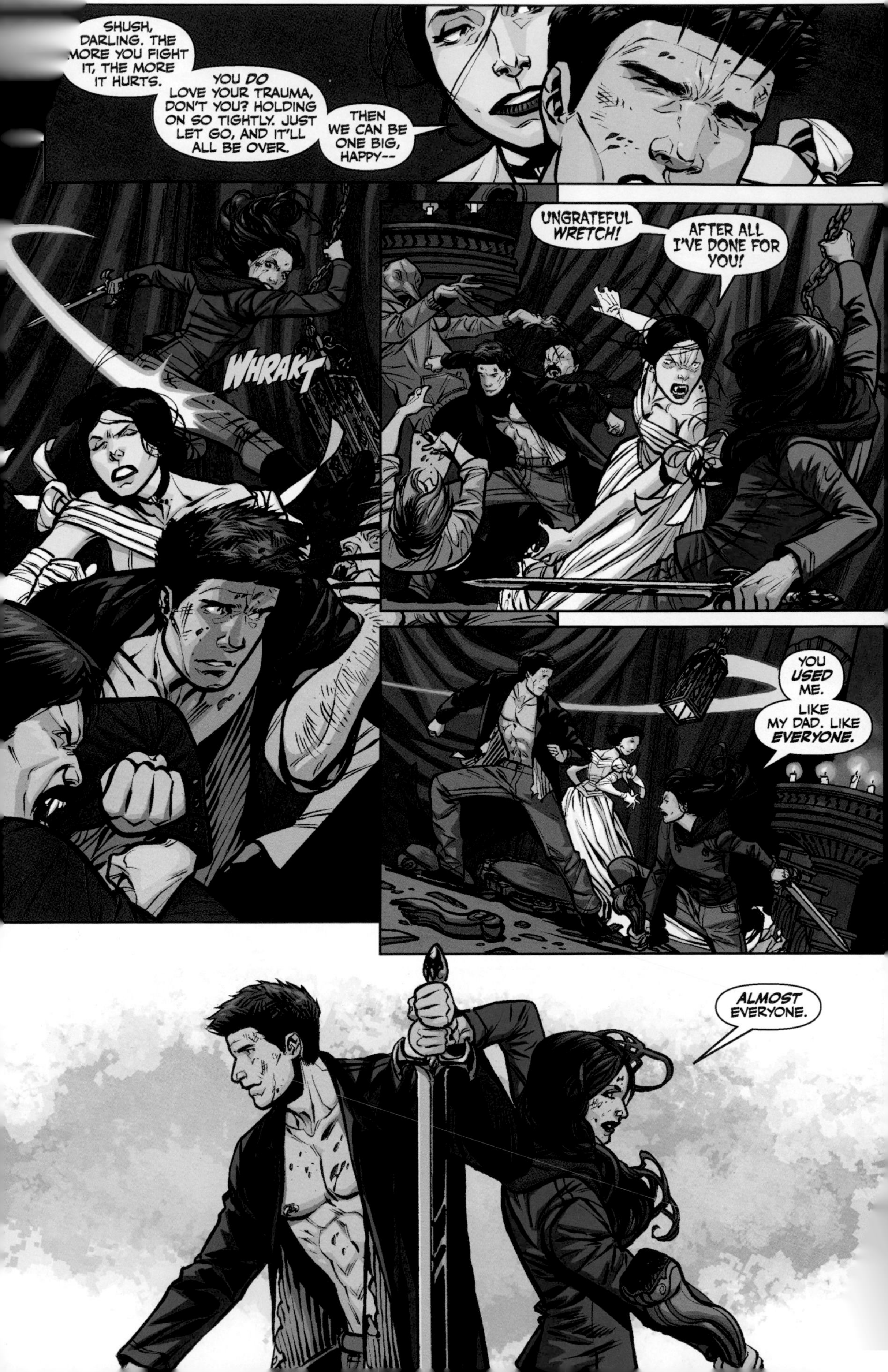

SHUSH, DARLING. THE MORE YOU FIGHT IT, THE MORE IT HURTS.
YOU DO LOVE YOUR TRAUMA, DON'T YOU? HOLDING ON SO TIGHTLY. JUST LET GO, AND IT'LL ALL BE OVER.
THEN WE CAN BE ONE BIG, HAPPY--
WHRAKT
UNGRATEFUL WRETCH!
AFTER ALL I'VE DONE FOR YOU!
YOU USED ME.
LIKE MY DAD. LIKE EVERYONE.
ALMOST EVERYONE.

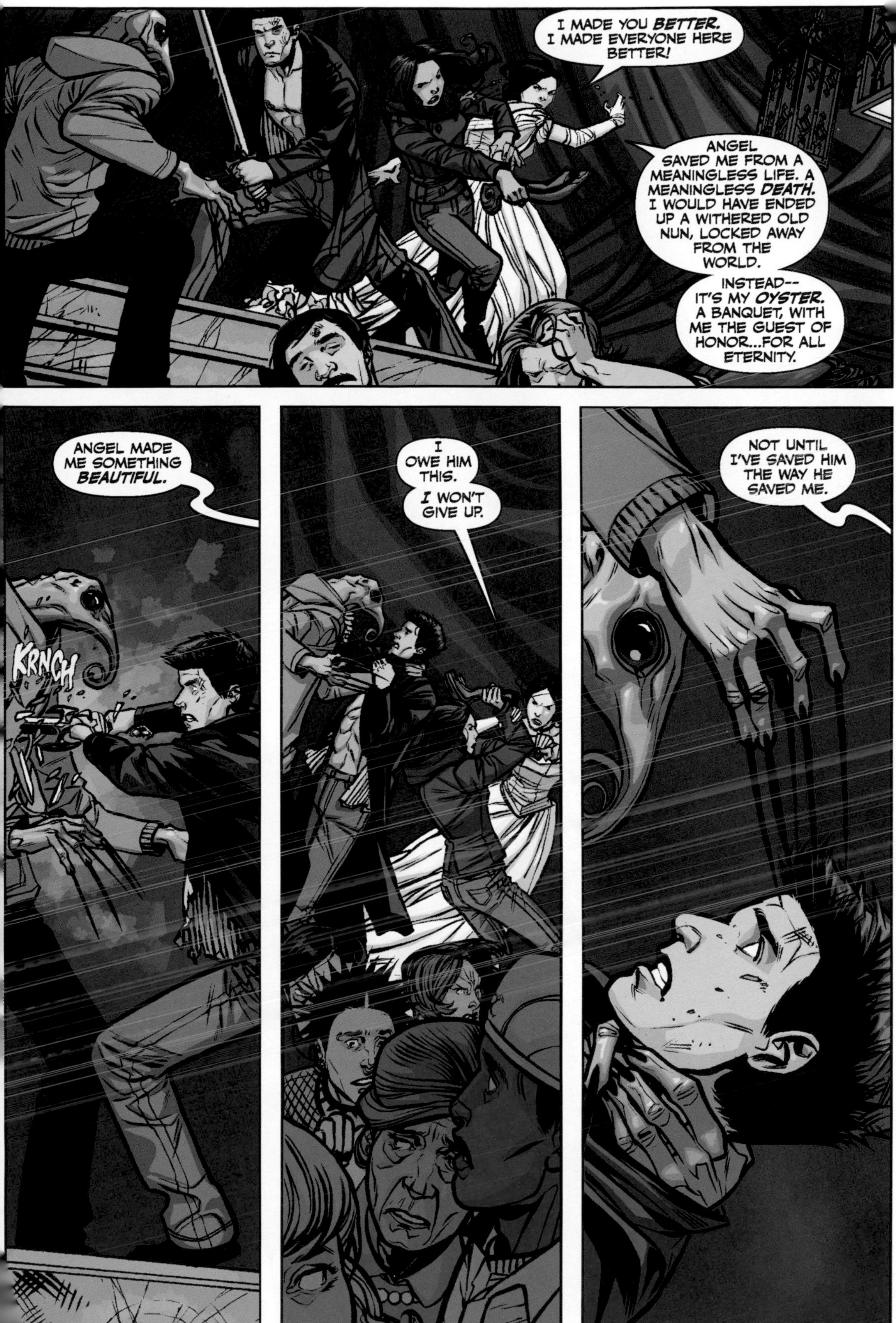
I MADE YOU BETTER. I MADE EVERYONE HERE BETTER!
ANGEL SAVED ME FROM A MEANINGLESS LIFE. A MEANINGLESS DEATH. I WOULD HAVE ENDED UP A WITHERED OLD NUN, LOCKED AWAY FROM THE WORLD.
INSTEAD-- IT'S MY OYSTER. A BANQUET, WITH ME THE GUEST OF HONOR...FOR ALL ETERNITY.
ANGEL MADE ME SOMETHING BEAUTIFUL.
KRNCH
I OWE HIM THIS.
I WON'T GIVE UP.
NOT UNTIL I'VE SAVED HIM THE WAY HE SAVED ME.

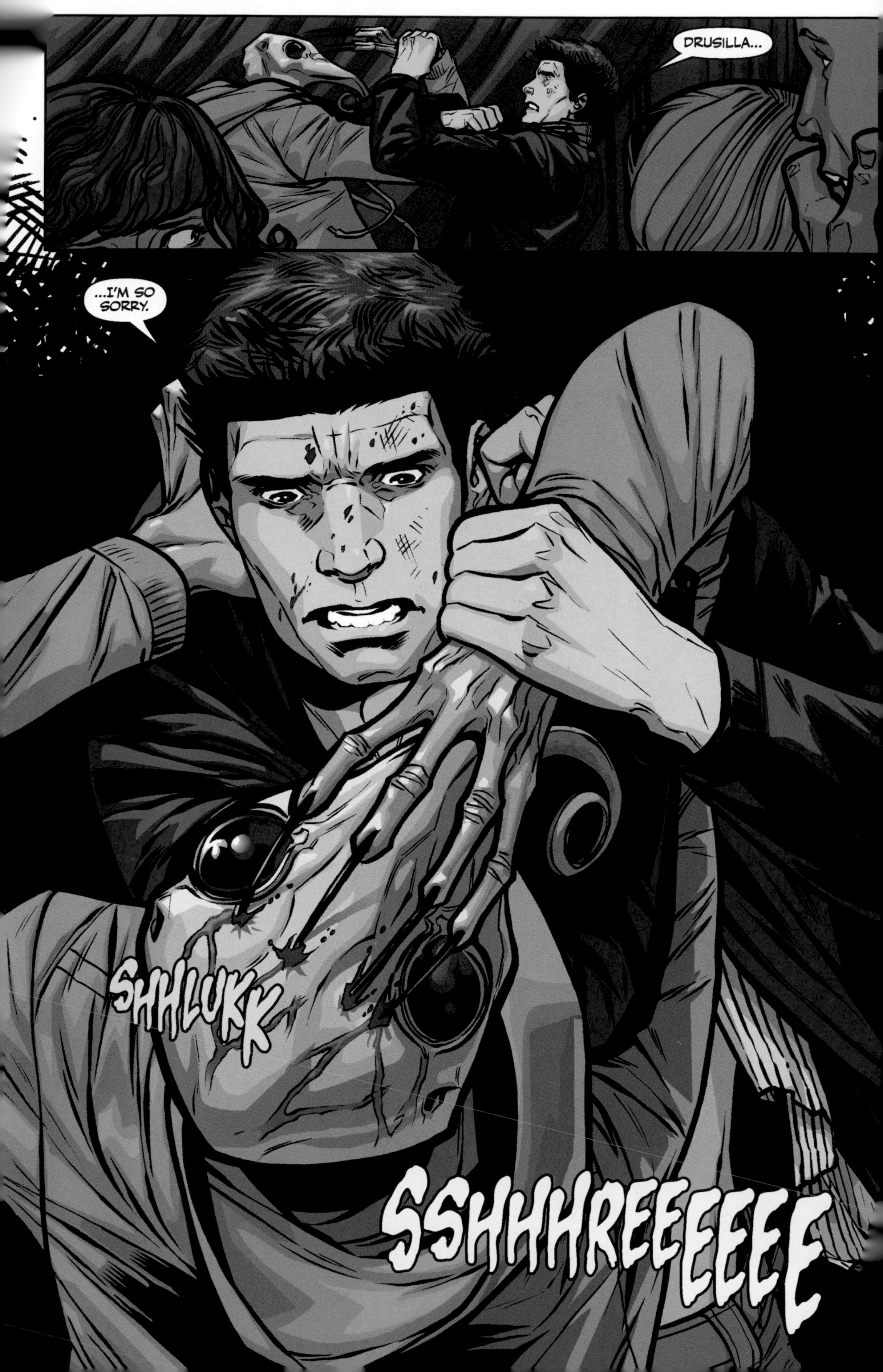
DRUSILLA...
...I'M SO SORRY.
SHHLUKK
SSHHHREEEEEEE

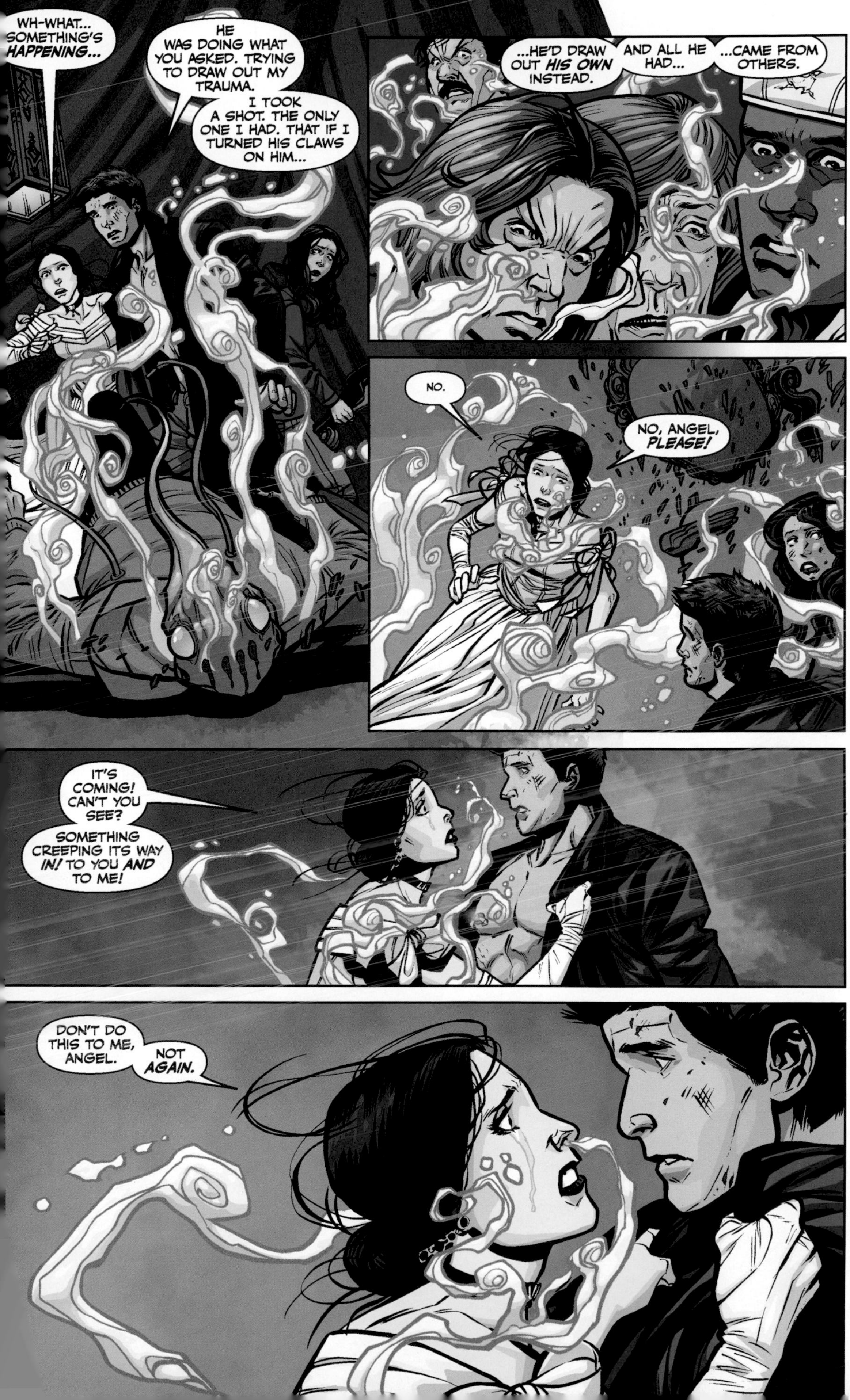
WH-WHAT... SOMETHING'S HAPPENING...
HE WAS DOING WHAT YOU ASKED. TRYING TO DRAW OUT MY TRAUMA.
I TOOK A SHOT. THE ONLY ONE I HAD. THAT IF I TURNED HIS CLAWS ON HIM...
...HE'D DRAW OUT HIS OWN INSTEAD.
AND ALL HE HAD...
...CAME FROM OTHERS.
NO.
NO, ANGEL, PLEASE!
IT'S COMING! CAN'T YOU SEE?
SOMETHING CREEPING ITS WAY IN! TO YOU AND TO ME!
DON'T DO THIS TO ME, ANGEL.
NOT AGAIN.

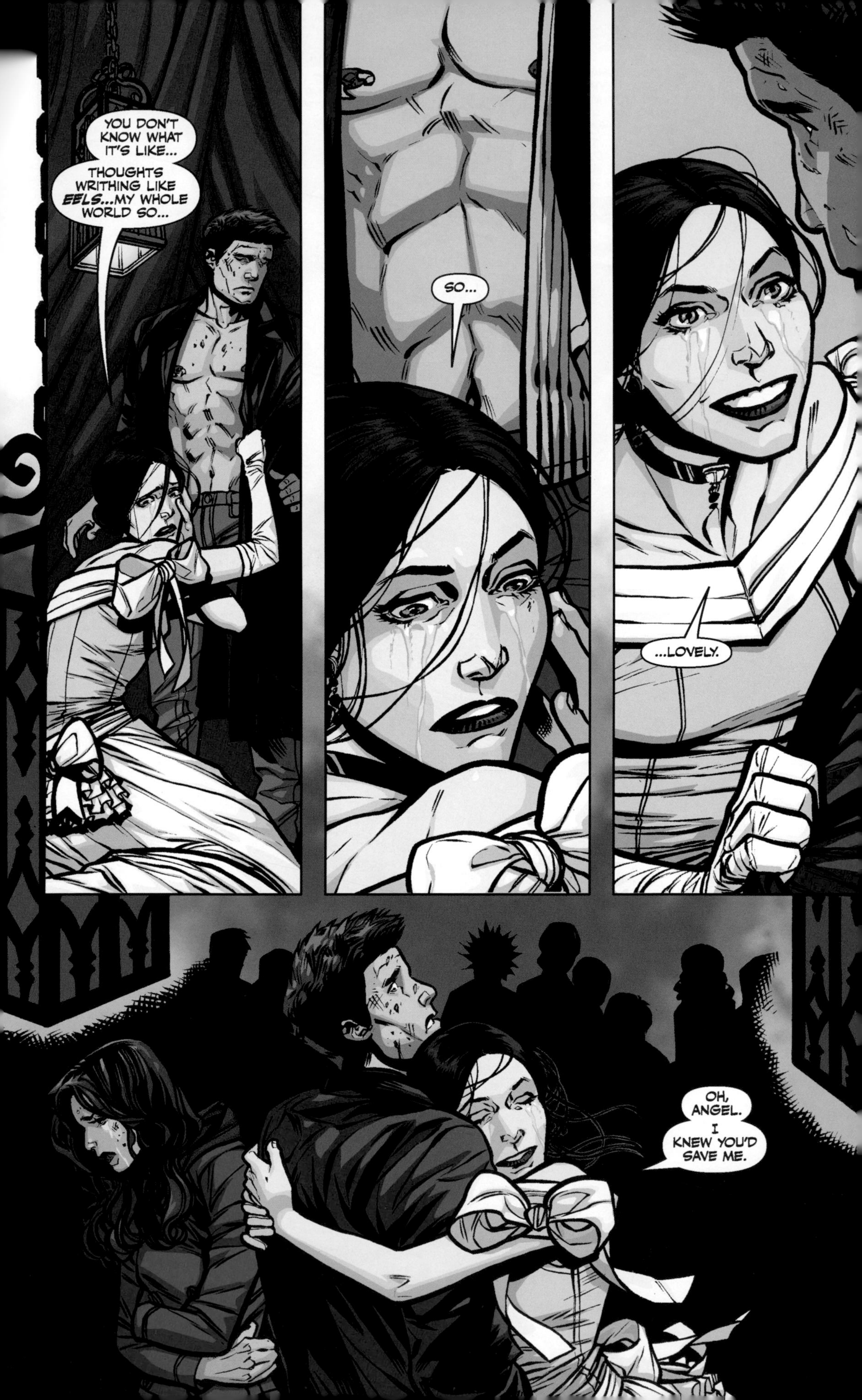
YOU DON'T KNOW WHAT IT'S LIKE...
THOUGHTS WRITHING LIKE EELS...MY WHOLE WORLD SO...
SO...
...LOVELY.
OH, ANGEL. I KNEW YOU'D SAVE ME.

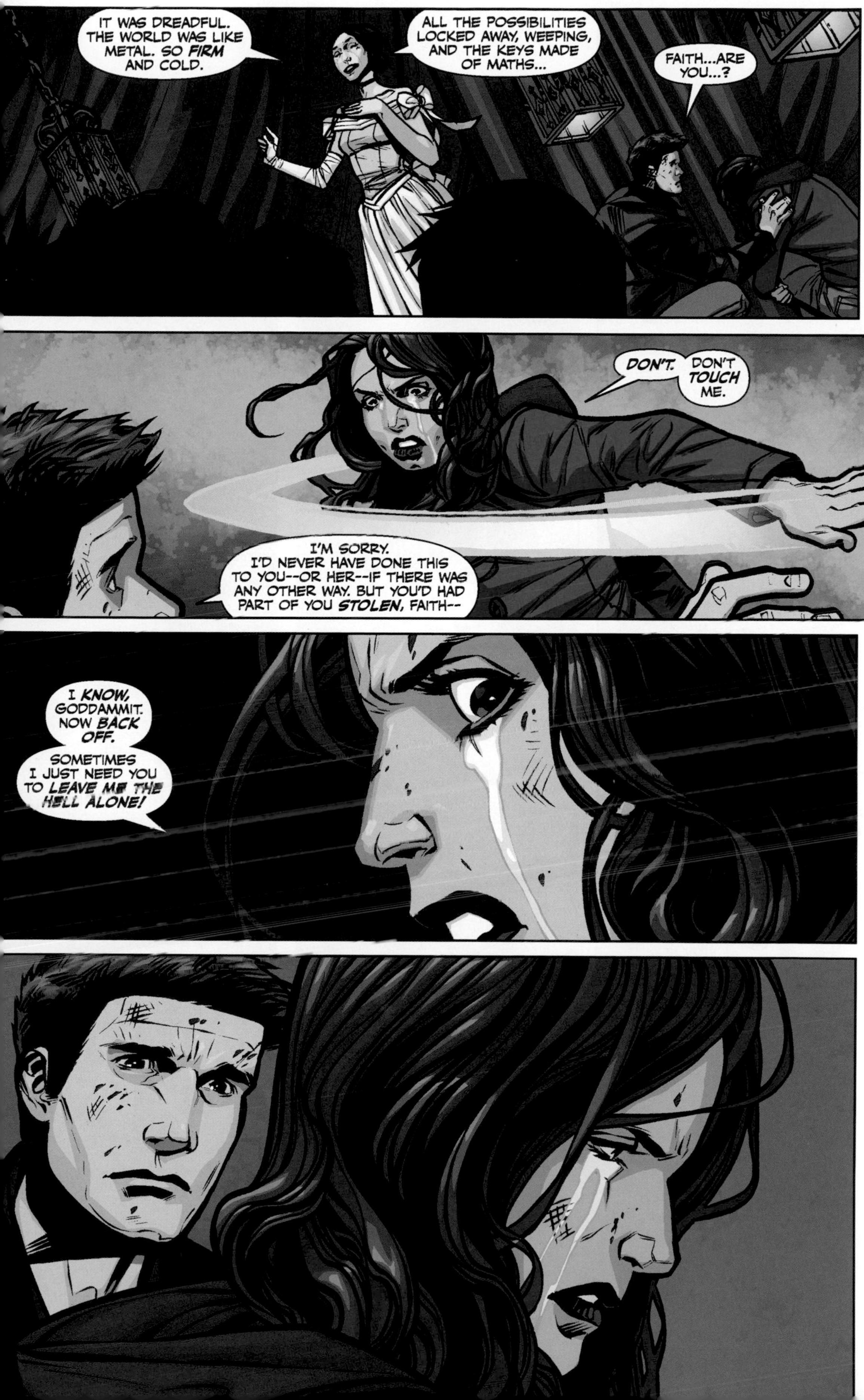
IT WAS DREADFUL. THE WORLD WAS LIKE METAL. SO FIRM AND COLD.
ALL THE POSSIBILITIES LOCKED AWAY, WEEPING, AND THE KEYS MADE OF MATHS...
FAITH...ARE YOU...?
DON'T. DON'T TOUCH ME.
I'M SORRY. I'D NEVER HAVE DONE THIS TO YOU--OR HER--IF THERE WAS ANY OTHER WAY. BUT YOU'D HAD PART OF YOU STOLEN, FAITH--
I KNOW, GODDAMMIT. NOW BACK OFF.
SOMETIMES I JUST NEED YOU TO LEAVE ME THE HELL ALONE!

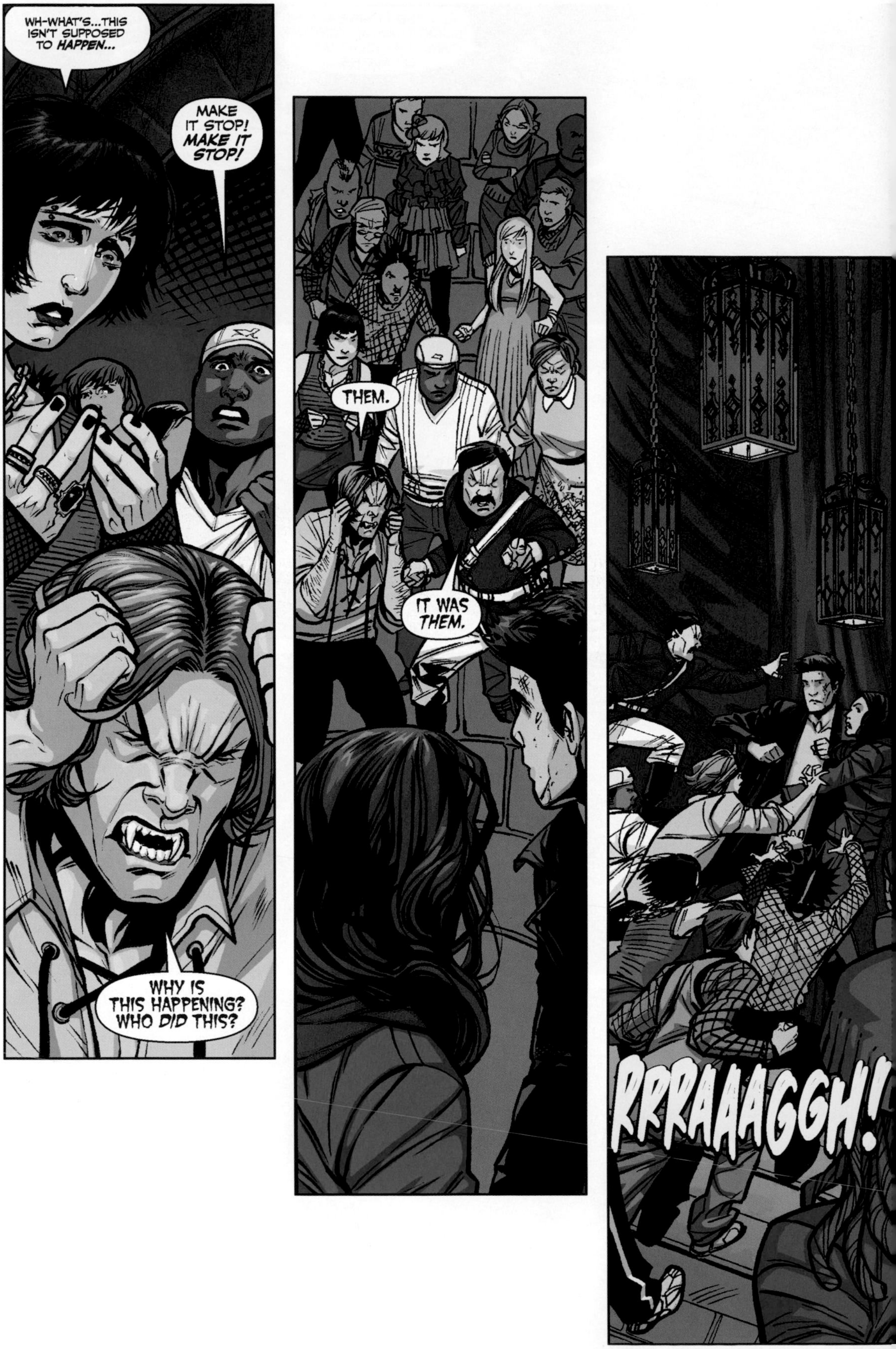
WH-WHAT'S...THIS ISN'T SUPPOSED TO HAPPEN...
MAKE IT STOP! MAKE IT STOP!
WHY IS THIS HAPPENING? WHO DID THIS?
THEM.
IT WAS THEM.
RRRAAAGGH!

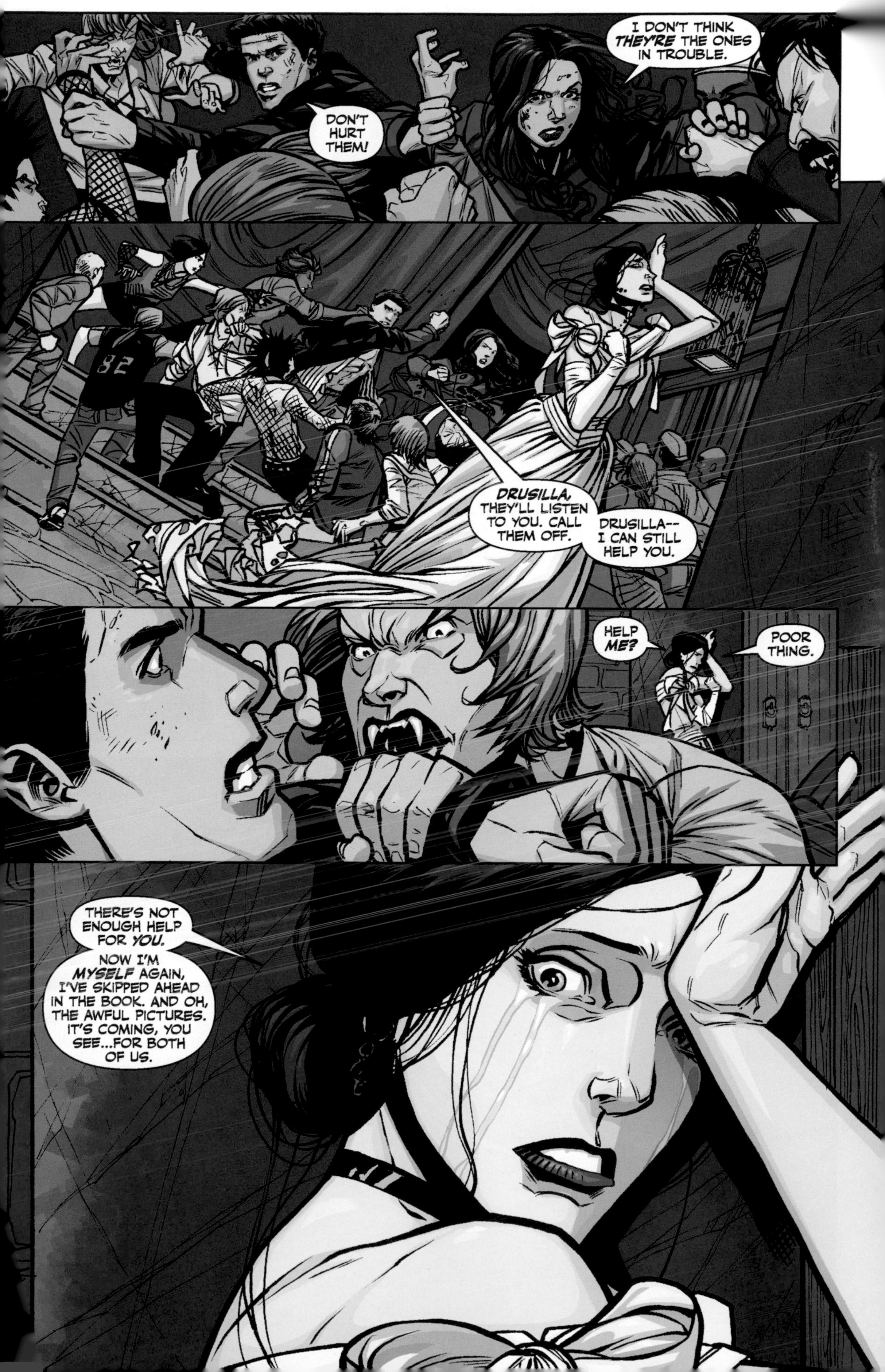
DON'T HURT THEM!
I DON'T THINK THEY'RE THE ONES IN TROUBLE.
DRUSILLA, THEY'LL LISTEN TO YOU. CALL THEM OFF.
DRUSILLA-- I CAN STILL HELP YOU.
HELP ME?
POOR THING.
THERE'S NOT ENOUGH HELP FOR YOU.
NOW I'M MYSELF AGAIN, I'VE SKIPPED AHEAD IN THE BOOK. AND OH, THE AWFUL PICTURES. IT'S COMING, YOU SEE...FOR BOTH OF US.

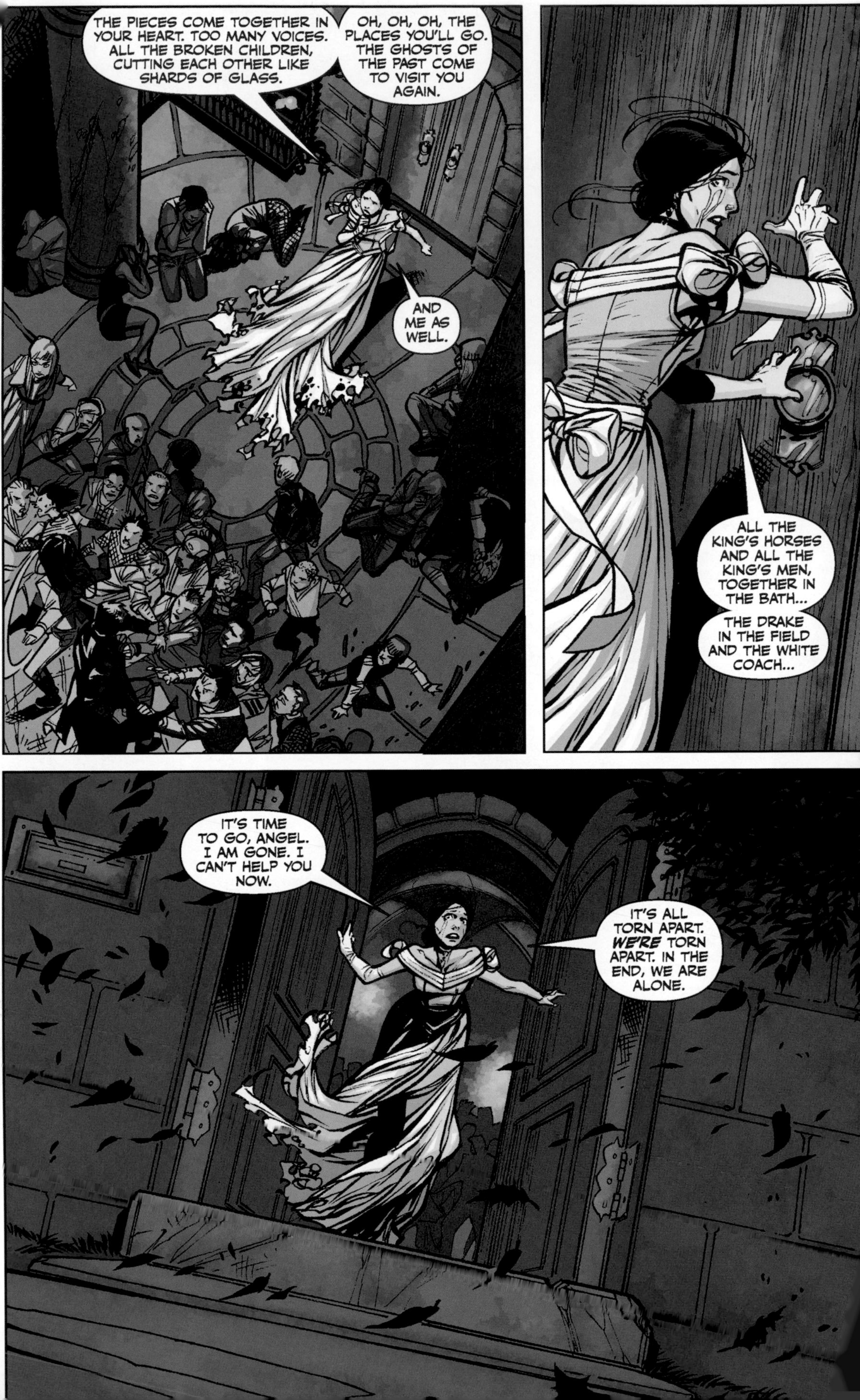
THE PIECES COME TOGETHER IN YOUR HEART. TOO MANY VOICES. ALL THE BROKEN CHILDREN, CUTTING EACH OTHER LIKE SHARDS OF GLASS.
OH, OH, OH, THE PLACES YOU'LL GO. THE GHOSTS OF THE PAST COME TO VISIT YOU AGAIN.
AND ME AS WELL.
ALL THE KING'S HORSES AND ALL THE KING'S MEN, TOGETHER IN THE BATH...
THE DRAKE IN THE FIELD AND THE WHITE COACH...
IT'S TIME TO GO, ANGEL. I AM GONE. I CAN'T HELP YOU NOW.
IT'S ALL TORN APART. *WE'RE* TORN APART. IN THE END, WE ARE ALONE.

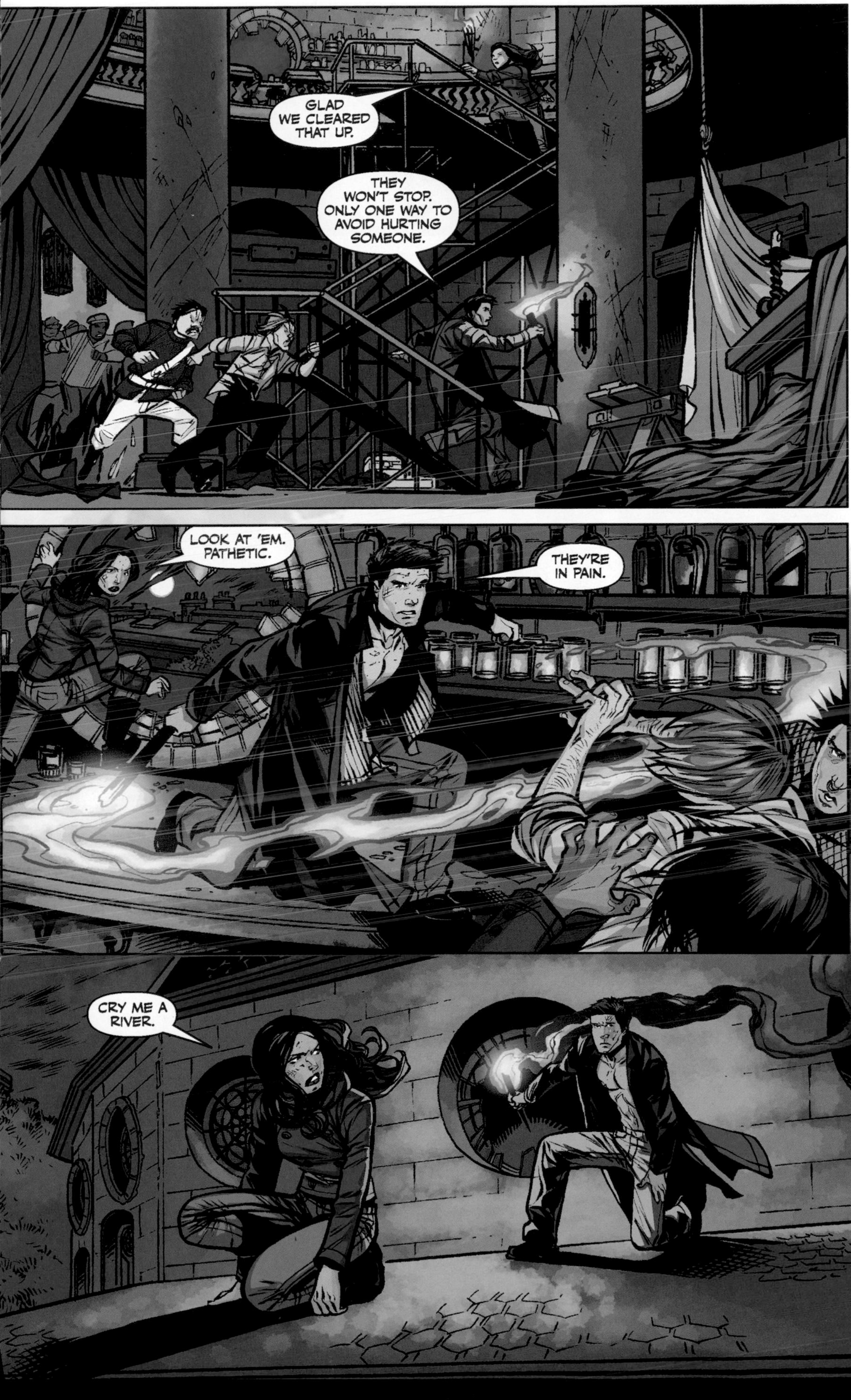
GLAD WE CLEARED THAT UP.
THEY WON'T STOP. ONLY ONE WAY TO AVOID HURTING SOMEONE.
LOOK AT 'EM. PATHETIC.
THEY'RE IN PAIN.
CRY ME A RIVER.

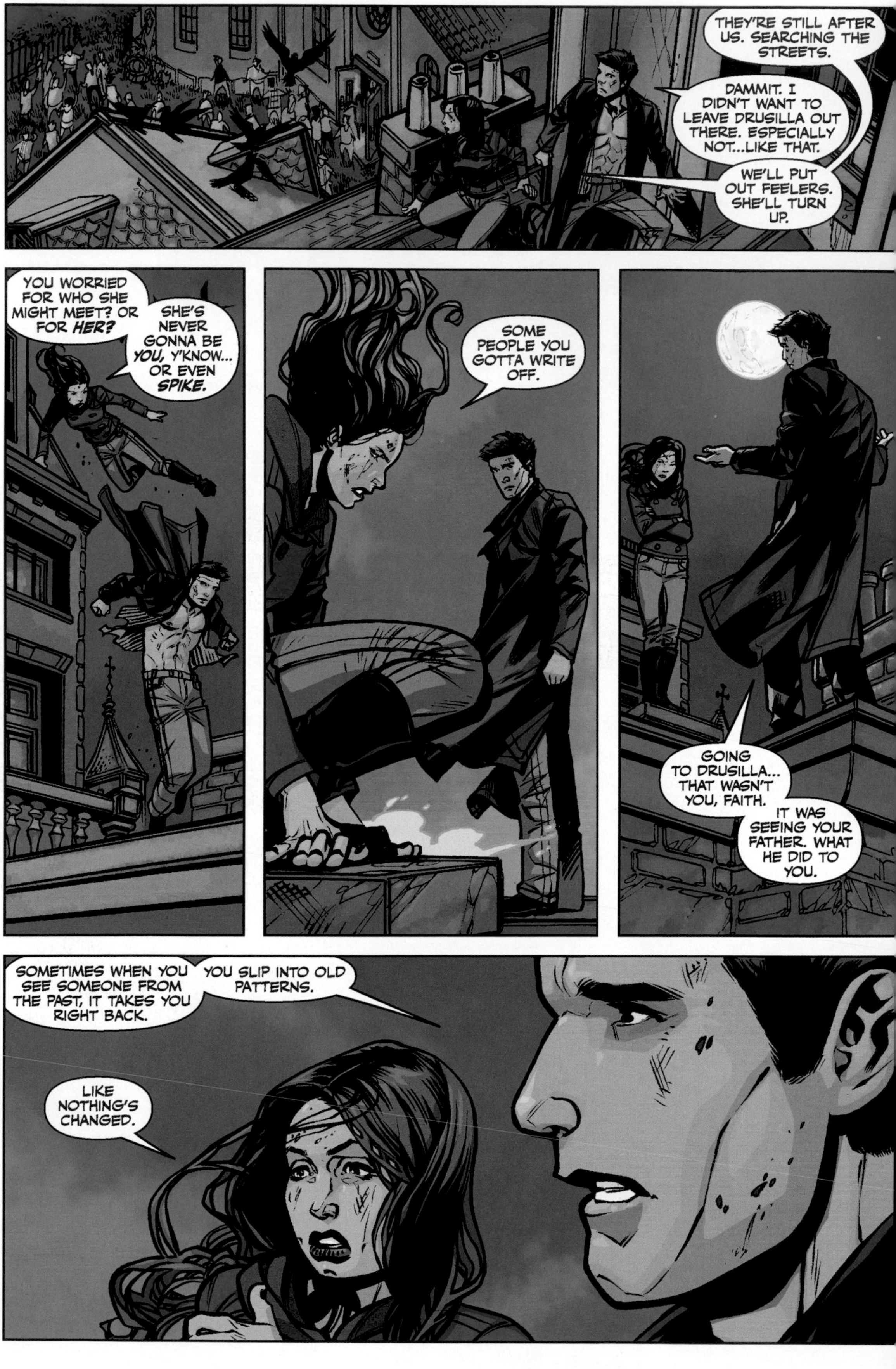
THEY'RE STILL AFTER US. SEARCHING THE STREETS.
DAMMIT. I DIDN'T WANT TO LEAVE DRUSILLA OUT THERE. ESPECIALLY NOT...LIKE THAT.
WE'LL PUT OUT FEELERS. SHE'LL TURN UP.
YOU WORRIED FOR WHO SHE MIGHT MEET? OR FOR *HER?*
SHE'S NEVER GONNA BE *YOU,* Y'KNOW... OR EVEN *SPIKE.*
SOME PEOPLE YOU GOTTA WRITE OFF.
GOING TO DRUSILLA... THAT WASN'T YOU, FAITH.
IT WAS SEEING YOUR FATHER. WHAT HE DID TO YOU.
SOMETIMES WHEN YOU SEE SOMEONE FROM THE PAST, IT TAKES YOU RIGHT BACK.
YOU SLIP INTO OLD PATTERNS.
LIKE NOTHING'S CHANGED.

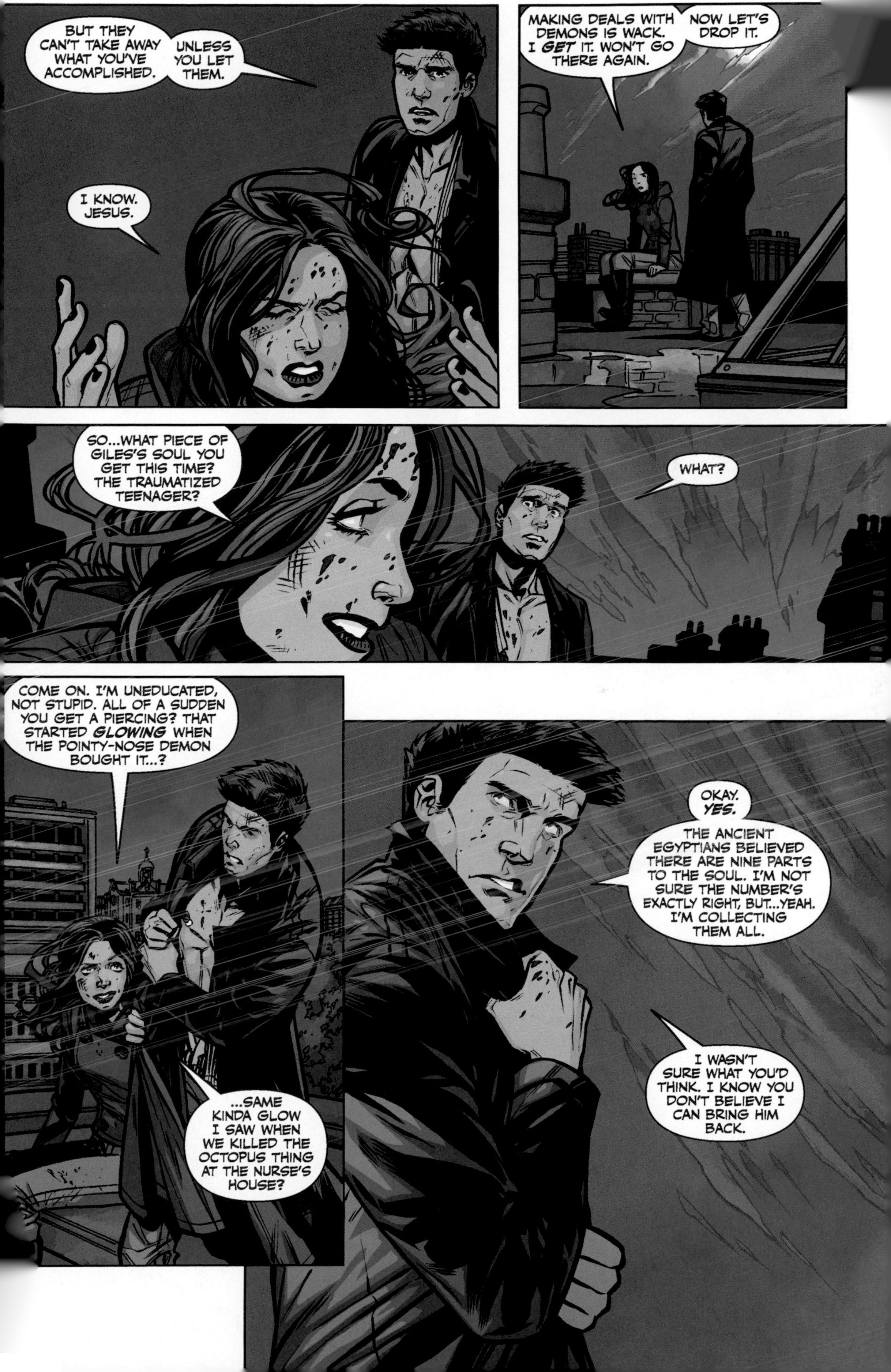
BUT THEY CAN'T TAKE AWAY WHAT YOU'VE ACCOMPLISHED.
UNLESS YOU LET THEM.
I KNOW. JESUS.
MAKING DEALS WITH DEMONS IS WACK. I *GET* IT. WON'T GO THERE AGAIN.
NOW LET'S DROP IT.
SO...WHAT PIECE OF GILES'S SOUL YOU GET THIS TIME? THE TRAUMATIZED TEENAGER?
WHAT?
COME ON. I'M UNEDUCATED, NOT STUPID. ALL OF A SUDDEN YOU GET A PIERCING? THAT STARTED *GLOWING* WHEN THE POINTY-NOSE DEMON BOUGHT IT...?
...SAME KINDA GLOW I SAW WHEN WE KILLED THE OCTOPUS THING AT THE NURSE'S HOUSE?
OKAY. *YES.*
THE ANCIENT EGYPTIANS BELIEVED THERE ARE NINE PARTS TO THE SOUL. I'M NOT SURE THE NUMBER'S EXACTLY RIGHT, BUT...YEAH. I'M COLLECTING THEM ALL.
I WASN'T SURE WHAT YOU'D THINK. I KNOW YOU DON'T BELIEVE I CAN BRING HIM BACK.

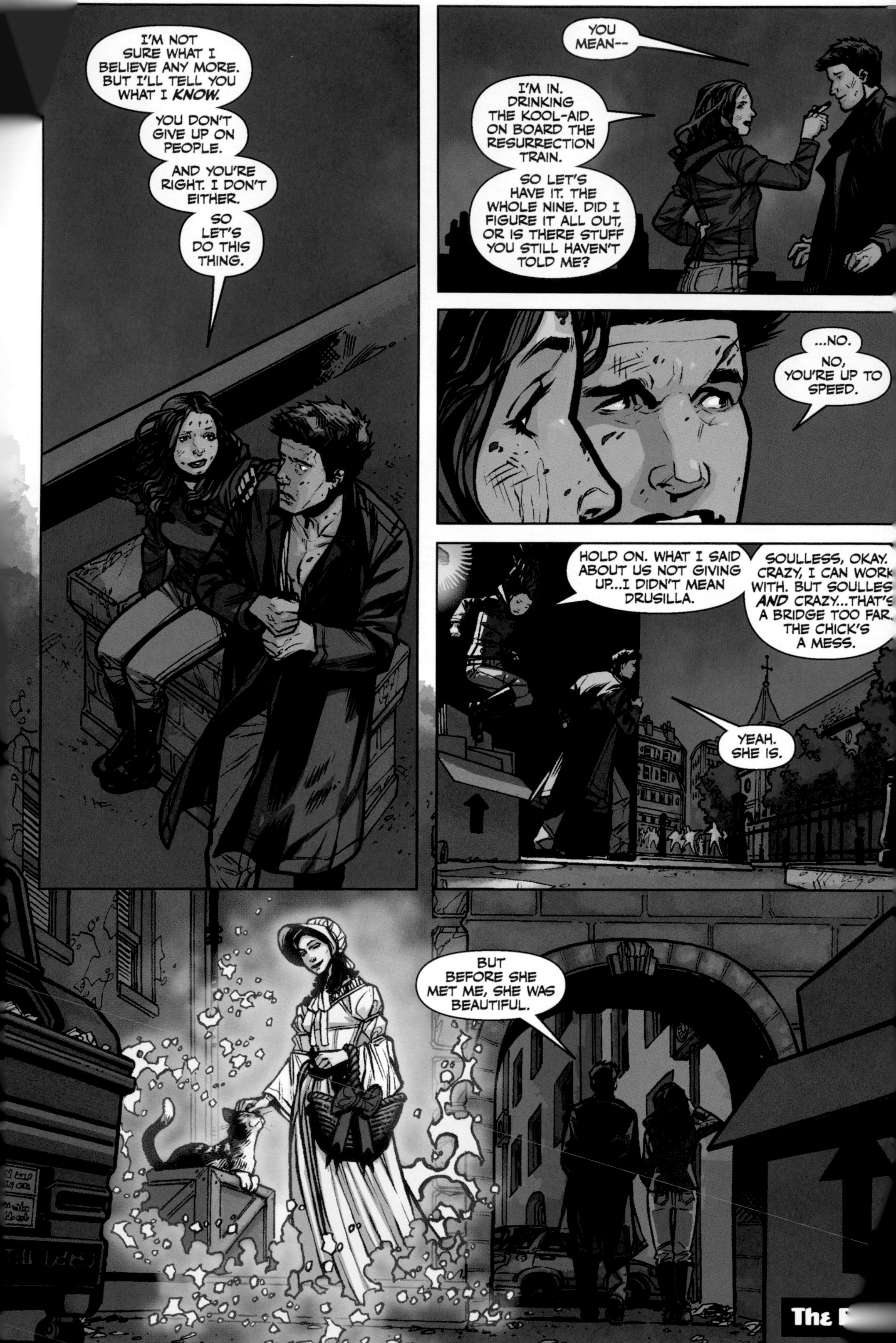
I'M NOT SURE WHAT I BELIEVE ANY MORE. BUT I'LL TELL YOU WHAT I *KNOW.*
YOU DON'T GIVE UP ON PEOPLE.
AND YOU'RE RIGHT. I DON'T EITHER.
SO LET'S DO THIS THING.
YOU MEAN--
I'M IN. DRINKING THE KOOL-AID. ON BOARD THE RESURRECTION TRAIN.
SO LET'S HAVE IT. THE WHOLE NINE. DID I FIGURE IT ALL OUT, OR IS THERE STUFF YOU STILL HAVEN'T TOLD ME?
...NO.
NO, YOU'RE UP TO SPEED.
HOLD ON. WHAT I SAID ABOUT US NOT GIVING UP...I DIDN'T MEAN DRUSILLA.
SOULLESS, OKAY. CRAZY, I CAN WORK WITH. BUT SOULLES *AND* CRAZY...THAT'S A BRIDGE TOO FAR. THE CHICK'S A MESS.
YEAH. SHE IS.
BUT BEFORE SHE MET ME, SHE WAS BEAUTIFUL.

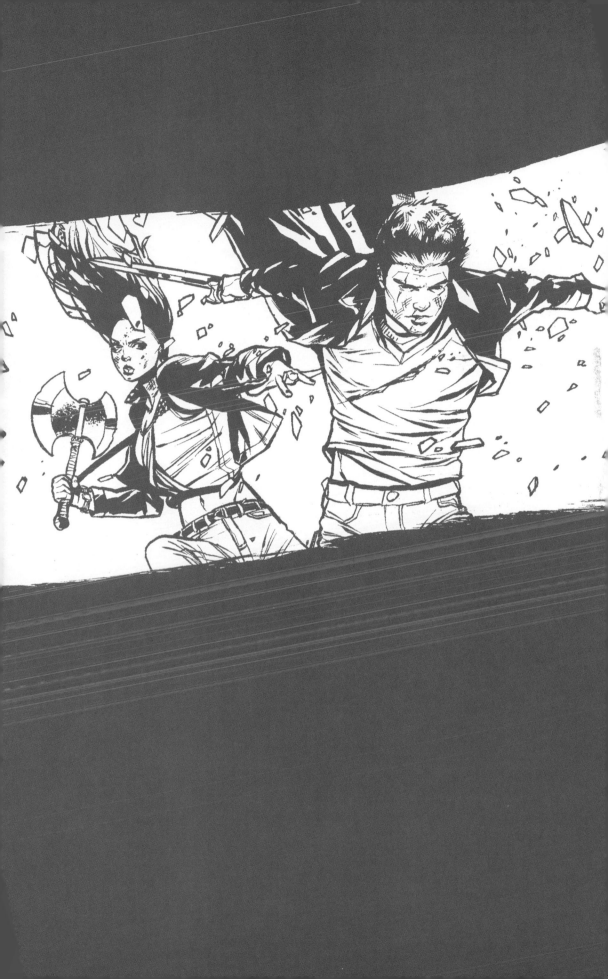

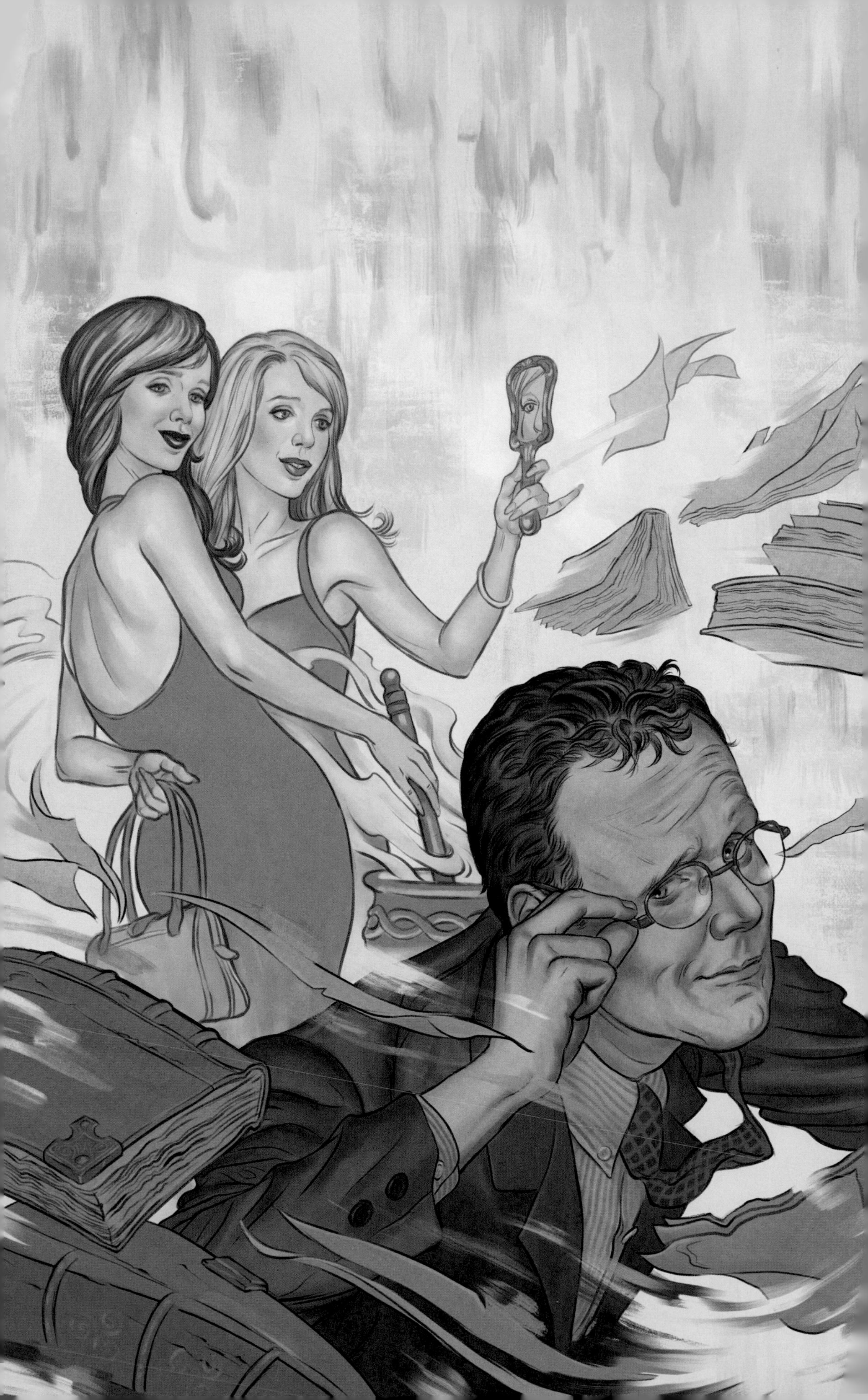

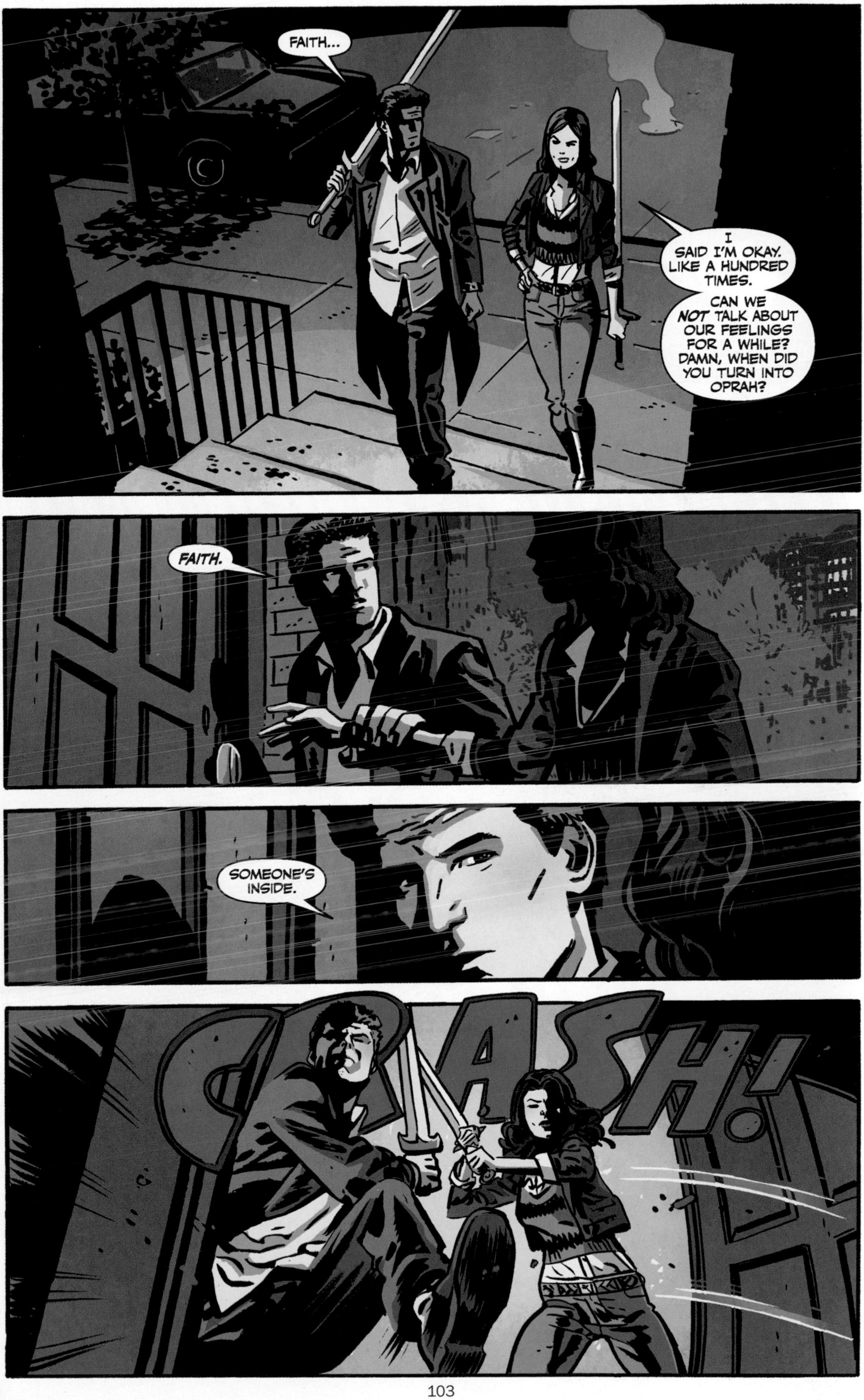
FAITH...
I SAID I'M OKAY. LIKE A HUNDRED TIMES.
CAN WE *NOT* TALK ABOUT OUR FEELINGS FOR A WHILE? DAMN, WHEN DID YOU TURN INTO OPRAH?
FAITH.
SOMEONE'S INSIDE.
CRASH!

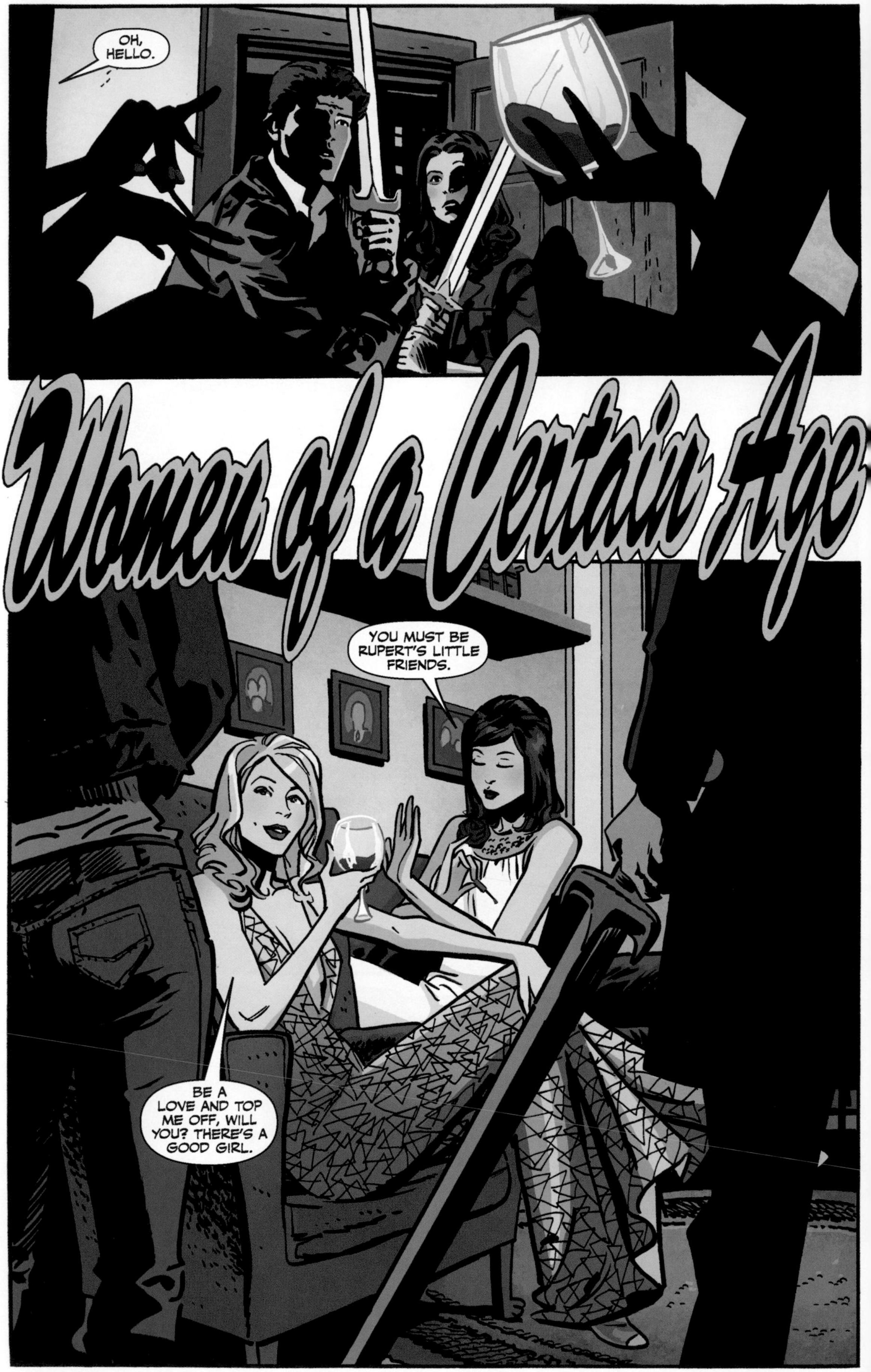
OH, HELLO.
Women of a Certain Age
YOU MUST BE RUPERT'S LITTLE FRIENDS.
BE A LOVE AND TOP ME OFF, WILL YOU? THERE'S A GOOD GIRL.

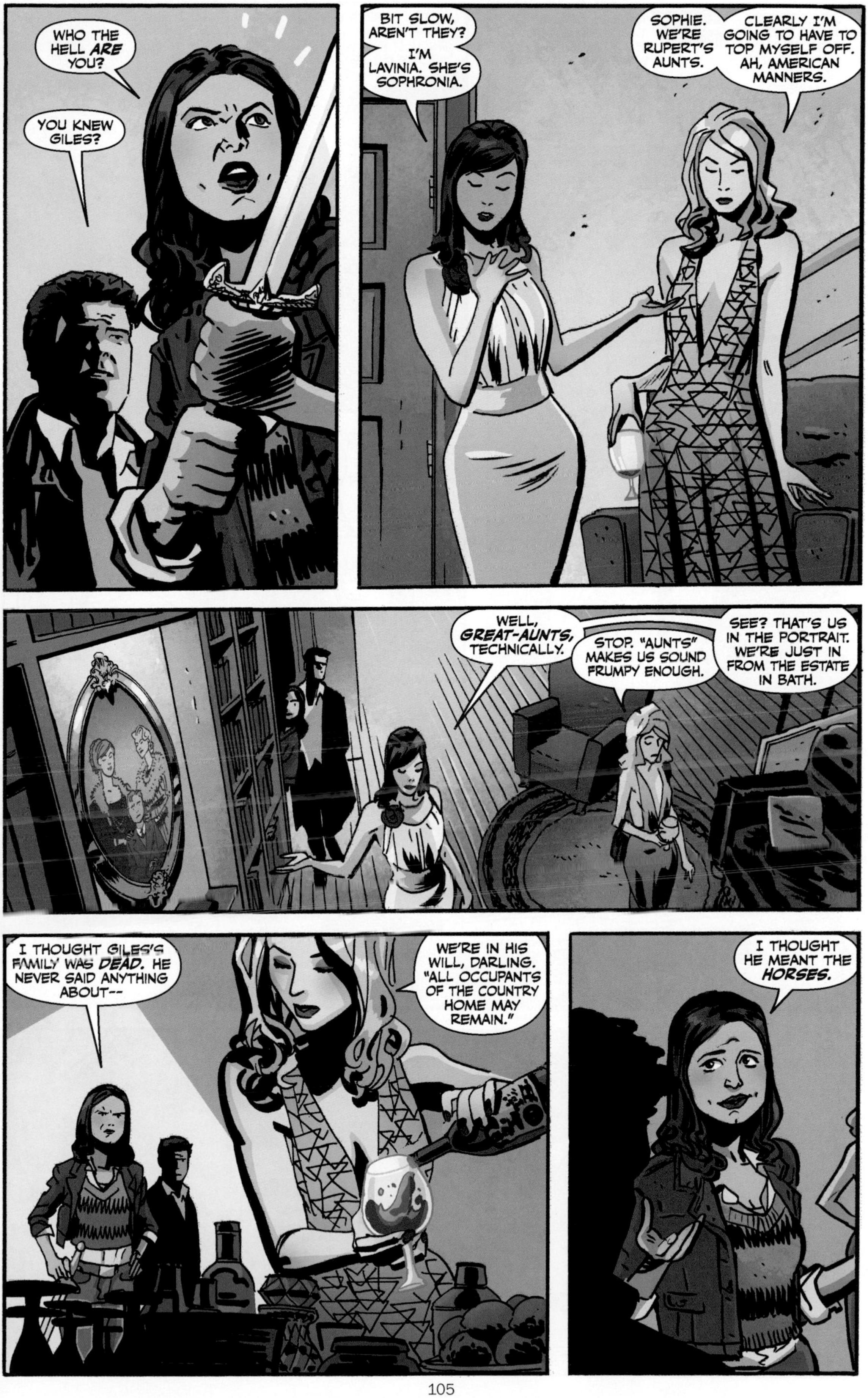
WHO THE HELL ARE YOU?
YOU KNEW GILES?
BIT SLOW, AREN'T THEY?
I'M LAVINIA. SHE'S SOPHRONIA.
SOPHIE. WE'RE RUPERT'S AUNTS.
CLEARLY I'M GOING TO HAVE TO TOP MYSELF OFF. AH, AMERICAN MANNERS.
WELL, GREAT-AUNTS, TECHNICALLY.
STOP. "AUNTS" MAKES US SOUND FRUMPY ENOUGH.
SEE? THAT'S US IN THE PORTRAIT. WE'RE JUST IN FROM THE ESTATE IN BATH.
I THOUGHT GILES'S FAMILY WAS DEAD. HE NEVER SAID ANYTHING ABOUT--
WE'RE IN HIS WILL, DARLING. "ALL OCCUPANTS OF THE COUNTRY HOME MAY REMAIN."
I THOUGHT HE MEANT THE HORSES.

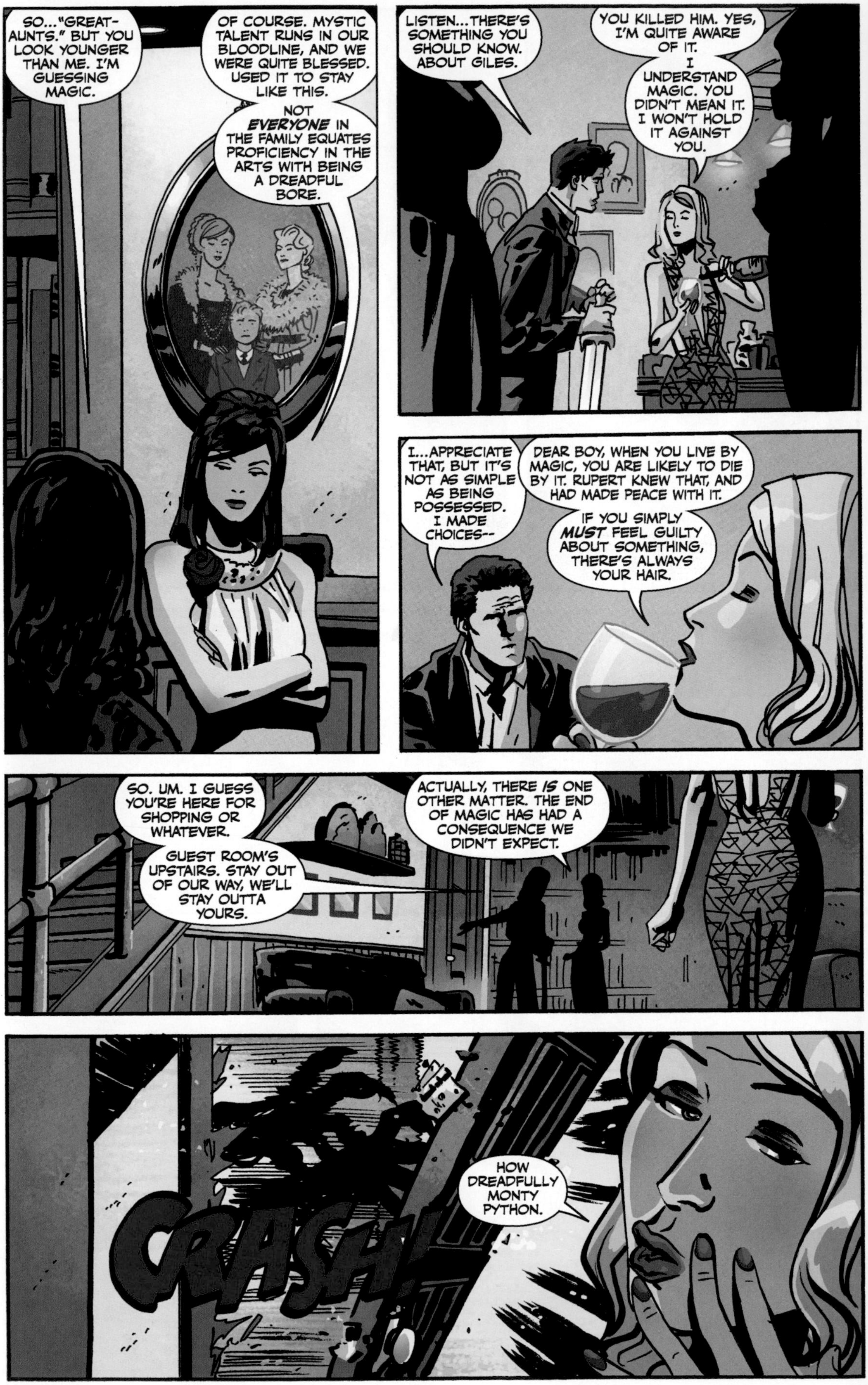
SO..."GREAT-AUNTS." BUT YOU LOOK YOUNGER THAN ME. I'M GUESSING MAGIC.
OF COURSE. MYSTIC TALENT RUNS IN OUR BLOODLINE, AND WE WERE QUITE BLESSED. USED IT TO STAY LIKE THIS.
NOT EVERYONE IN THE FAMILY EQUATES PROFICIENCY IN THE ARTS WITH BEING A DREADFUL BORE.
LISTEN...THERE'S SOMETHING YOU SHOULD KNOW. ABOUT GILES.
YOU KILLED HIM. YES, I'M QUITE AWARE OF IT.
I UNDERSTAND MAGIC. YOU DIDN'T MEAN IT. I WON'T HOLD IT AGAINST YOU.
I...APPRECIATE THAT, BUT IT'S NOT AS SIMPLE AS BEING POSSESSED. I MADE CHOICES--
DEAR BOY, WHEN YOU LIVE BY MAGIC, YOU ARE LIKELY TO DIE BY IT. RUPERT KNEW THAT, AND HAD MADE PEACE WITH IT.
IF YOU SIMPLY MUST FEEL GUILTY ABOUT SOMETHING, THERE'S ALWAYS YOUR HAIR.
SO. UM. I GUESS YOU'RE HERE FOR SHOPPING OR WHATEVER.
GUEST ROOM'S UPSTAIRS. STAY OUT OF OUR WAY, WE'LL STAY OUTTA YOURS.
ACTUALLY, THERE IS ONE OTHER MATTER. THE END OF MAGIC HAS HAD A CONSEQUENCE WE DIDN'T EXPECT.
CRASH!
HOW DREADFULLY MONTY PYTHON.

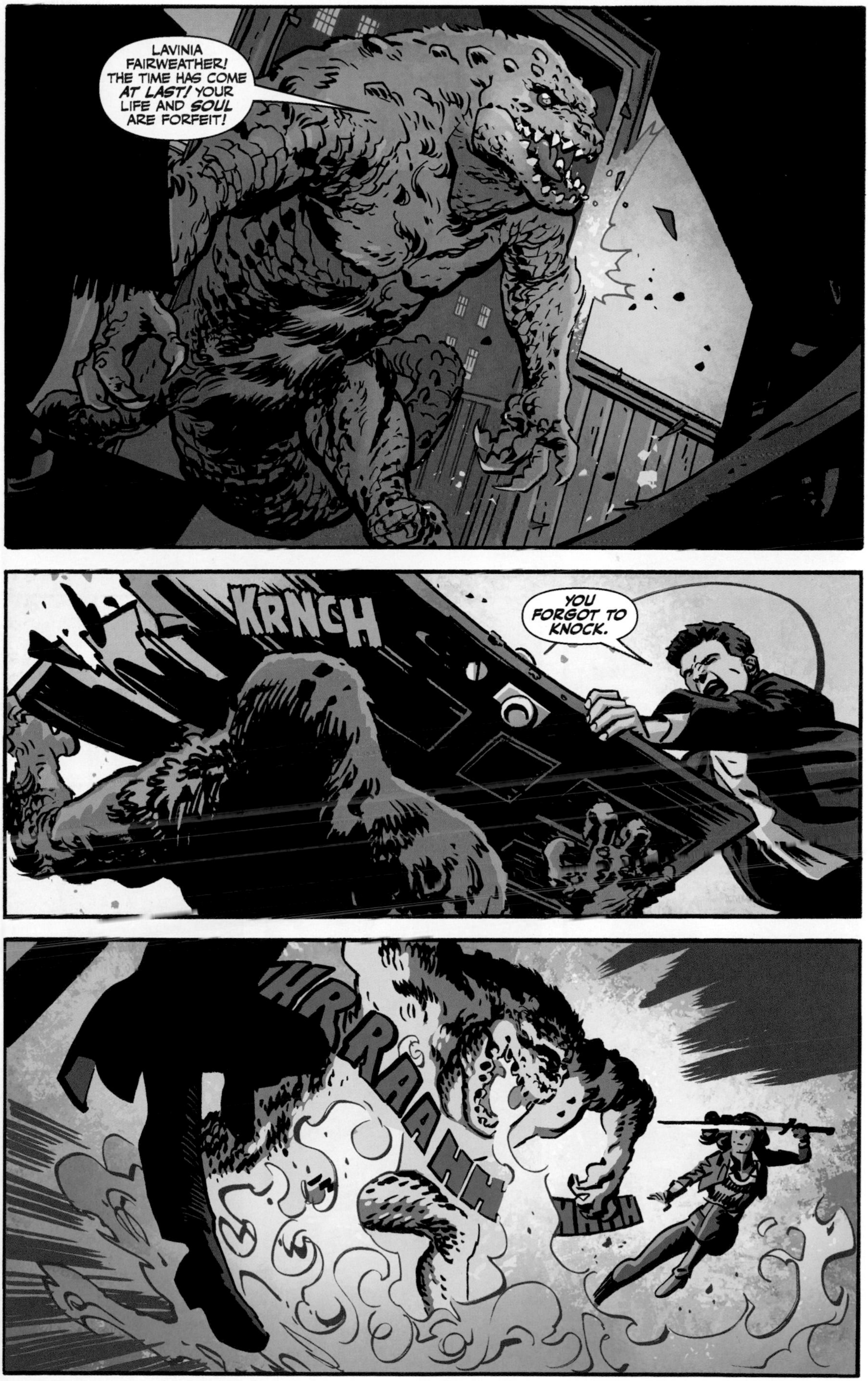
LAVINIA FAIRWEATHER! THE TIME HAS COME *AT LAST!* YOUR LIFE AND *SOUL* ARE FORFEIT!
KRNCH
YOU FORGOT TO KNOCK.
HRRAAHH

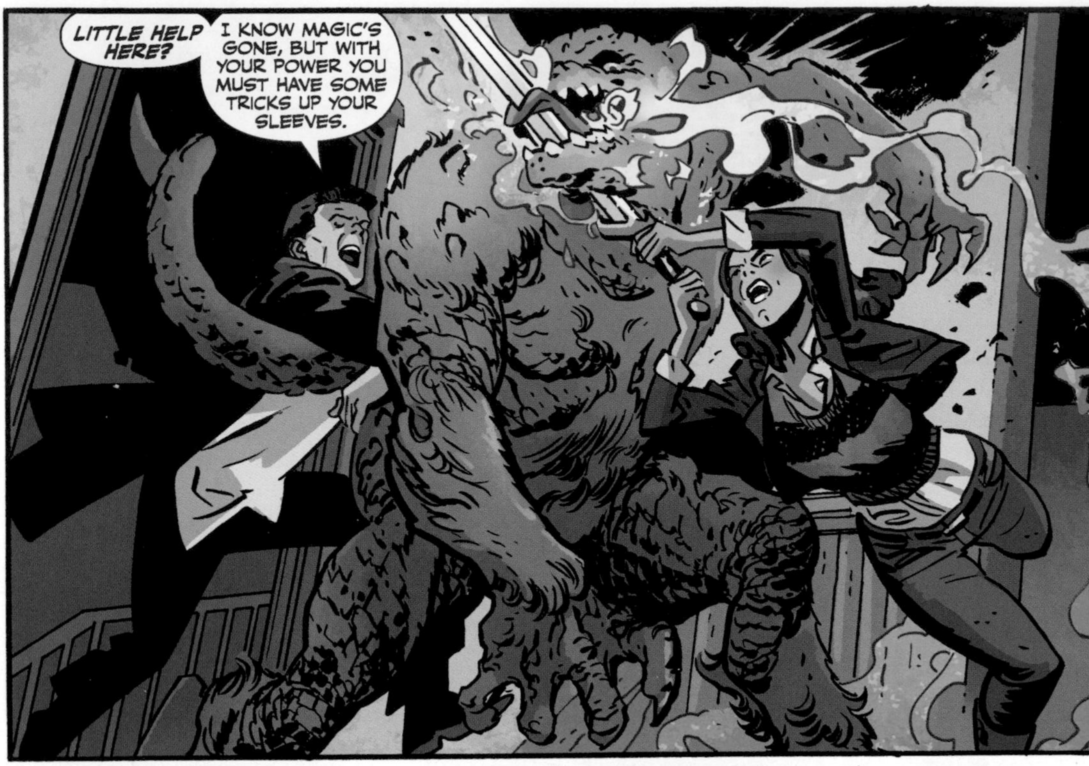
LITTLE HELP HERE?
I KNOW MAGIC'S GONE, BUT WITH YOUR POWER YOU MUST HAVE SOME TRICKS UP YOUR SLEEVES.
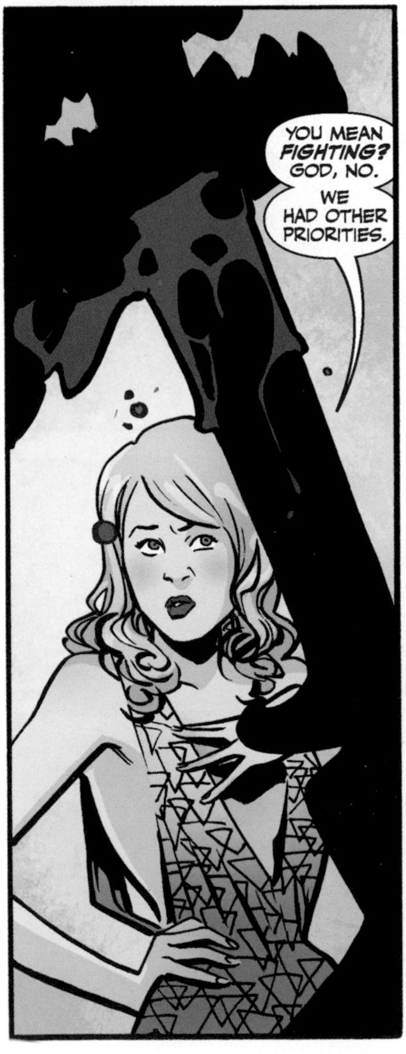
YOU MEAN FIGHTING? GOD, NO.
WE HAD OTHER PRIORITIES.
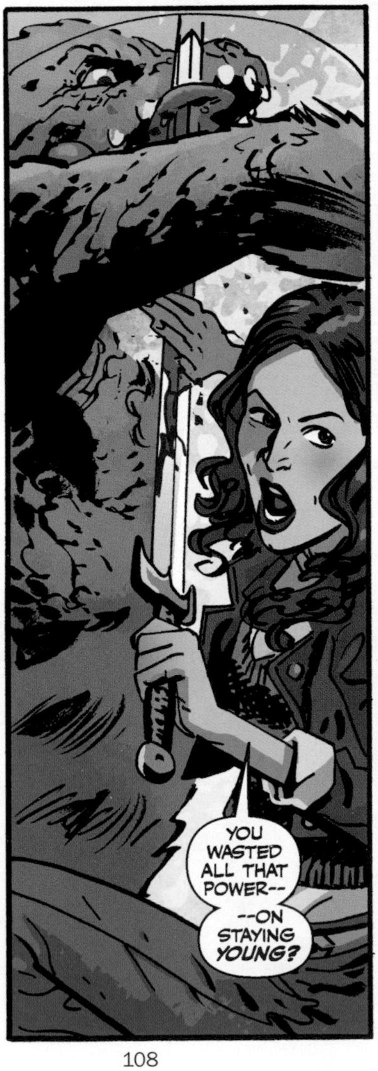
YOU WASTED ALL THAT POWER--
--ON STAYING YOUNG?
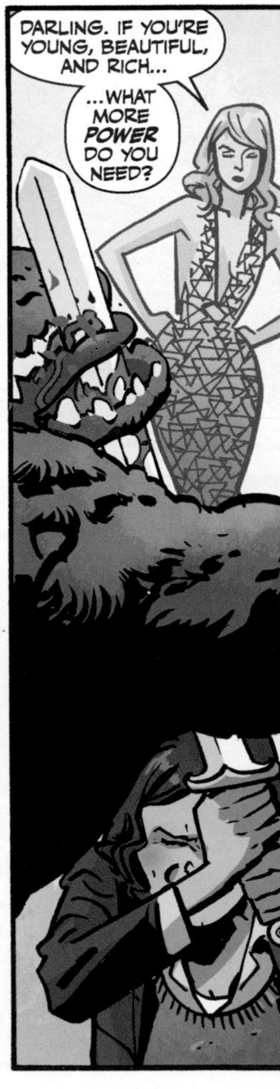
DARLING. IF YOU'RE YOUNG, BEAUTIFUL, AND RICH...
...WHAT MORE POWER DO YOU NEED?

ON THREE.

ONE...

...TWO...

THREE!

SHKK

OKAY, WHAT THE HELL WAS THAT ABOUT?

OH...I KIND OF PROMISED HIM MY SOUL. IN EXCHANGE FOR A SALVE THAT BANISHES CELLULITE. WORKED LIKE A CHARM.

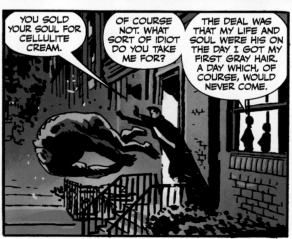

YOU SOLD YOUR SOUL FOR CELLULITE CREAM.

OF COURSE NOT. WHAT SORT OF IDIOT DO YOU TAKE ME FOR?

THE DEAL WAS THAT MY LIFE AND SOUL WERE HIS ON THE DAY I GOT MY FIRST GRAY HAIR. A DAY WHICH, OF COURSE, WOULD NEVER COME.

BUT THEN MAGIC WENT AWAY. AND, WELL, YESTERDAY THERE WAS THIS.

I CAN'T LOOK.

IT'S STILL HIDEOUS.

I DYED MINE.

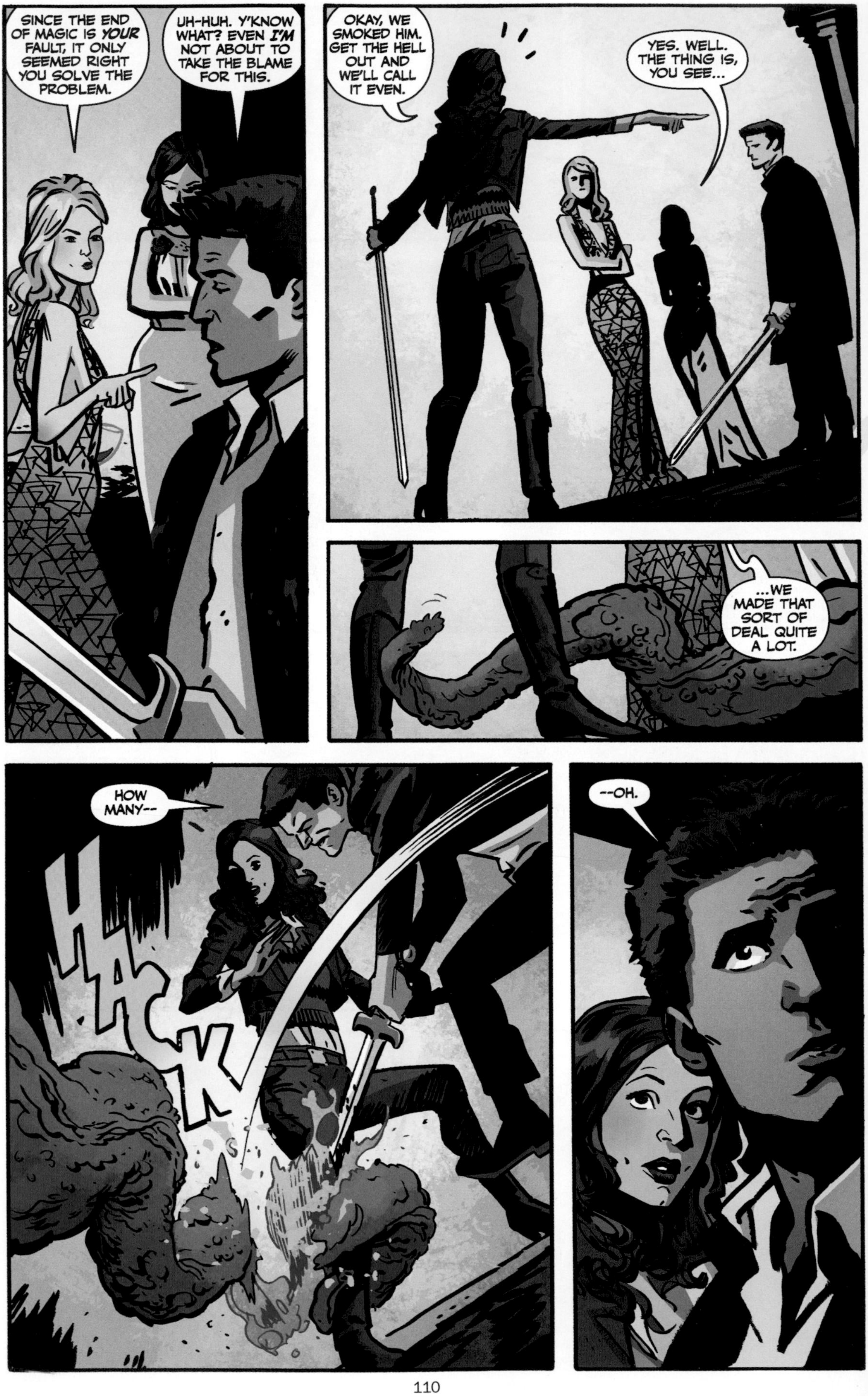
SINCE THE END OF MAGIC IS YOUR FAULT, IT ONLY SEEMED RIGHT YOU SOLVE THE PROBLEM.
UH-HUH. Y'KNOW WHAT? EVEN I'M NOT ABOUT TO TAKE THE BLAME FOR THIS.
OKAY, WE SMOKED HIM. GET THE HELL OUT AND WE'LL CALL IT EVEN.
YES. WELL. THE THING IS, YOU SEE...
...WE MADE THAT SORT OF DEAL QUITE A LOT.
HOW MANY--
HACK
--OH.

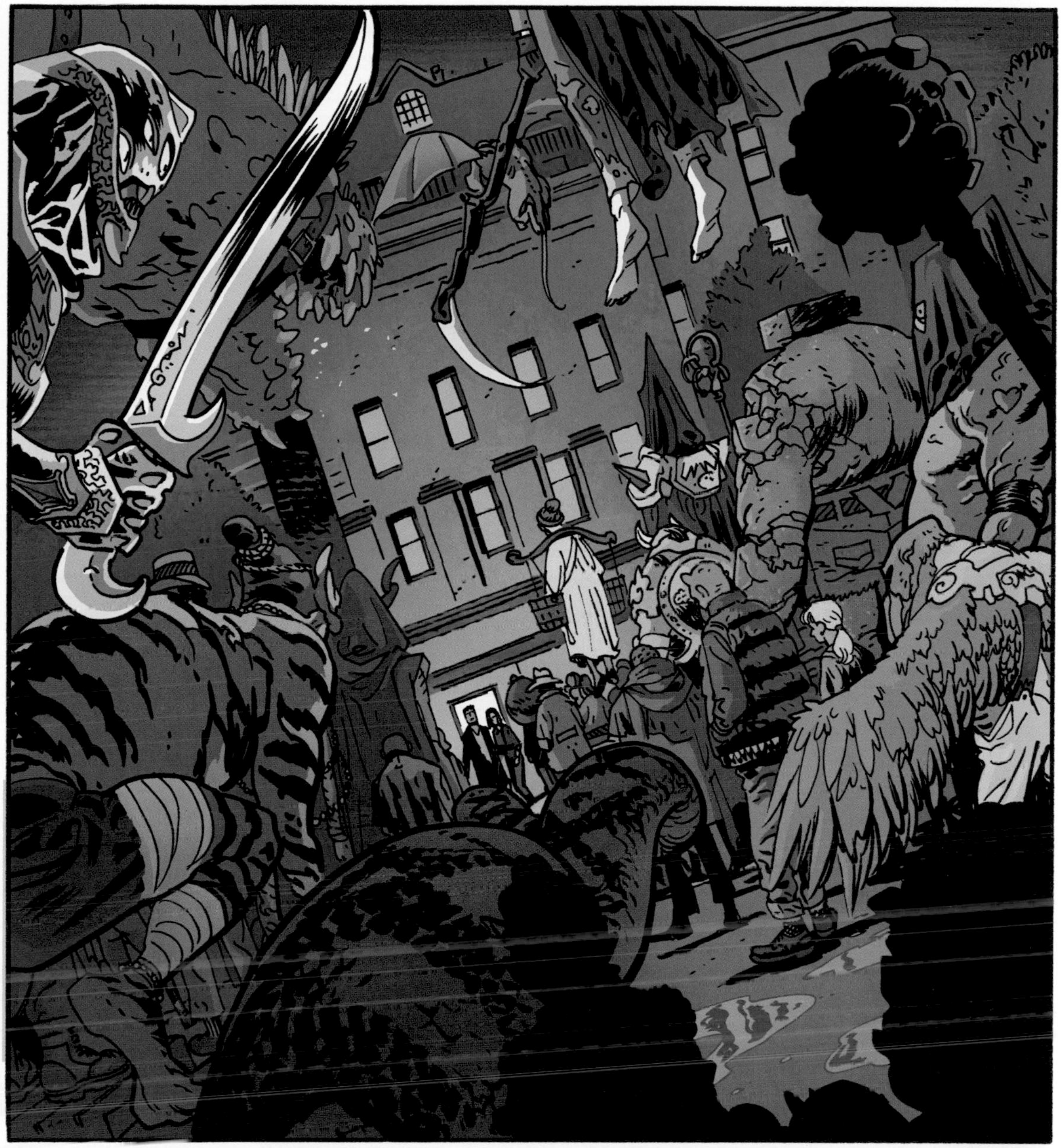

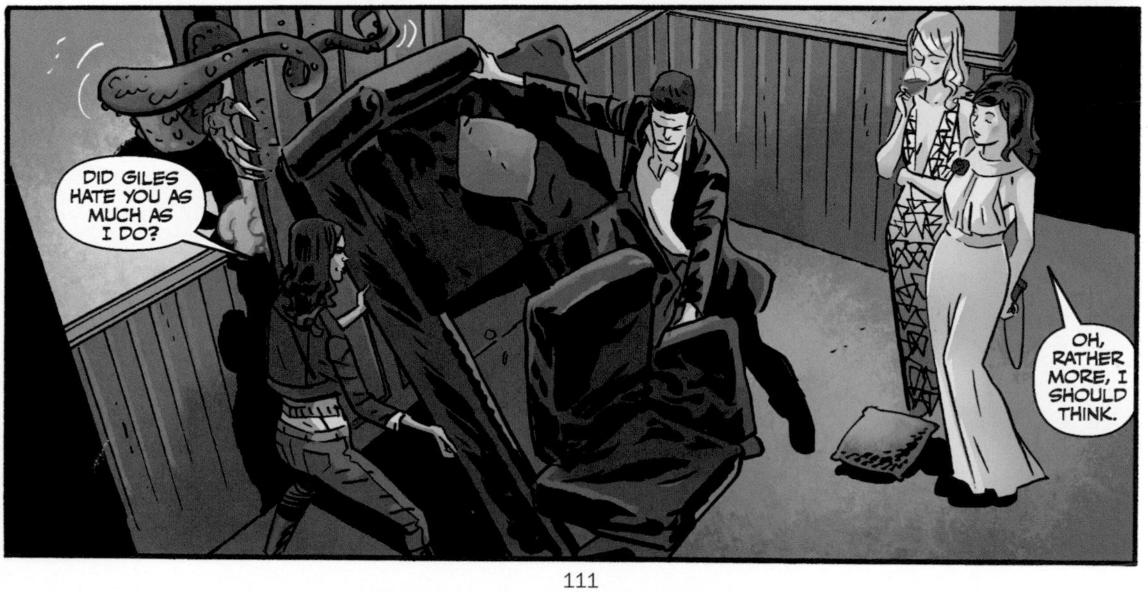
DID GILES HATE YOU AS MUCH AS I DO?
OH, RATHER MORE, I SHOULD THINK.

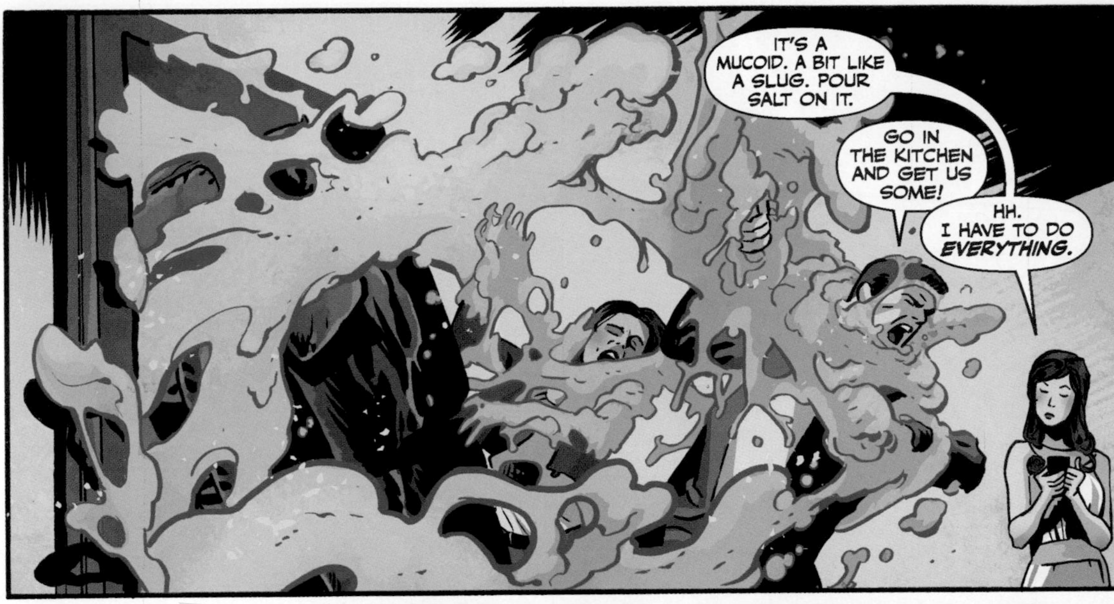
IT'S A MUCOID. A BIT LIKE A SLUG. POUR SALT ON IT.
GO IN THE KITCHEN AND GET US SOME!
HH. I HAVE TO DO *EVERYTHING*.

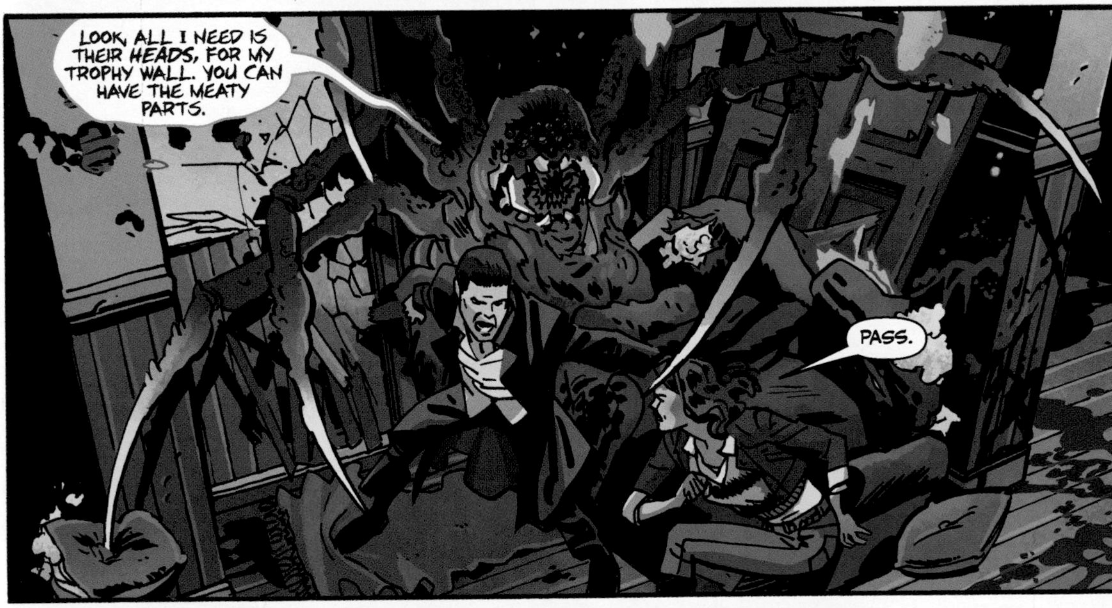
LOOK, ALL I NEED IS THEIR *HEADS*, FOR MY TROPHY WALL. YOU CAN HAVE THE MEATY PARTS.
PASS.

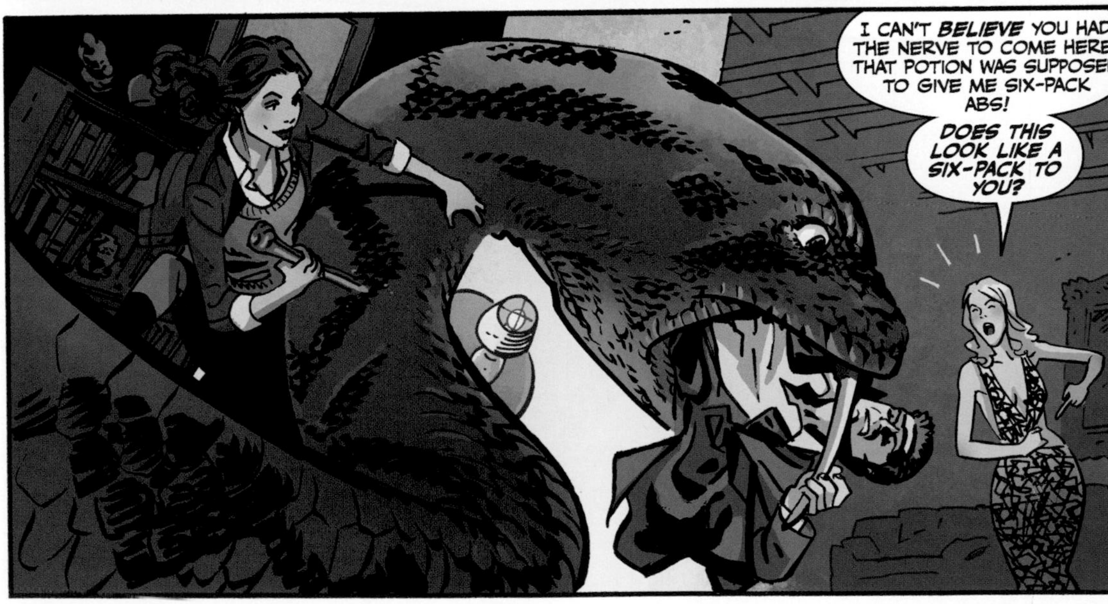
I CAN'T ***BELIEVE*** YOU HAD THE NERVE TO COME HERE! THAT POTION WAS SUPPOSED TO GIVE ME SIX-PACK ABS!
DOES THIS LOOK LIKE A SIX-PACK TO YOU?

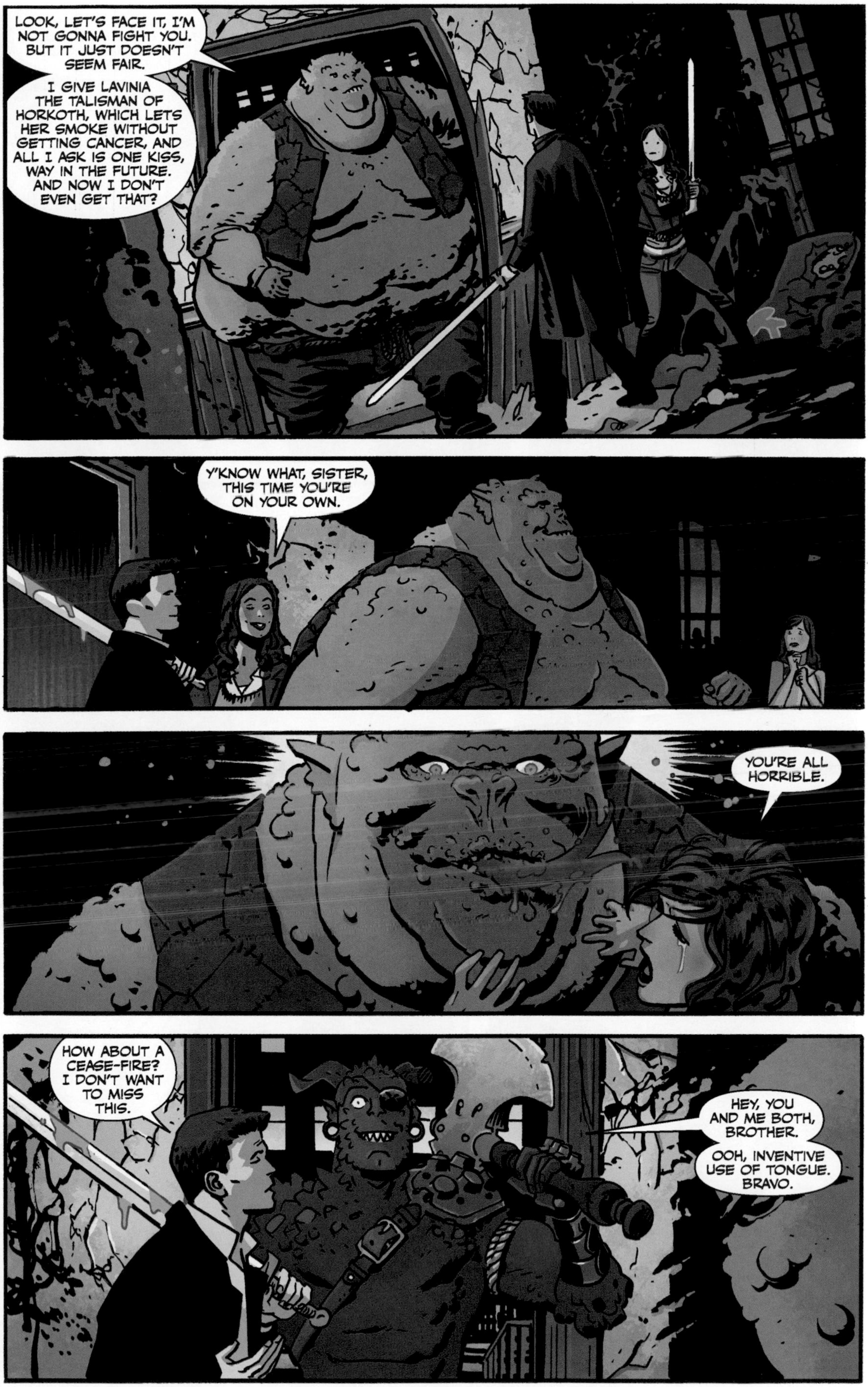
LOOK, LET'S FACE IT, I'M NOT GONNA FIGHT YOU. BUT IT JUST DOESN'T SEEM FAIR.
I GIVE LAVINIA THE TALISMAN OF HORKOTH, WHICH LETS HER SMOKE WITHOUT GETTING CANCER, AND ALL I ASK IS ONE KISS, WAY IN THE FUTURE. AND NOW I DON'T EVEN GET THAT?
Y'KNOW WHAT, SISTER, THIS TIME YOU'RE ON YOUR OWN.
YOU'RE ALL HORRIBLE.
HOW ABOUT A CEASE-FIRE? I DON'T WANT TO MISS THIS.
HEY, YOU AND ME BOTH, BROTHER.
OOH, INVENTIVE USE OF TONGUE. BRAVO.

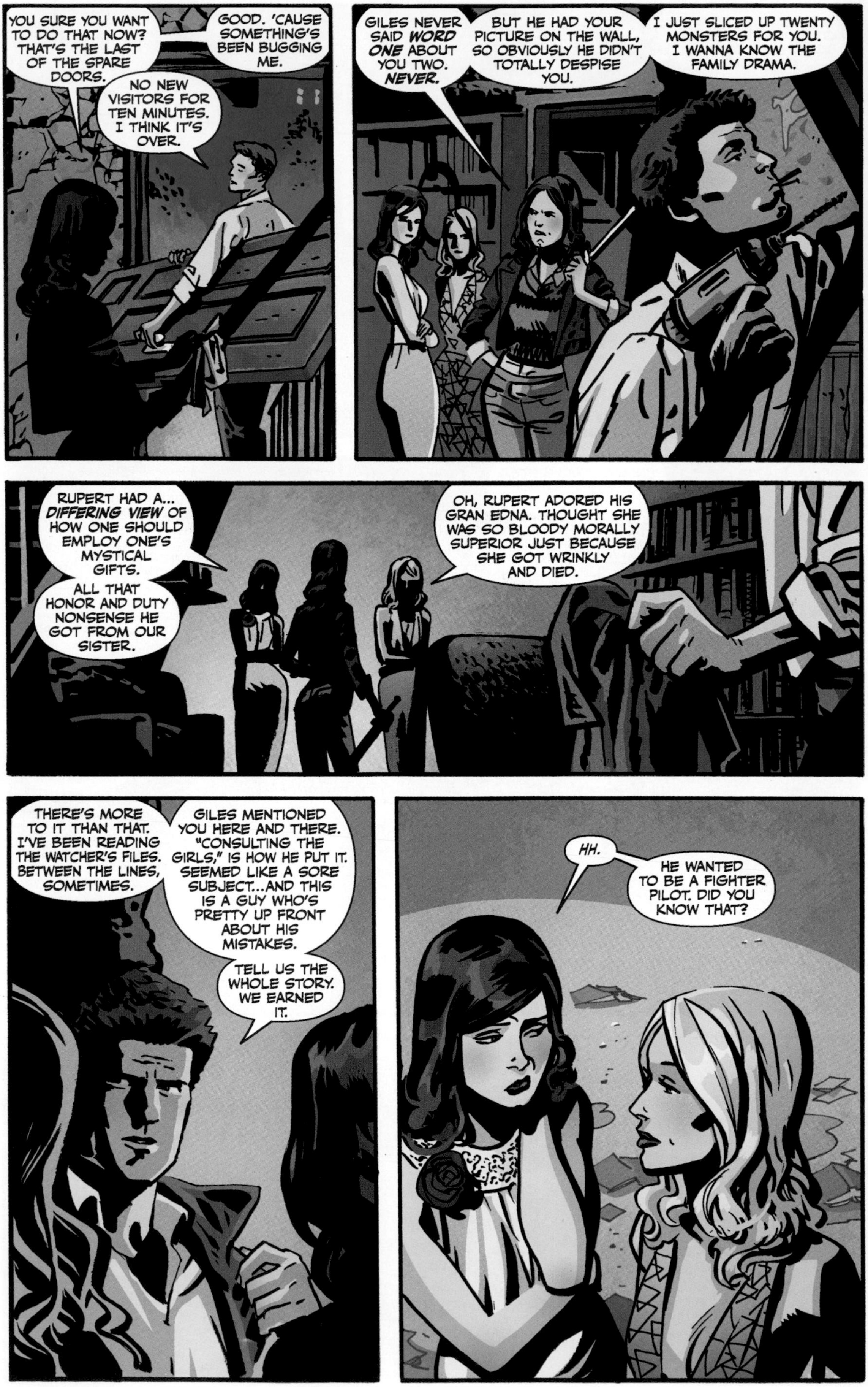
YOU SURE YOU WANT TO DO THAT NOW? THAT'S THE LAST OF THE SPARE DOORS.
GOOD. 'CAUSE SOMETHING'S BEEN BUGGING ME.
NO NEW VISITORS FOR TEN MINUTES. I THINK IT'S OVER.
GILES NEVER SAID *WORD ONE* ABOUT YOU TWO. *NEVER.*
BUT HE HAD YOUR PICTURE ON THE WALL, SO OBVIOUSLY HE DIDN'T TOTALLY DESPISE YOU.
I JUST SLICED UP TWENTY MONSTERS FOR YOU. I WANNA KNOW THE FAMILY DRAMA.
RUPERT HAD A... *DIFFERING VIEW* OF HOW ONE SHOULD EMPLOY ONE'S MYSTICAL GIFTS.
ALL THAT HONOR AND DUTY NONSENSE HE GOT FROM OUR SISTER.
OH, RUPERT ADORED HIS GRAN EDNA. THOUGHT SHE WAS SO BLOODY MORALLY SUPERIOR JUST BECAUSE SHE GOT WRINKLY AND DIED.
THERE'S MORE TO IT THAN THAT. I'VE BEEN READING THE WATCHER'S FILES. BETWEEN THE LINES, SOMETIMES.
GILES MENTIONED YOU HERE AND THERE. "CONSULTING THE GIRLS," IS HOW HE PUT IT. SEEMED LIKE A SORE SUBJECT...AND THIS IS A GUY WHO'S PRETTY UP FRONT ABOUT HIS MISTAKES.
TELL US THE WHOLE STORY. WE EARNED IT.
HH.
HE WANTED TO BE A FIGHTER PILOT. DID YOU KNOW THAT?

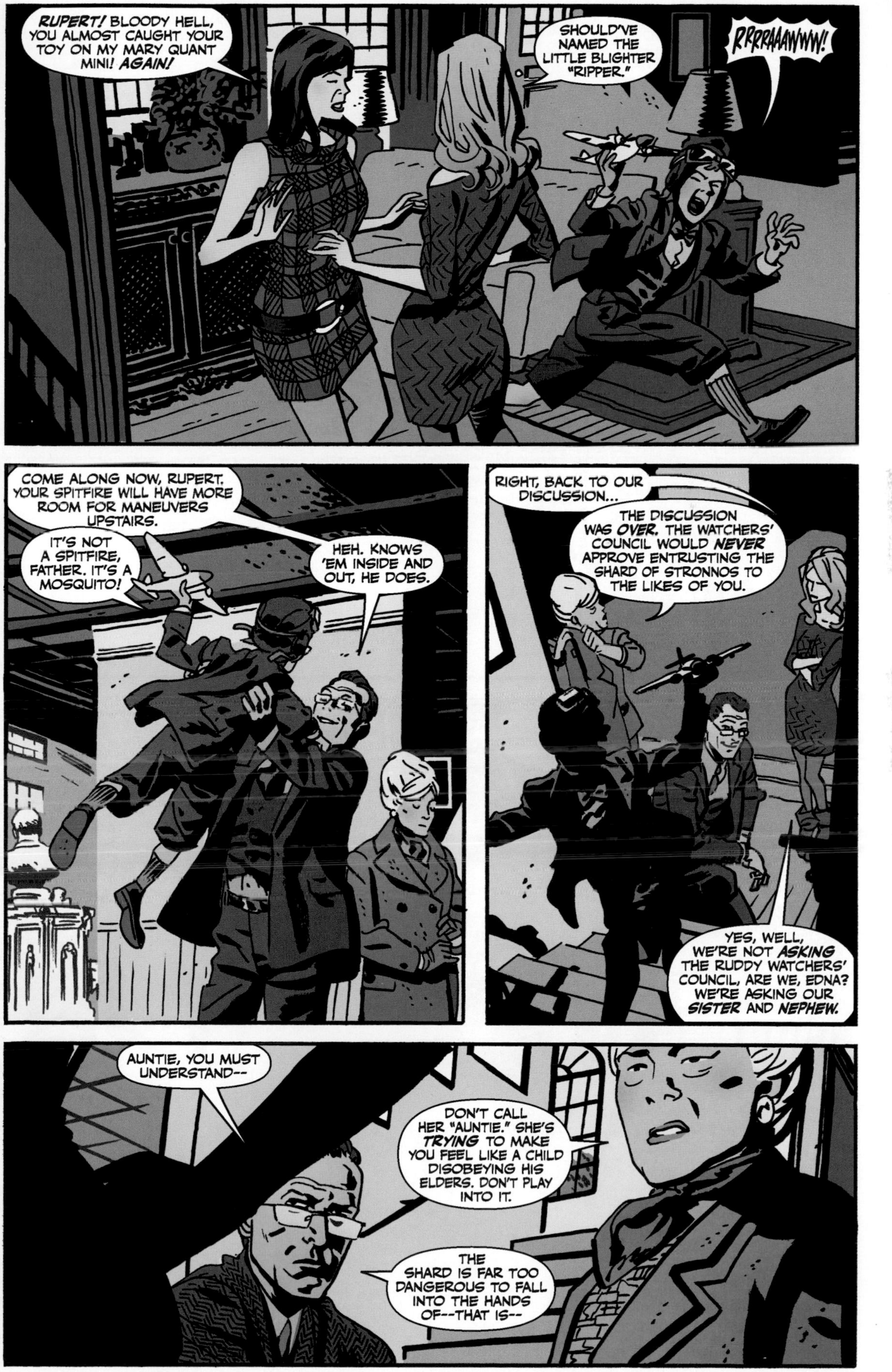
RUPERT! BLOODY HELL, YOU ALMOST CAUGHT YOUR TOY ON MY MARY QUANT MINI! AGAIN!
SHOULD'VE NAMED THE LITTLE BLIGHTER "RIPPER."
RRRRAAAWWW!
COME ALONG NOW, RUPERT. YOUR SPITFIRE WILL HAVE MORE ROOM FOR MANEUVERS UPSTAIRS.
IT'S NOT A SPITFIRE, FATHER. IT'S A MOSQUITO!
HEH. KNOWS 'EM INSIDE AND OUT, HE DOES.
RIGHT, BACK TO OUR DISCUSSION...
THE DISCUSSION WAS OVER. THE WATCHERS' COUNCIL WOULD NEVER APPROVE ENTRUSTING THE SHARD OF STRONNOS TO THE LIKES OF YOU.
YES, WELL, WE'RE NOT ASKING THE RUDDY WATCHERS' COUNCIL, ARE WE, EDNA? WE'RE ASKING OUR SISTER AND NEPHEW.
AUNTIE, YOU MUST UNDERSTAND--
DON'T CALL HER "AUNTIE." SHE'S TRYING TO MAKE YOU FEEL LIKE A CHILD DISOBEYING HIS ELDERS. DON'T PLAY INTO IT.
THE SHARD IS FAR TOO DANGEROUS TO FALL INTO THE HANDS OF--THAT IS--

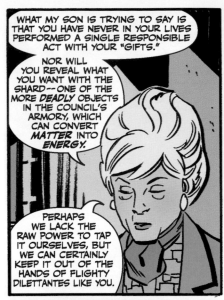

WHAT MY SON IS TRYING TO SAY IS THAT YOU HAVE NEVER IN YOUR LIVES PERFORMED A SINGLE RESPONSIBLE ACT WITH YOUR "GIFTS."

NOR WILL YOU REVEAL WHAT YOU WANT WITH THE SHARD--ONE OF THE MORE *DEADLY* OBJECTS IN THE COUNCIL'S ARMORY, WHICH CAN CONVERT *MATTER* INTO *ENERGY*.

PERHAPS WE LACK THE RAW POWER TO TAP IT OURSELVES, BUT WE CAN CERTAINLY KEEP IT OUT OF THE HANDS OF FLIGHTY DILETTANTES LIKE YOU.

WE HAVE A *GRAND AND NOBLE* PURPOSE, I'LL HAVE YOU KNOW.

OH? WHAT? REMOVING THAT EXTRA TEN POUNDS YOU'VE ACCUMULATED AROUND YOUR MIDDLE?

TAKE THAT *BACK*, YOU WRINKLED OLD *PRUNE!*

HRRMPH... AWFULLY BRIGHT IN HERE...

WHAT THE DEVIL--

THE FAIRWEATHER SISTERS SPEAK THE TRUTH.

YOU SEE, THE SHARD CAN ALSO MAKE *ENERGY* INTO *MATTER*.

THEY HOPE TO TRANSFORM THEIR LOVERS BACK TO FLESH...SEEING AS I HAVE MADE THEM BEINGS OF *LIGHT*, TRAPPED WITHIN THEIR VAIN PARAMOURS' *MIRRORS*.

A *LIGHT DEMON*. GET BACK...

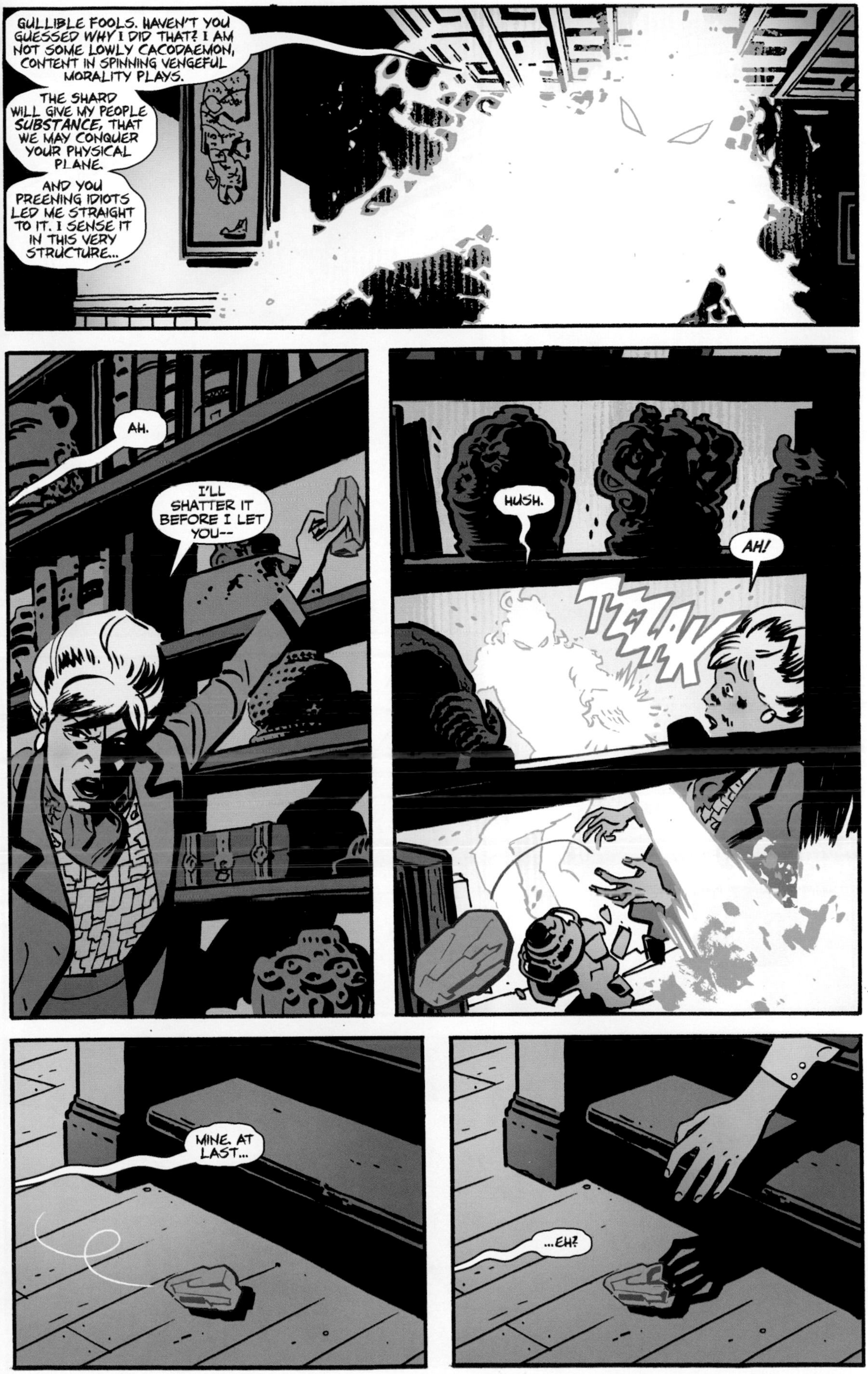

GULLIBLE FOOLS. HAVEN'T YOU GUESSED WHY I DID THAT? I AM NOT SOME LOWLY CACODAEMON, CONTENT IN SPINNING VENGEFUL MORALITY PLAYS.
THE SHARD WILL GIVE MY PEOPLE SUBSTANCE, THAT WE MAY CONQUER YOUR PHYSICAL PLANE.
AND YOU PREENING IDIOTS LED ME STRAIGHT TO IT. I SENSE IT IN THIS VERY STRUCTURE...
AH.
I'LL SHATTER IT BEFORE I LET YOU--
HUSH.
AH!
TZZK
MINE. AT LAST...
...EH?

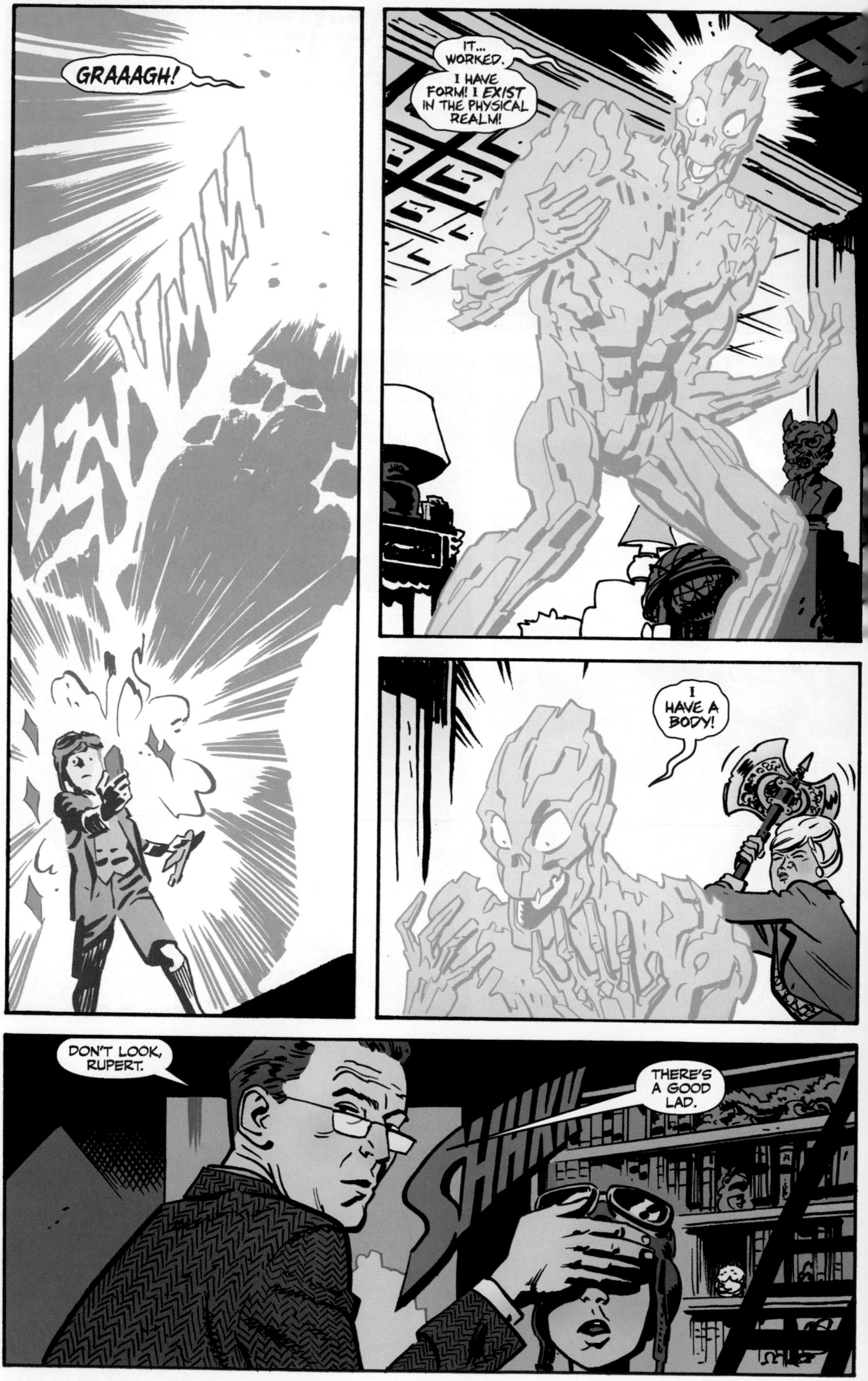
GRAAAGH!
IT... WORKED. I HAVE FORM! I EXIST IN THE PHYSICAL REALM!
I HAVE A BODY!
DON'T LOOK, RUPERT.
THERE'S A GOOD LAD.

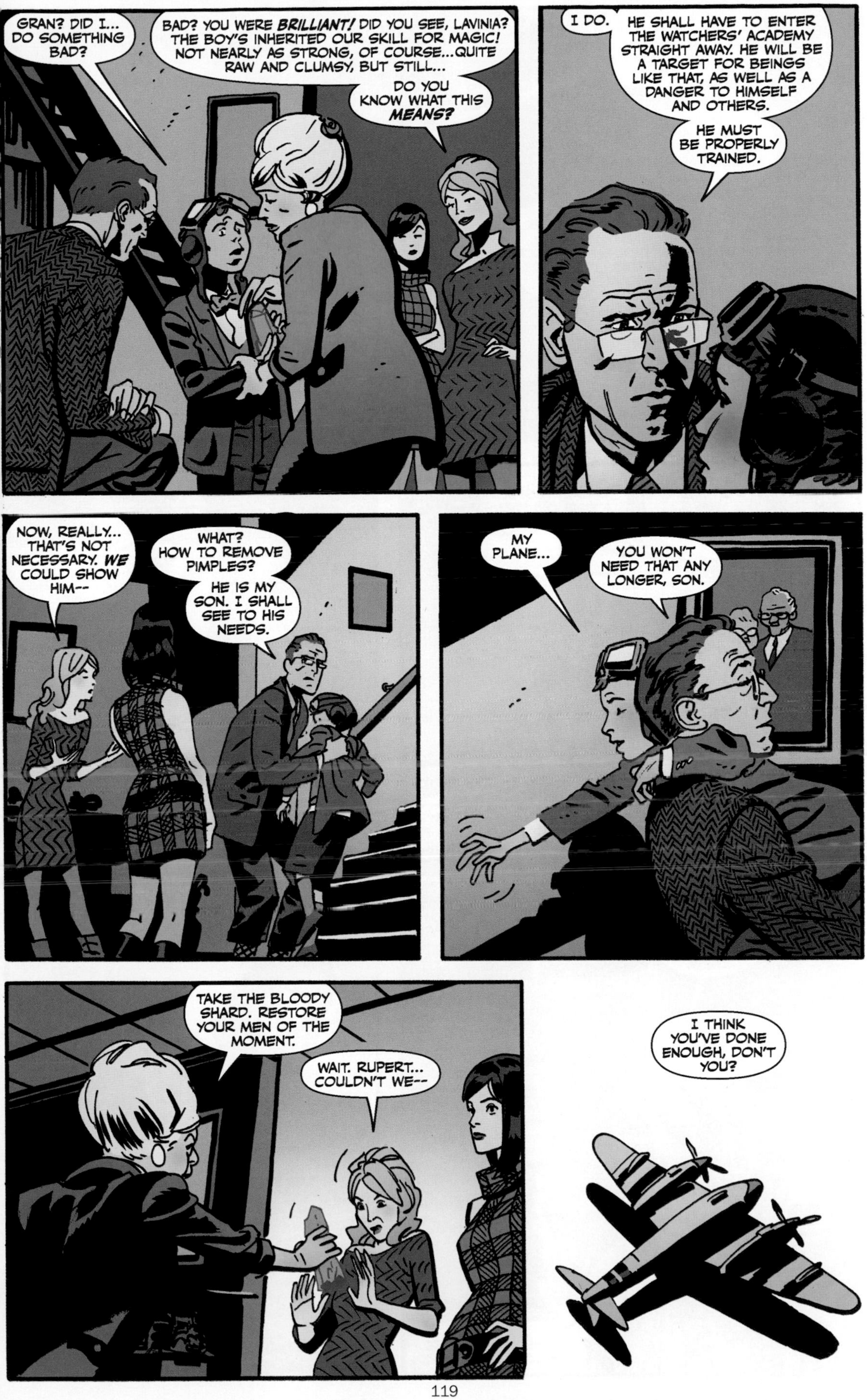
GRAN? DID I... DO SOMETHING BAD?
BAD? YOU WERE BRILLIANT! DID YOU SEE, LAVINIA? THE BOY'S INHERITED OUR SKILL FOR MAGIC! NOT NEARLY AS STRONG, OF COURSE...QUITE RAW AND CLUMSY, BUT STILL...
DO YOU KNOW WHAT THIS MEANS?
I DO.
HE SHALL HAVE TO ENTER THE WATCHERS' ACADEMY STRAIGHT AWAY. HE WILL BE A TARGET FOR BEINGS LIKE THAT, AS WELL AS A DANGER TO HIMSELF AND OTHERS.
HE MUST BE PROPERLY TRAINED.
NOW, REALLY... THAT'S NOT NECESSARY. WE COULD SHOW HIM--
WHAT? HOW TO REMOVE PIMPLES?
HE IS MY SON. I SHALL SEE TO HIS NEEDS.
MY PLANE...
YOU WON'T NEED THAT ANY LONGER, SON.
TAKE THE BLOODY SHARD. RESTORE YOUR MEN OF THE MOMENT.
WAIT. RUPERT... COULDN'T WE--
I THINK YOU'VE DONE ENOUGH, DON'T YOU?

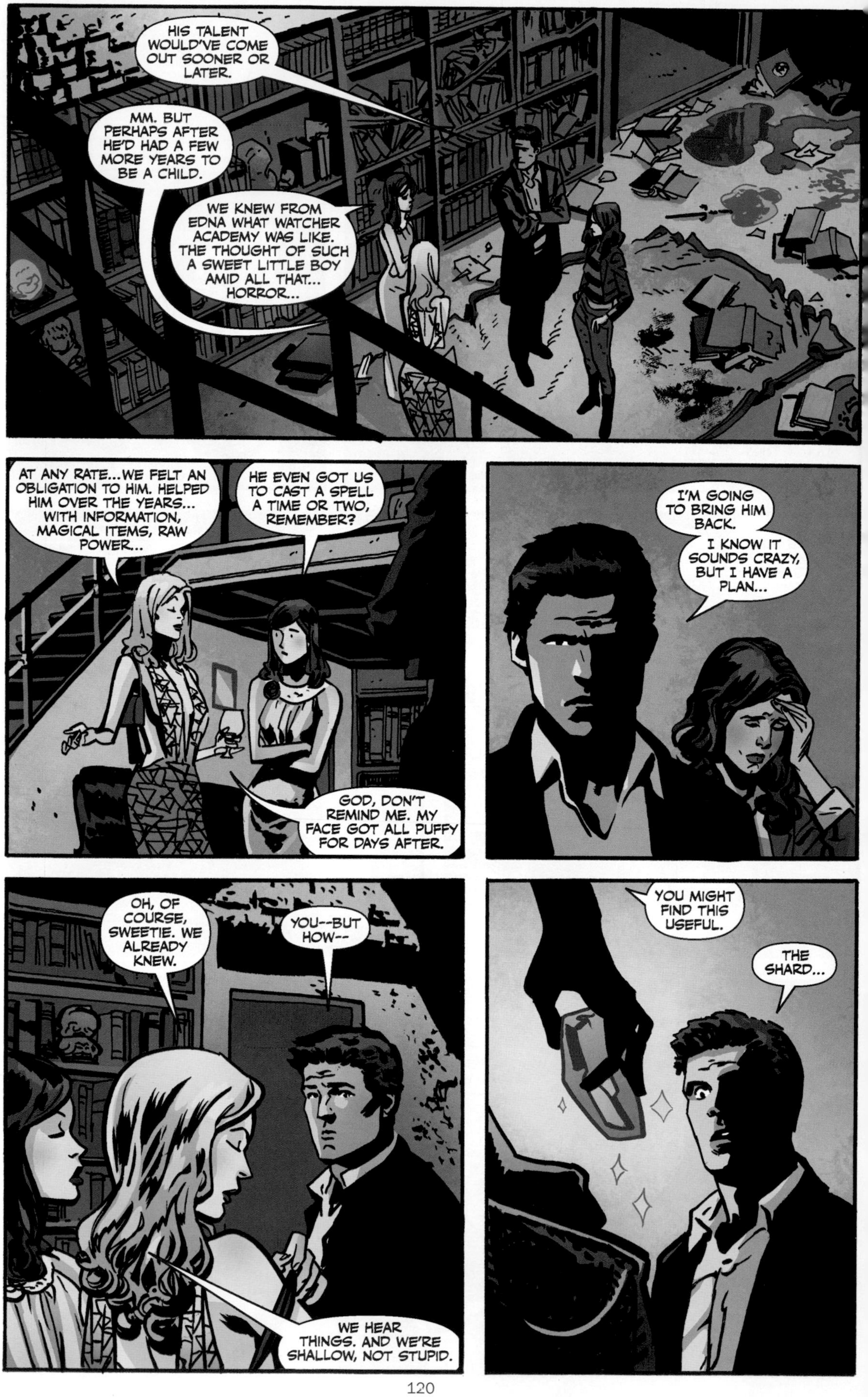
HIS TALENT WOULD'VE COME OUT SOONER OR LATER.
MM. BUT PERHAPS AFTER HE'D HAD A FEW MORE YEARS TO BE A CHILD.
WE KNEW FROM EDNA WHAT WATCHER ACADEMY WAS LIKE. THE THOUGHT OF SUCH A SWEET LITTLE BOY AMID ALL THAT... HORROR...
AT ANY RATE...WE FELT AN OBLIGATION TO HIM. HELPED HIM OVER THE YEARS... WITH INFORMATION, MAGICAL ITEMS, RAW POWER...
HE EVEN GOT US TO CAST A SPELL A TIME OR TWO, REMEMBER?
GOD, DON'T REMIND ME. MY FACE GOT ALL PUFFY FOR DAYS AFTER.
I'M GOING TO BRING HIM BACK.
I KNOW IT SOUNDS CRAZY, BUT I HAVE A PLAN...
OH, OF COURSE, SWEETIE. WE ALREADY KNEW.
YOU--BUT HOW--
WE HEAR THINGS. AND WE'RE SHALLOW, NOT STUPID.
YOU MIGHT FIND THIS USEFUL.
THE SHARD...

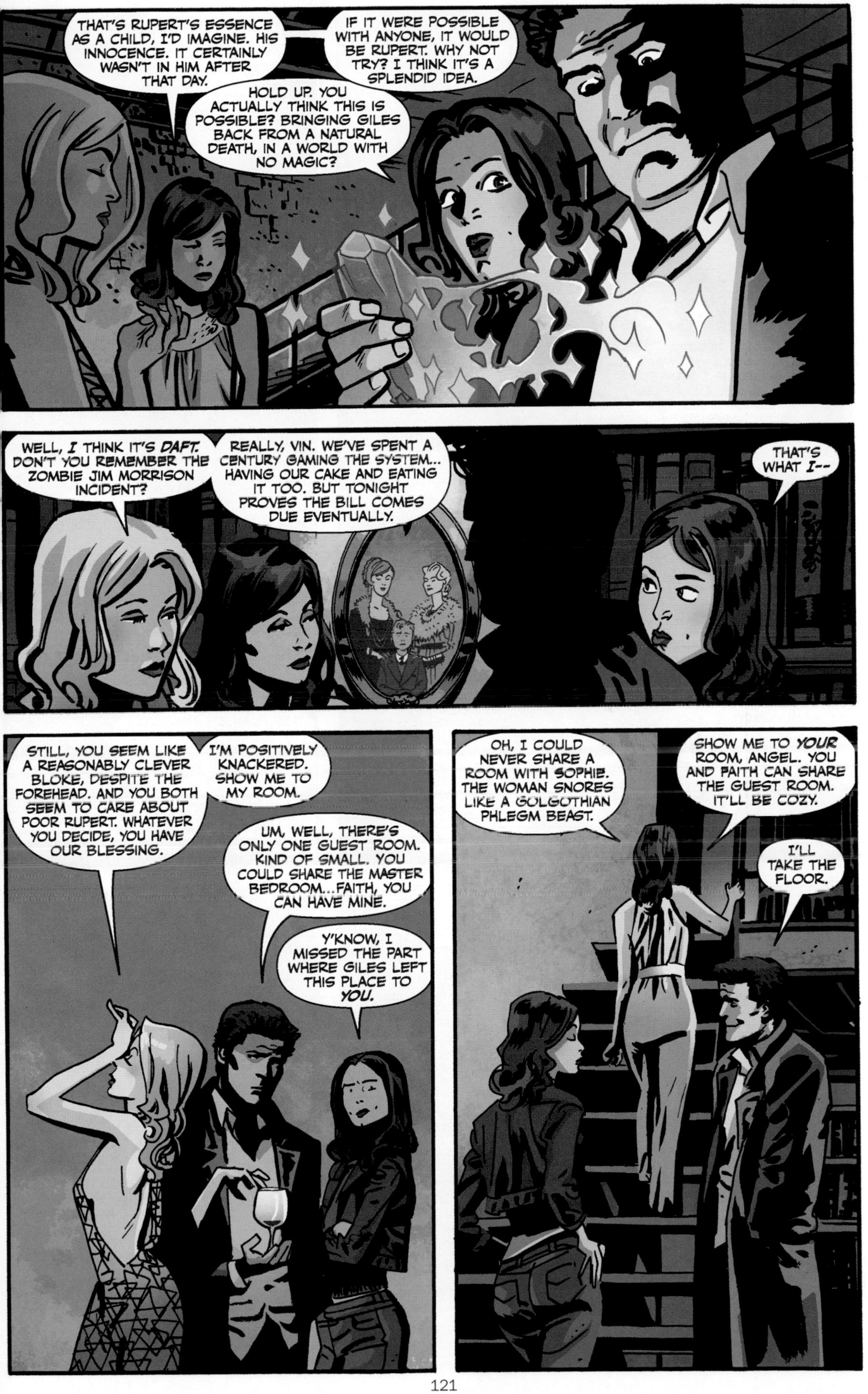

THAT'S RUPERT'S ESSENCE AS A CHILD, I'D IMAGINE. HIS INNOCENCE. IT CERTAINLY WASN'T IN HIM AFTER THAT DAY.
IF IT WERE POSSIBLE WITH ANYONE, IT WOULD BE RUPERT. WHY NOT TRY? I THINK IT'S A SPLENDID IDEA.
HOLD UP. YOU ACTUALLY THINK THIS IS POSSIBLE? BRINGING GILES BACK FROM A NATURAL DEATH, IN A WORLD WITH NO MAGIC?
WELL, I THINK IT'S DAFT. DON'T YOU REMEMBER THE ZOMBIE JIM MORRISON INCIDENT?
REALLY, VIN. WE'VE SPENT A CENTURY GAMING THE SYSTEM... HAVING OUR CAKE AND EATING IT TOO. BUT TONIGHT PROVES THE BILL COMES DUE EVENTUALLY.
THAT'S WHAT I--
STILL, YOU SEEM LIKE A REASONABLY CLEVER BLOKE, DESPITE THE FOREHEAD. AND YOU BOTH SEEM TO CARE ABOUT POOR RUPERT. WHATEVER YOU DECIDE, YOU HAVE OUR BLESSING.
I'M POSITIVELY KNACKERED. SHOW ME TO MY ROOM.
UM, WELL, THERE'S ONLY ONE GUEST ROOM. KIND OF SMALL. YOU COULD SHARE THE MASTER BEDROOM... FAITH, YOU CAN HAVE MINE.
Y'KNOW, I MISSED THE PART WHERE GILES LEFT THIS PLACE TO YOU.
OH, I COULD NEVER SHARE A ROOM WITH SOPHIE. THE WOMAN SNORES LIKE A GOLGOTHIAN PHLEGM BEAST.
SHOW ME TO YOUR ROOM, ANGEL. YOU AND FAITH CAN SHARE THE GUEST ROOM. IT'LL BE COZY.
I'LL TAKE THE FLOOR.

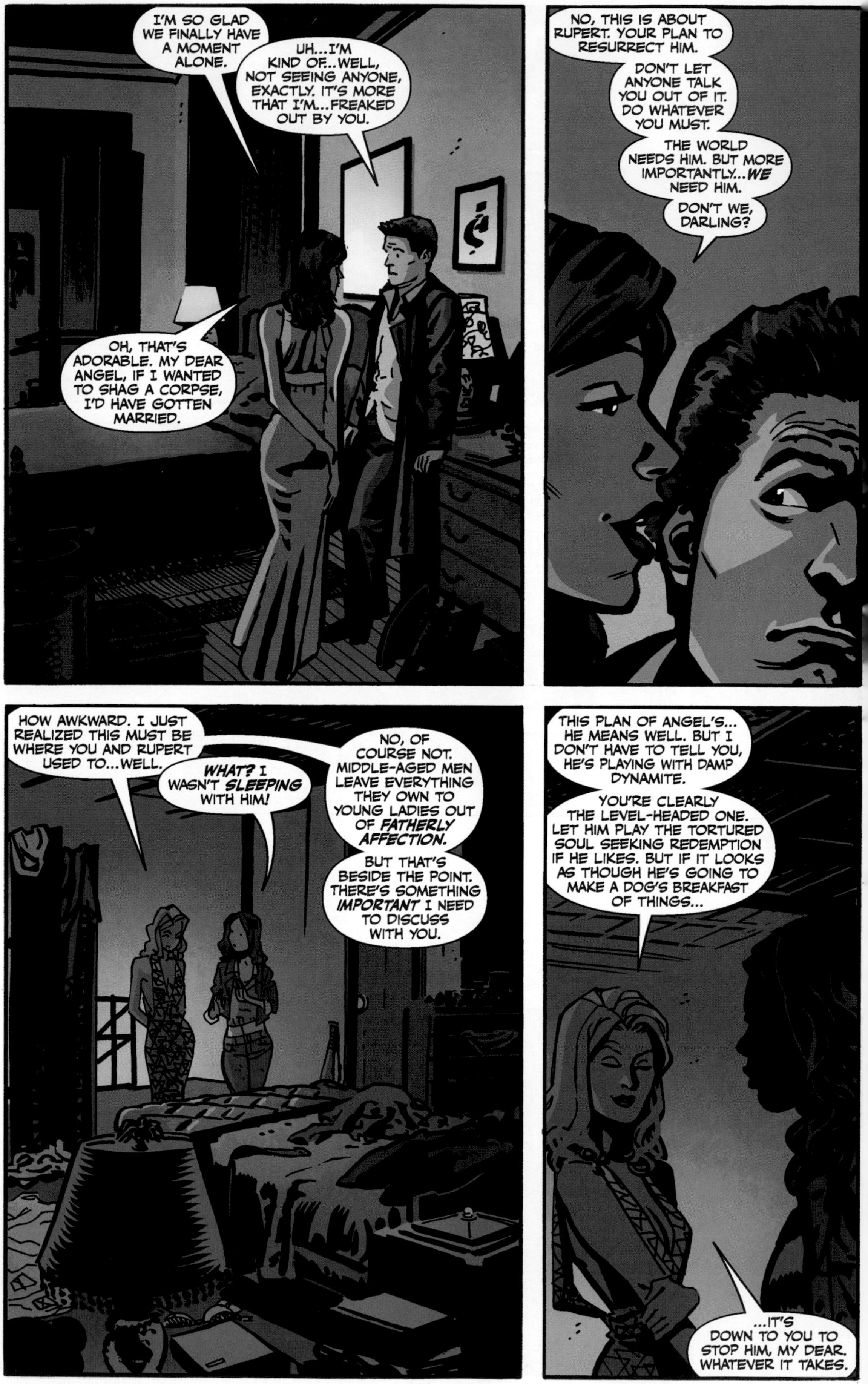
I'M SO GLAD WE FINALLY HAVE A MOMENT ALONE.
UH...I'M KIND OF...WELL, NOT SEEING ANYONE, EXACTLY. IT'S MORE THAT I'M...FREAKED OUT BY YOU.
OH, THAT'S ADORABLE. MY DEAR ANGEL, IF I WANTED TO SHAG A CORPSE, I'D HAVE GOTTEN MARRIED.
NO, THIS IS ABOUT RUPERT. YOUR PLAN TO RESURRECT HIM.
DON'T LET ANYONE TALK YOU OUT OF IT. DO WHATEVER YOU MUST.
THE WORLD NEEDS HIM. BUT MORE IMPORTANTLY...WE NEED HIM.
DON'T WE, DARLING?
HOW AWKWARD. I JUST REALIZED THIS MUST BE WHERE YOU AND RUPERT USED TO...WELL.
WHAT? I WASN'T SLEEPING WITH HIM!
NO, OF COURSE NOT. MIDDLE-AGED MEN LEAVE EVERYTHING THEY OWN TO YOUNG LADIES OUT OF FATHERLY AFFECTION.
BUT THAT'S BESIDE THE POINT. THERE'S SOMETHING IMPORTANT I NEED TO DISCUSS WITH YOU.
THIS PLAN OF ANGEL'S... HE MEANS WELL. BUT I DON'T HAVE TO TELL YOU, HE'S PLAYING WITH DAMP DYNAMITE.
YOU'RE CLEARLY THE LEVEL-HEADED ONE. LET HIM PLAY THE TORTURED SOUL SEEKING REDEMPTION IF HE LIKES. BUT IF IT LOOKS AS THOUGH HE'S GOING TO MAKE A DOG'S BREAKFAST OF THINGS...
...IT'S DOWN TO YOU TO STOP HIM, MY DEAR. WHATEVER IT TAKES.

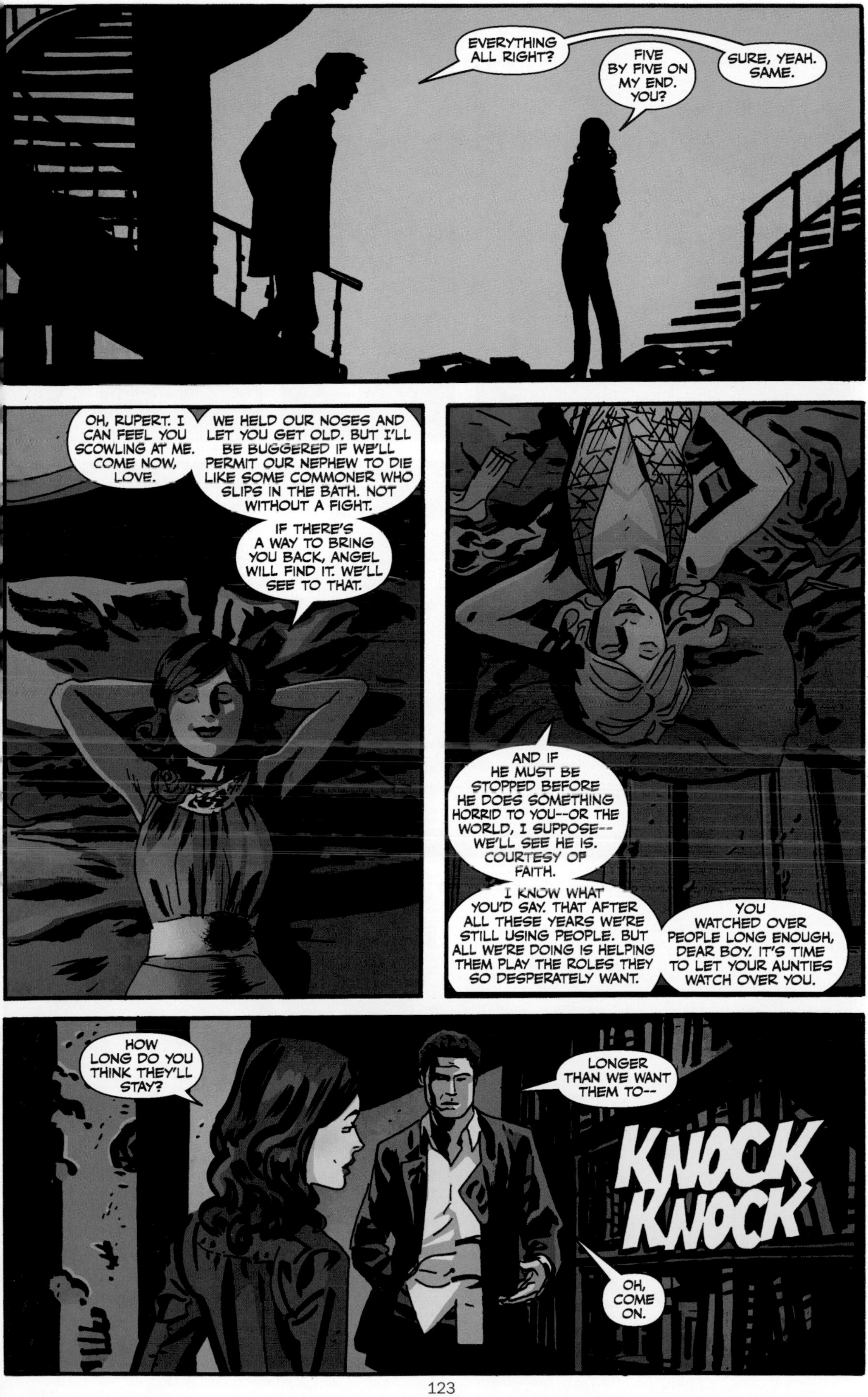
EVERYTHING ALL RIGHT?
FIVE BY FIVE ON MY END. YOU?
SURE, YEAH. SAME.
OH, RUPERT. I CAN FEEL YOU SCOWLING AT ME. COME NOW, LOVE.
WE HELD OUR NOSES AND LET YOU GET OLD. BUT I'LL BE BUGGERED IF WE'LL PERMIT OUR NEPHEW TO DIE LIKE SOME COMMONER WHO SLIPS IN THE BATH. NOT WITHOUT A FIGHT.
IF THERE'S A WAY TO BRING YOU BACK, ANGEL WILL FIND IT. WE'LL SEE TO THAT.
AND IF HE MUST BE STOPPED BEFORE HE DOES SOMETHING HORRID TO YOU--OR THE WORLD, I SUPPOSE--WE'LL SEE HE IS. COURTESY OF FAITH.
I KNOW WHAT YOU'D SAY. THAT AFTER ALL THESE YEARS WE'RE STILL USING PEOPLE. BUT ALL WE'RE DOING IS HELPING THEM PLAY THE ROLES THEY SO DESPERATELY WANT.
YOU WATCHED OVER PEOPLE LONG ENOUGH, DEAR BOY. IT'S TIME TO LET YOUR AUNTIES WATCH OVER YOU.
HOW LONG DO YOU THINK THEY'LL STAY?
LONGER THAN WE WANT THEM TO--
KNOCK KNOCK
OH, COME ON.

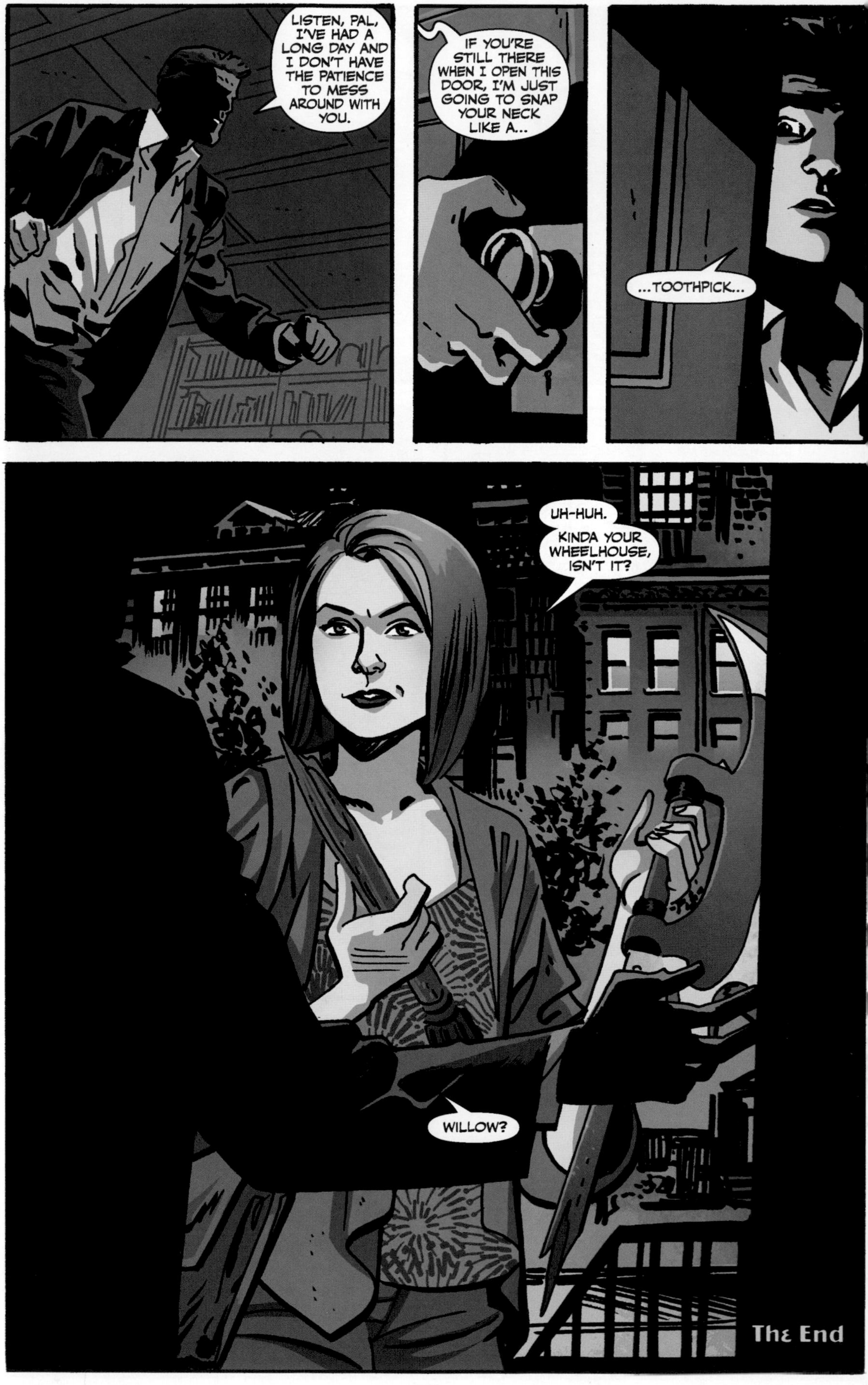
LISTEN, PAL, I'VE HAD A LONG DAY AND I DON'T HAVE THE PATIENCE TO MESS AROUND WITH YOU.
IF YOU'RE STILL THERE WHEN I OPEN THIS DOOR, I'M JUST GOING TO SNAP YOUR NECK LIKE A...
...TOOTHPICK...
UH-HUH.
KINDA YOUR WHEELHOUSE, ISN'T IT?
WILLOW?
The End

ANGEL & FAITH COVER GALLERY AND SKETCHBOOK

WITH NOTES FROM
REBEKAH ISAACS

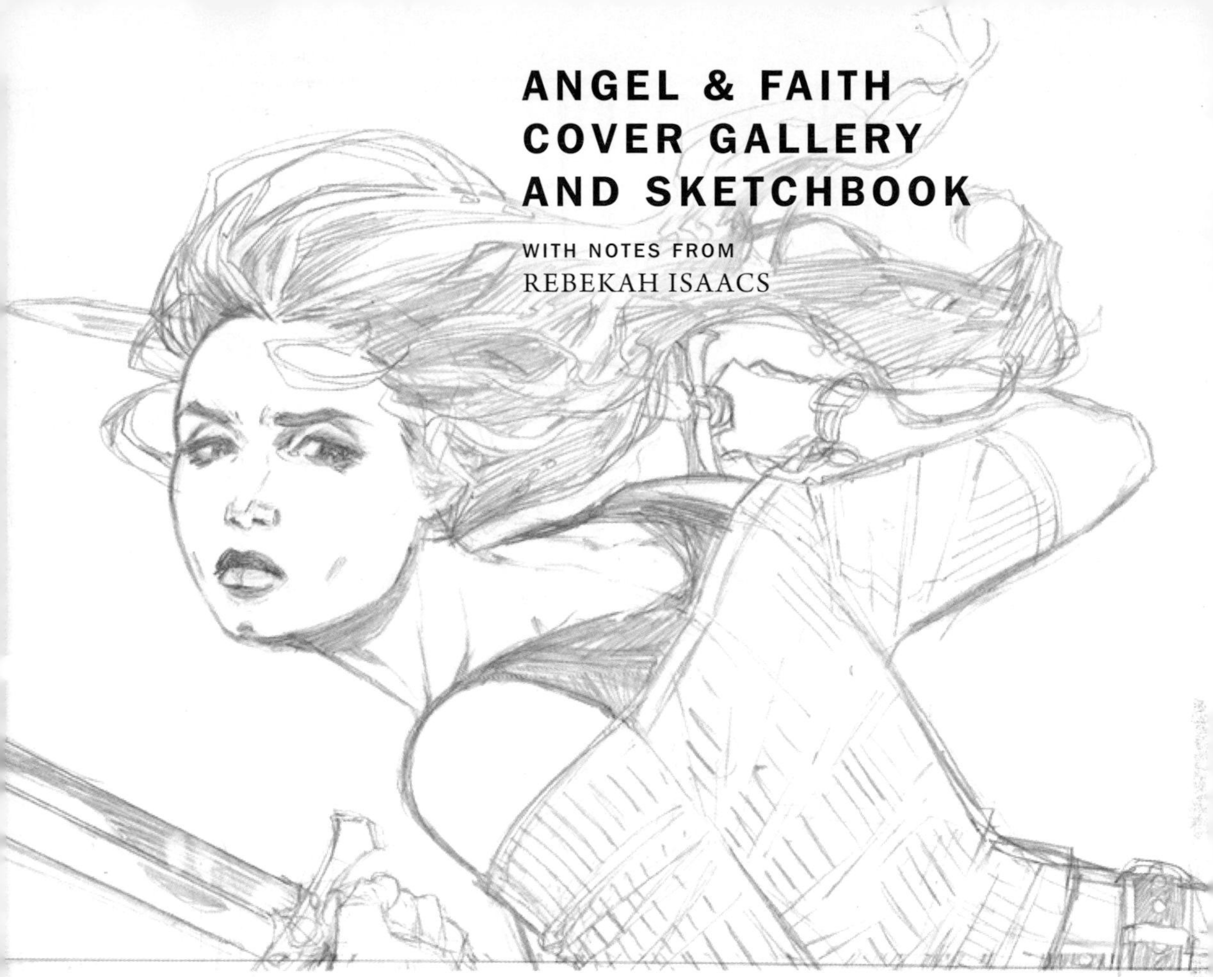

Variant cover pencils for Angel & Faith #6.

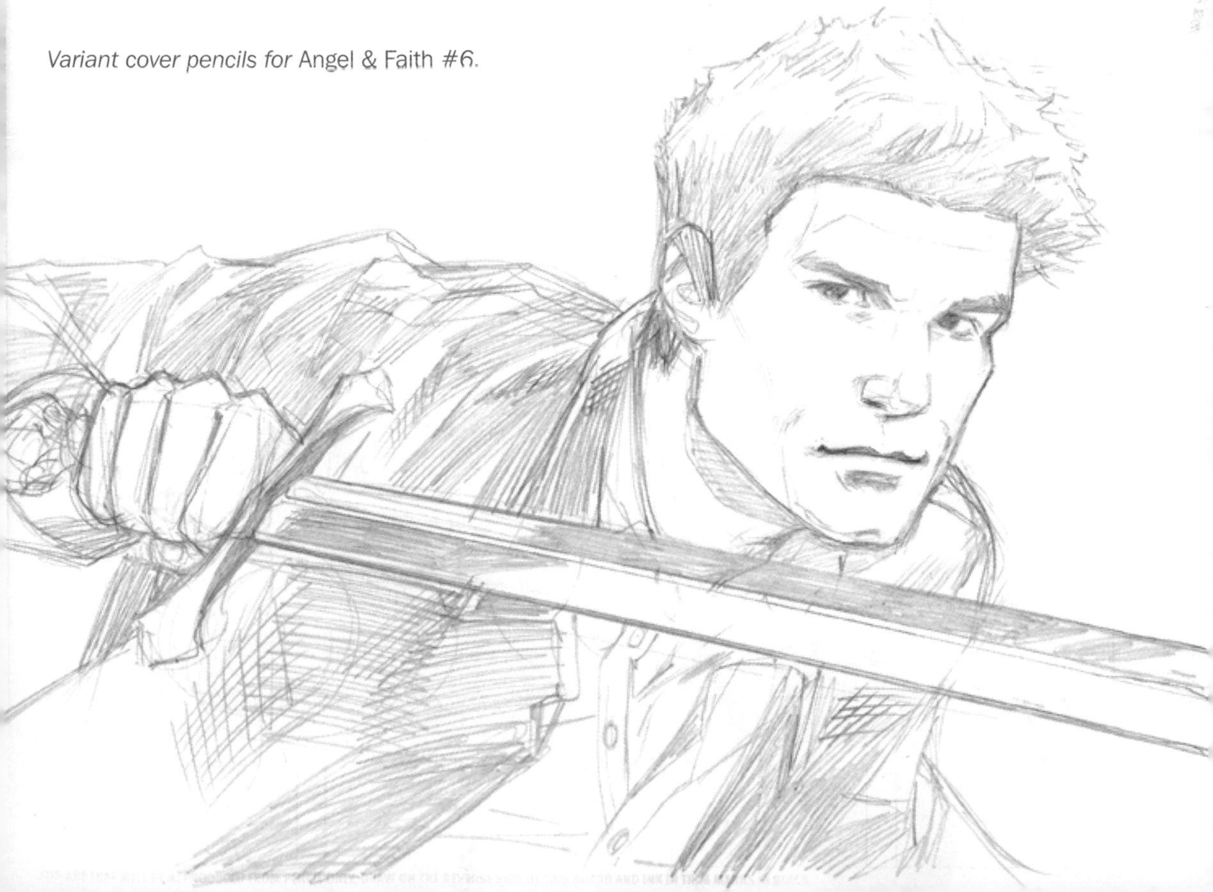

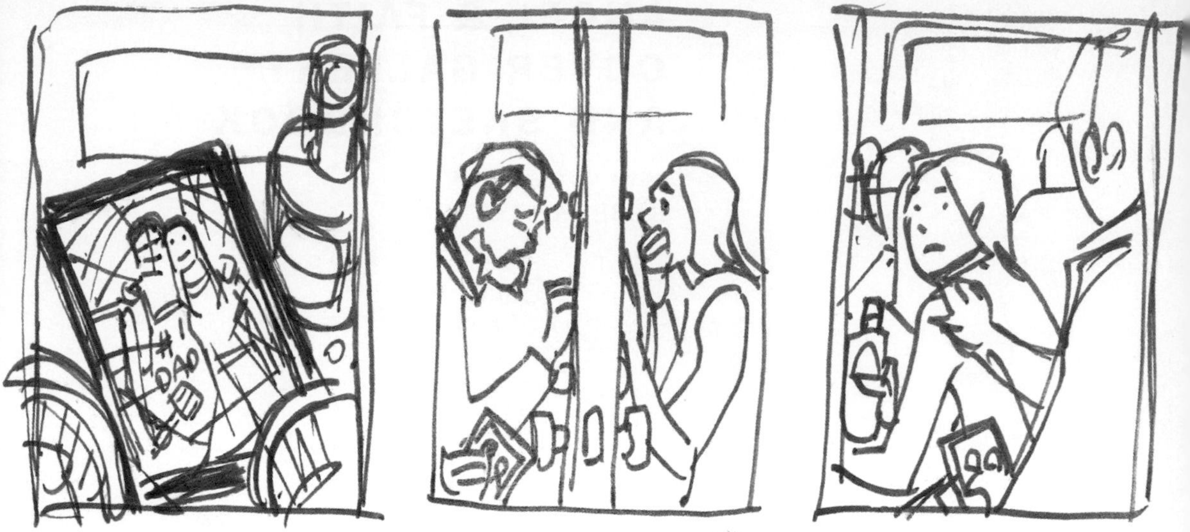

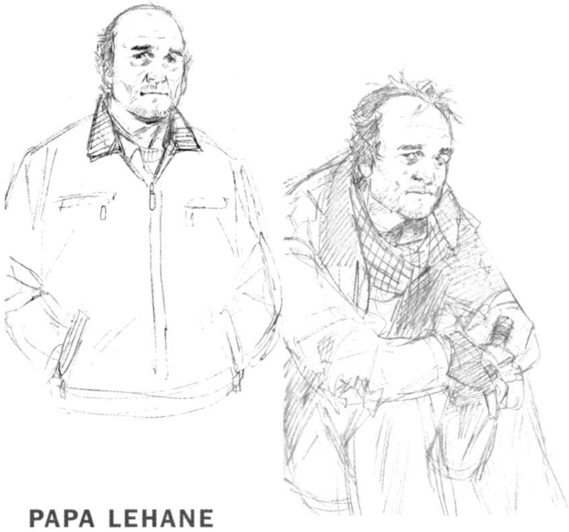

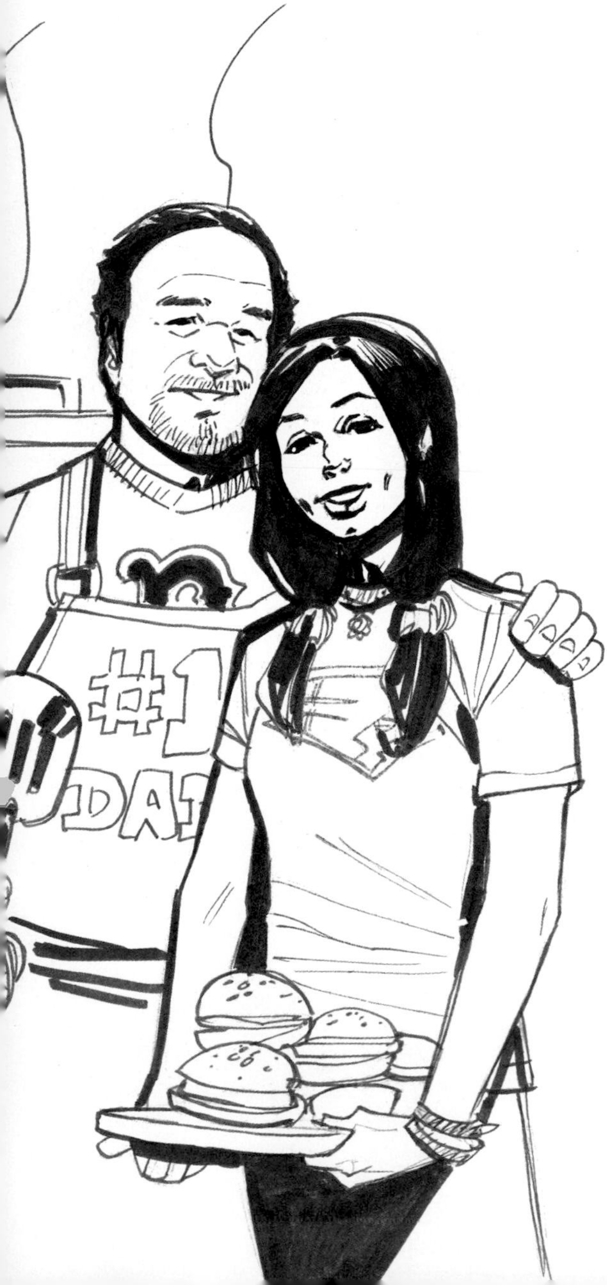

PAPA LEHANE

For Pat Lehane, Faith's father, I wanted to use a real person as a starting point to make him feel more real. It's too easy to make new characters feel generic and bland otherwise. Knowing that Eliza has Albanian roots, I did a Google search for other actors with similar heritage, and the Belushi brothers came up very quickly. I thought Jim had the perfect look, and if he'd been cast in such a role on the show I would've had no trouble believing it. It wasn't requested that I draw him in flashback during his past days of heavy alcoholism, and we never see him this way in the book, but imagining it and putting it on paper helped me get a better feel for the character in present day.

Above: *Cover ideas for the* Angel & Faith #7 *variant cover.*

Opposite: *Variant cover to* Angel & Faith #7.

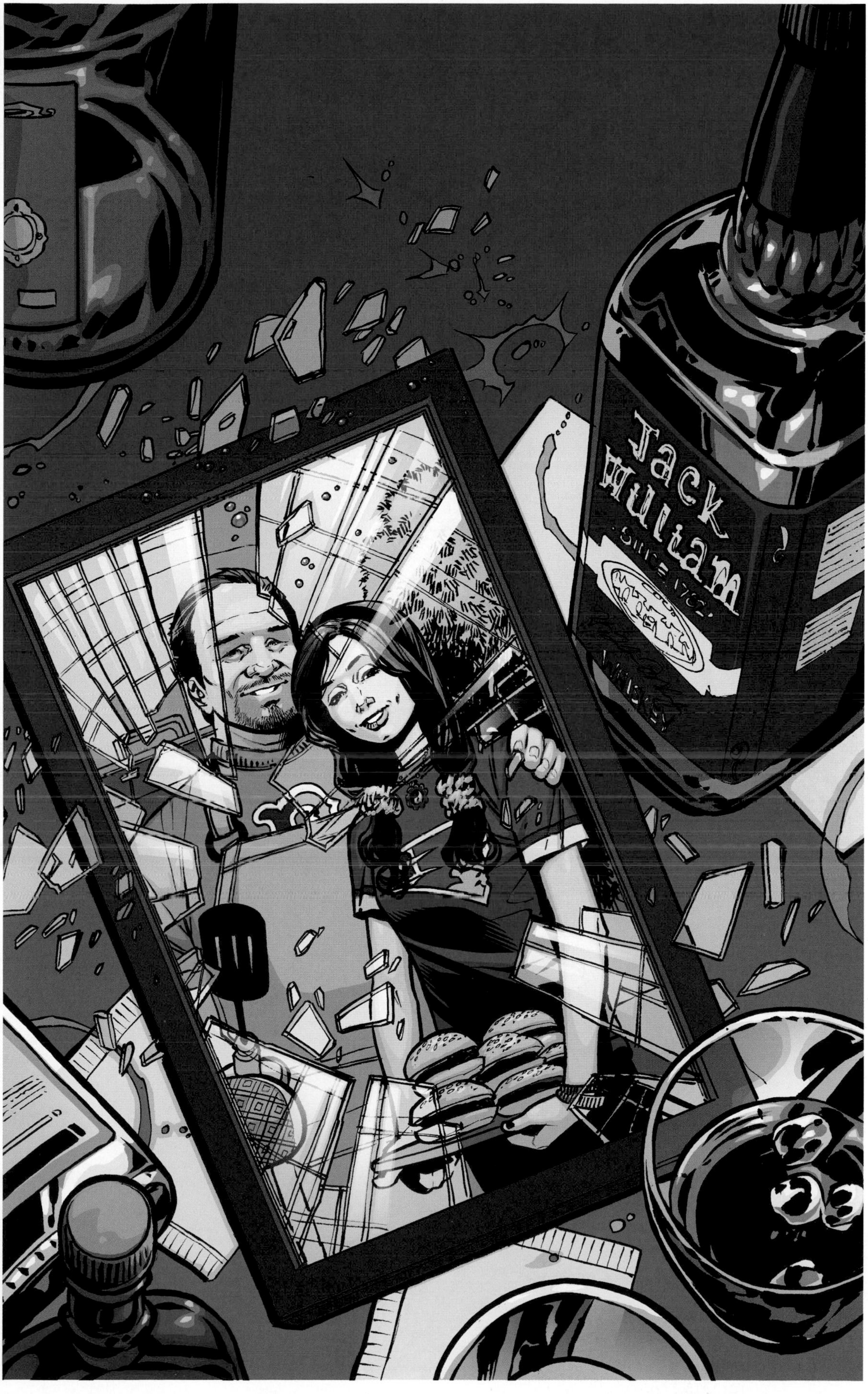
Jack

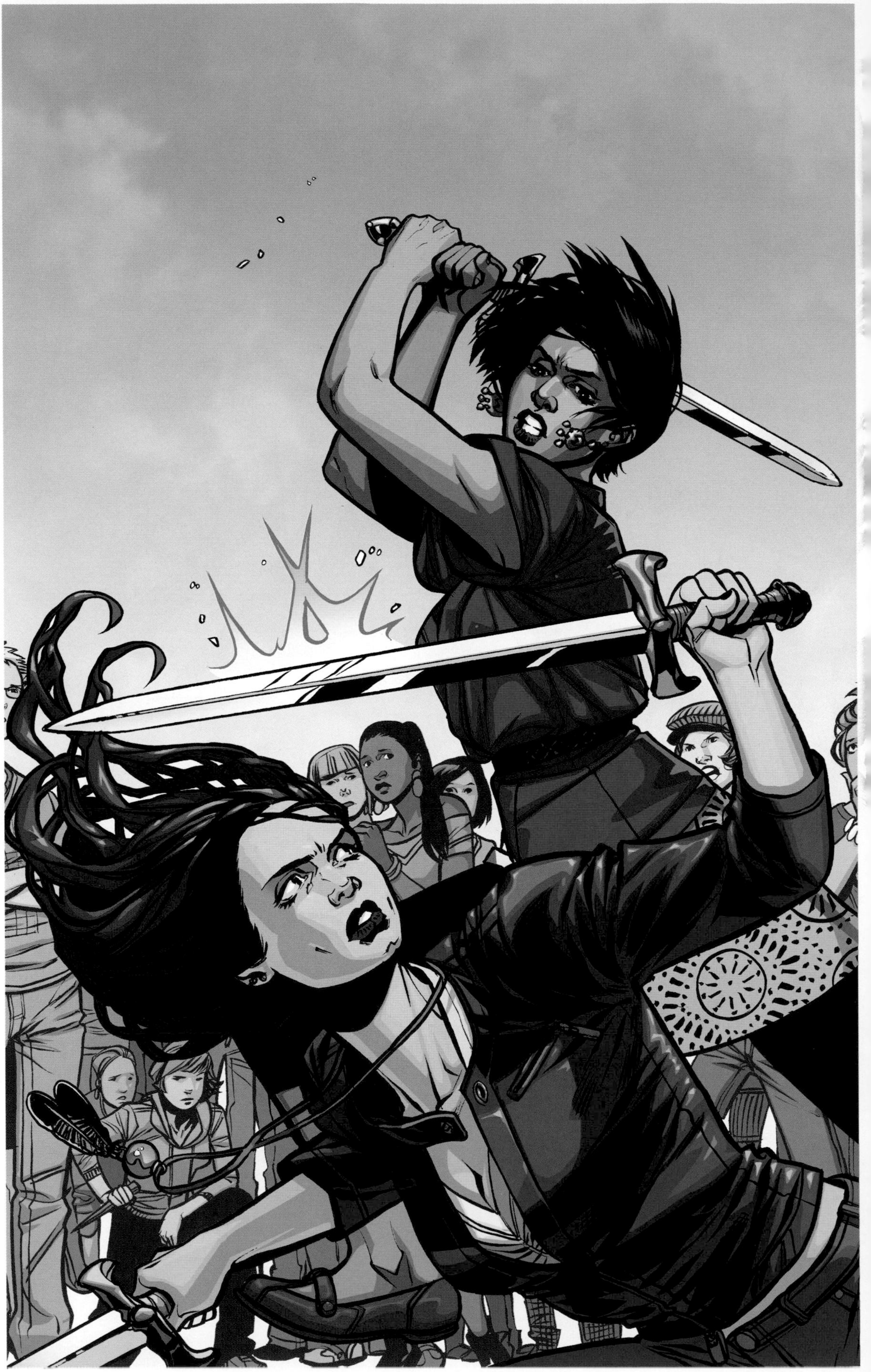

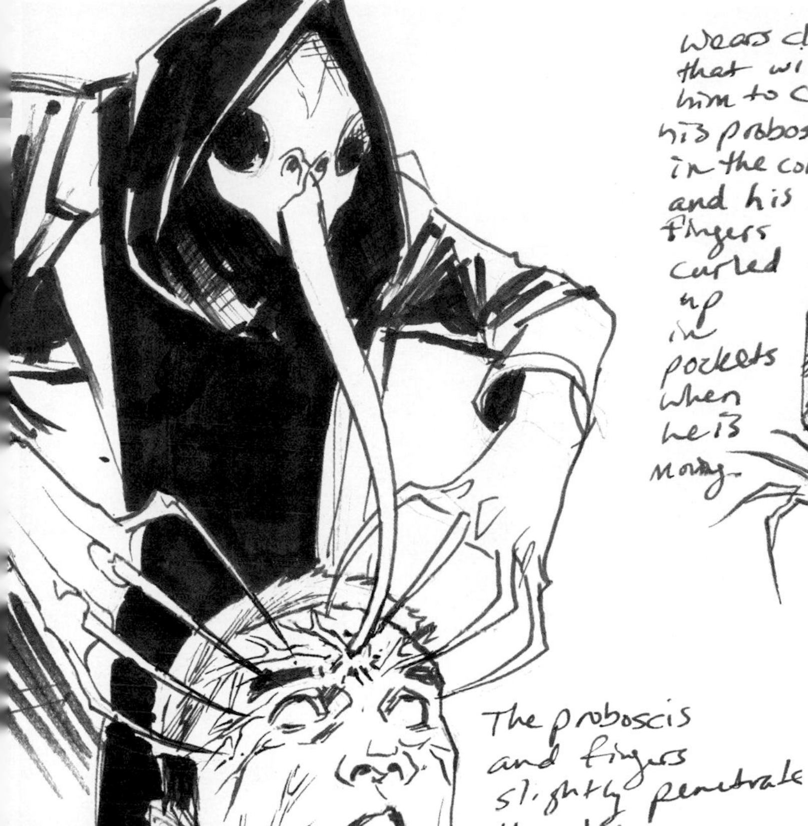
The proboscis and fingers slightly penetrate the skin

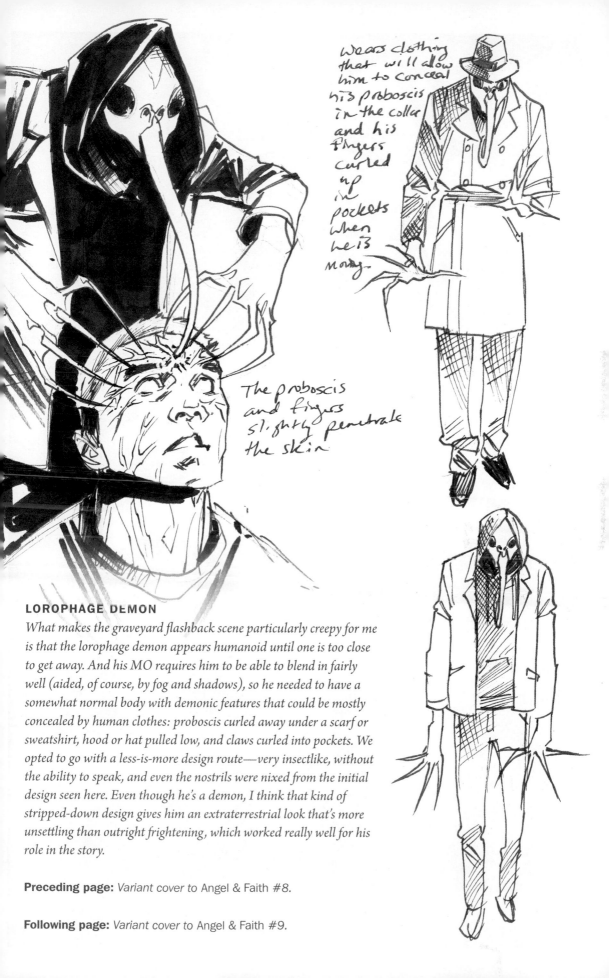

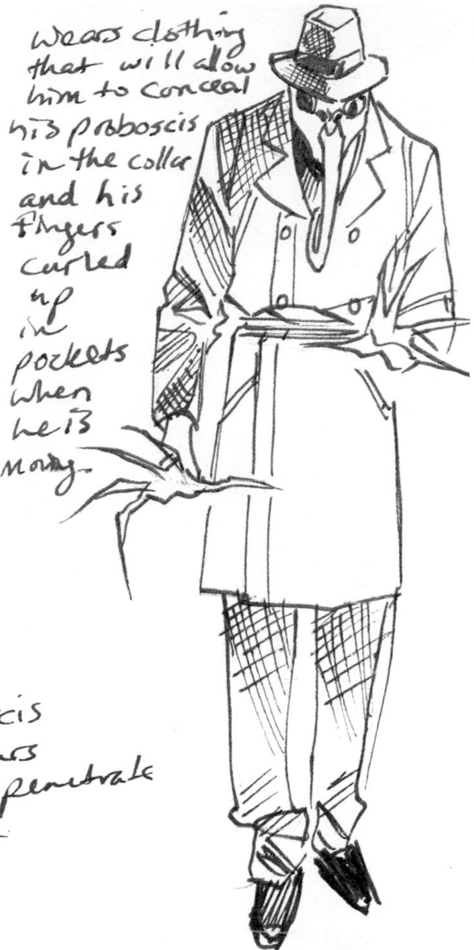
Wears clothing that will allow him to conceal his proboscis in the collar and his fingers curled up in pockets when he is moving.

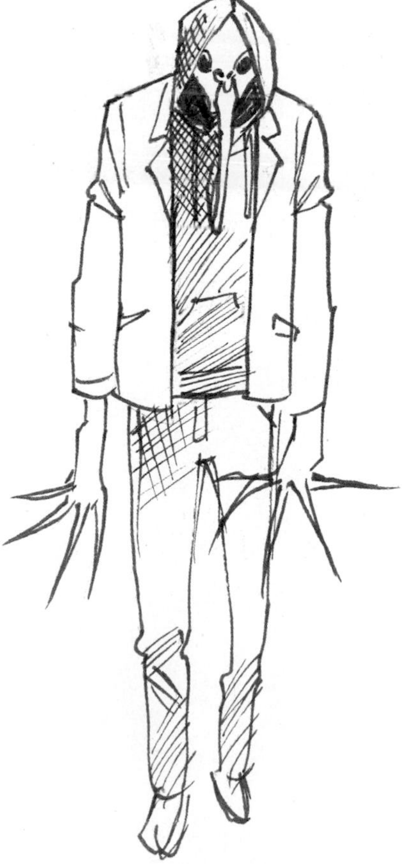

LOROPHAGE DEMON

What makes the graveyard flashback scene particularly creepy for me is that the lorophage demon appears humanoid until one is too close to get away. And his MO requires him to be able to blend in fairly well (aided, of course, by fog and shadows), so he needed to have a somewhat normal body with demonic features that could be mostly concealed by human clothes: proboscis curled away under a scarf or sweatshirt, hood or hat pulled low, and claws curled into pockets. We opted to go with a less-is-more design route—very insectlike, without the ability to speak, and even the nostrils were nixed from the initial design seen here. Even though he's a demon, I think that kind of stripped-down design gives him an extraterrestrial look that's more unsettling than outright frightening, which worked really well for his role in the story.

Preceding page: *Variant cover to* Angel & Faith *#8.*

Following page: *Variant cover to* Angel & Faith *#9.*

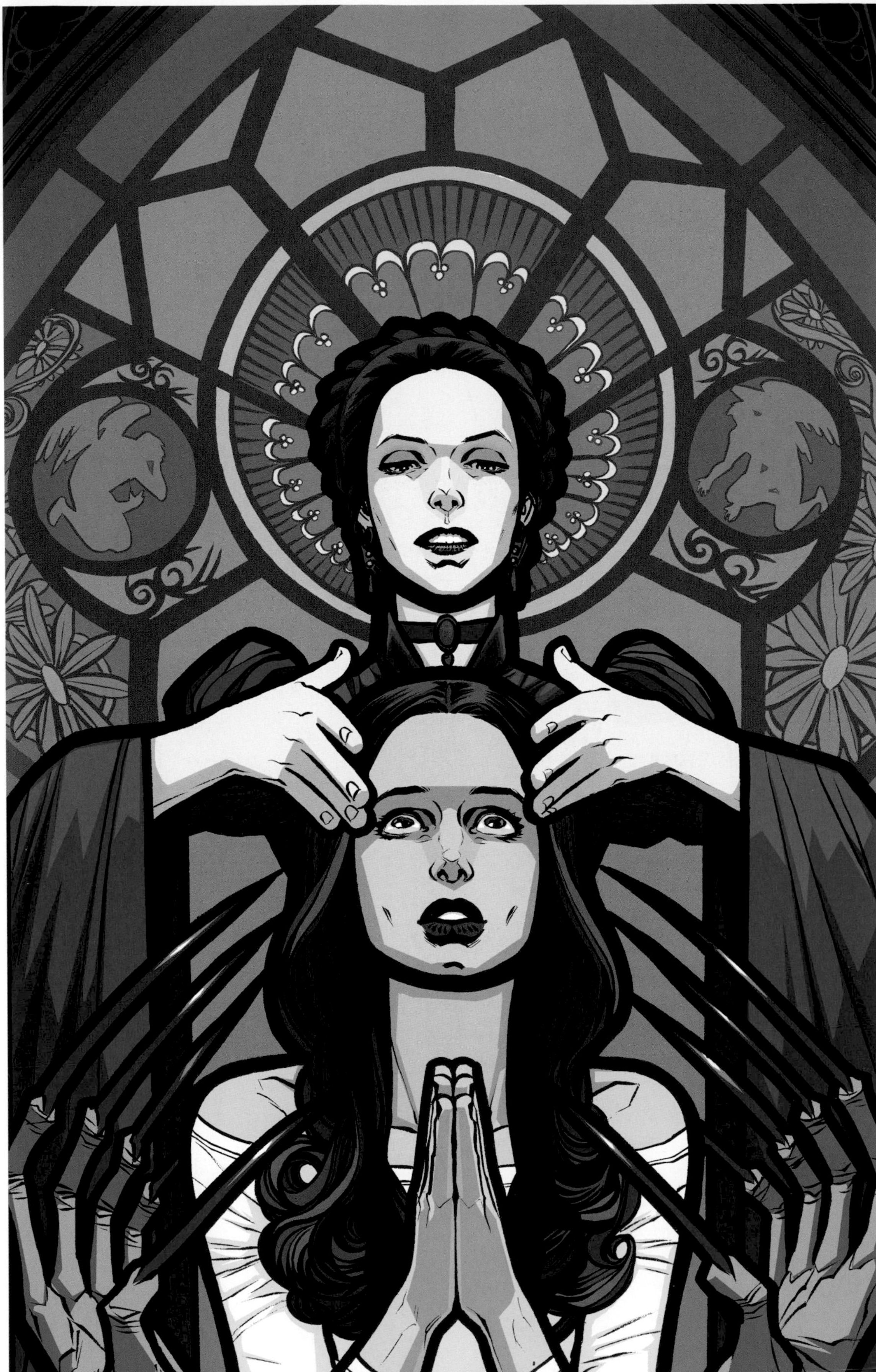

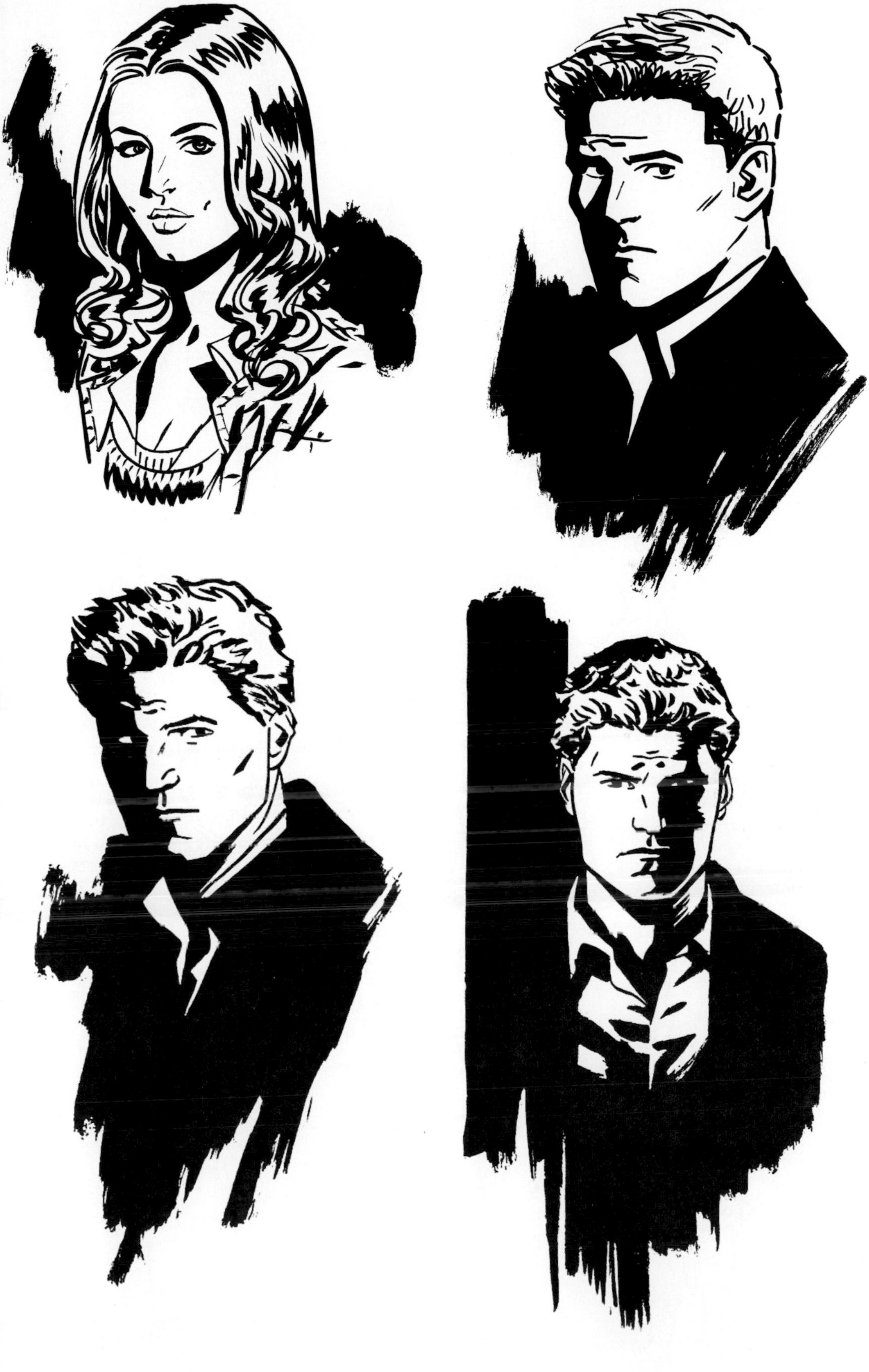

Likeness tryouts for Faith and Angel by issue #10's artist, Chris Samnee.

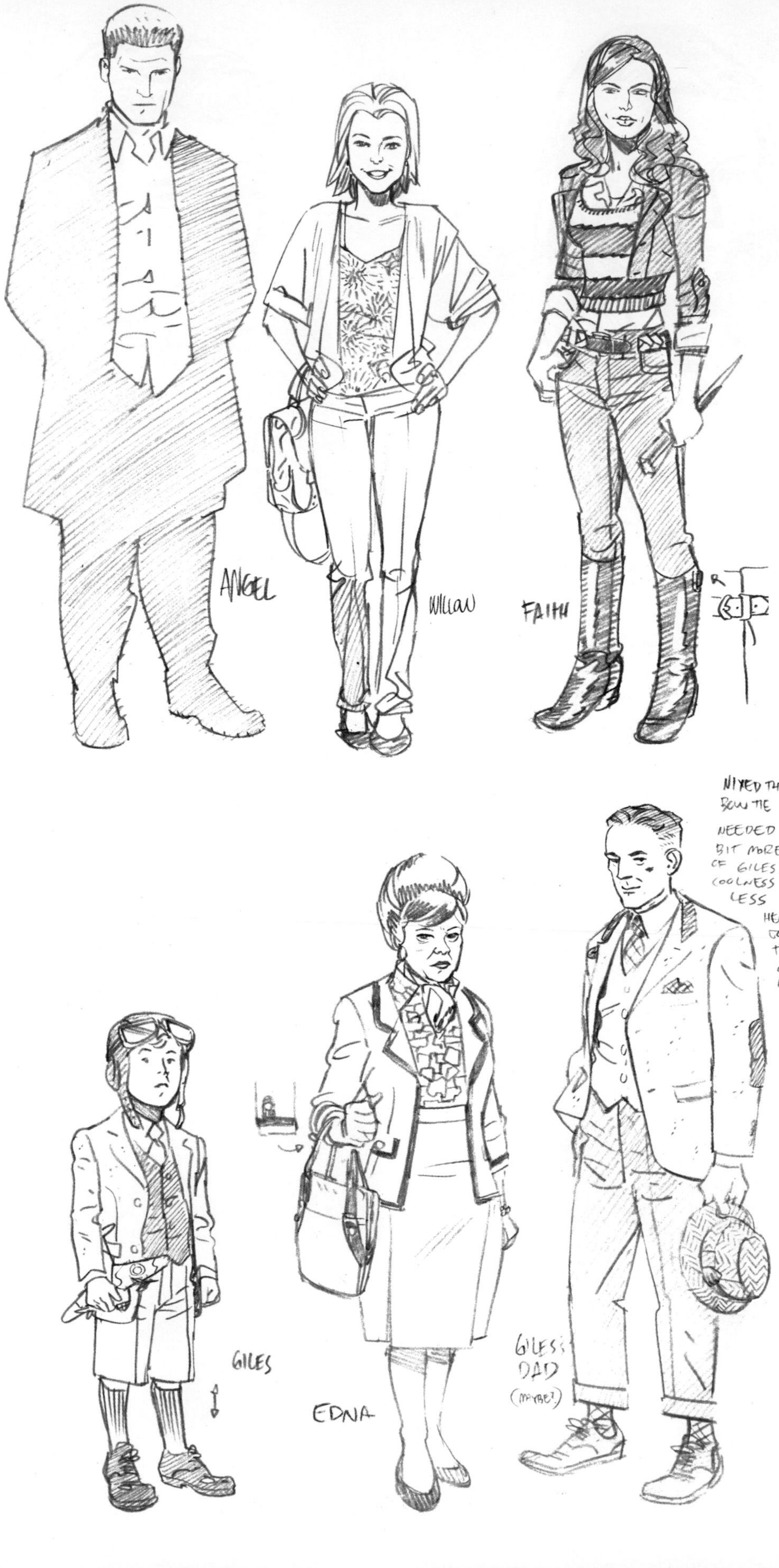
ANGEL
WILLOW
FAITH
NIXED THE BOW TIE
NEEDED A BIT MORE OF GILES'S COOLNESS & LESS HENRY JONES TWEEDY OLD MAN
GILES
EDNA
GILES'S DAD (MAYBE?)

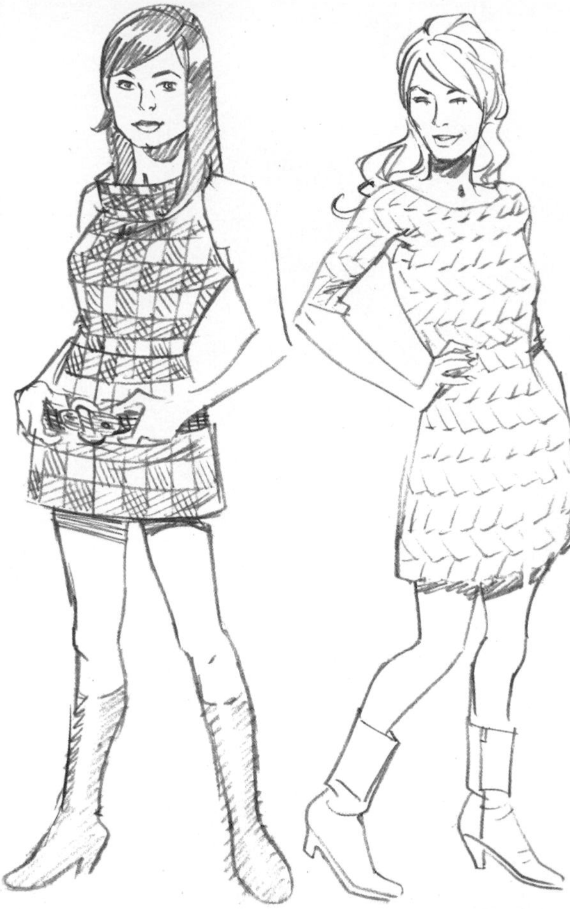

While Chris Samnee began work on Angel & Faith *#10, Rebekah Isaacs was working ahead on issue #11, where Willow plays an integral role in the story arc. The characters needed to have coordinating outfits throughout the series that each artist could refer to. Samnee created this visual to best track the main characters' fashionable ensembles.*

Samnee explored Giles's backstory (as well as introduced Willow to the series) in this special standalone issue that paints a vivid portrait of Giles's childhood and further establishes his bond with his two ageless aunts—Sophronia and Lavinia.

Following page: Angel & Faith #10 *variant cover.*

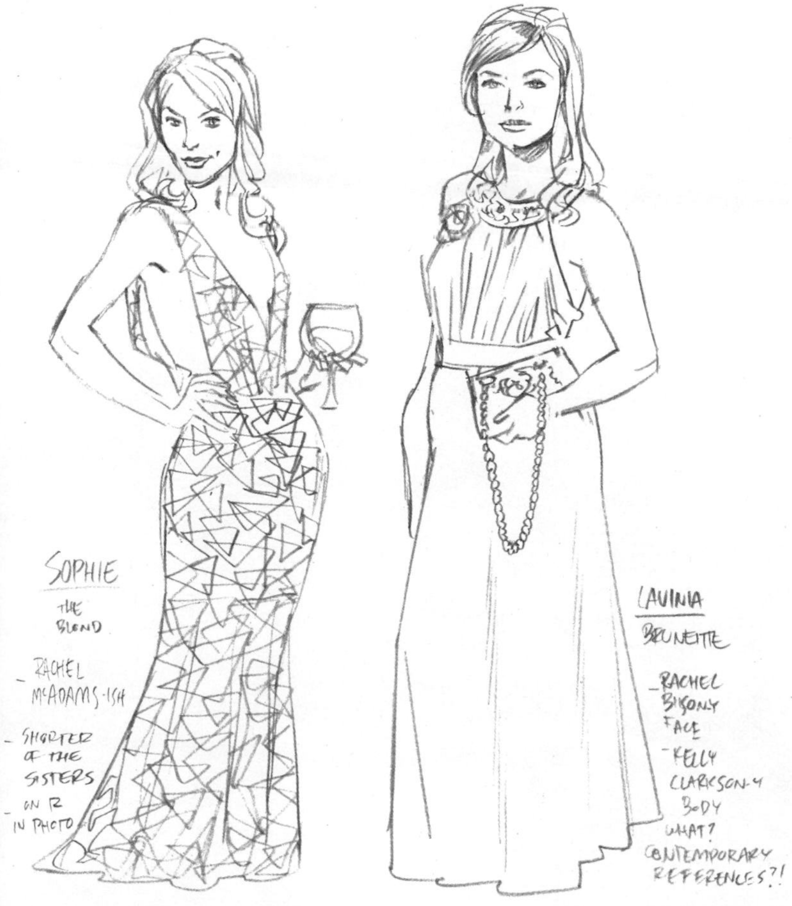
SOPHIE
THE BLOND
_RACHEL McADAMS-ISH
_SHORTER OF THE SISTERS
_ON R IN PHOTO
LAVINIA
BRUNETTE
_RACHEL BILSON-Y FACE
_KELLY CLARKSON-Y BODY
WHAT? CONTEMPORARY REFERENCES?!

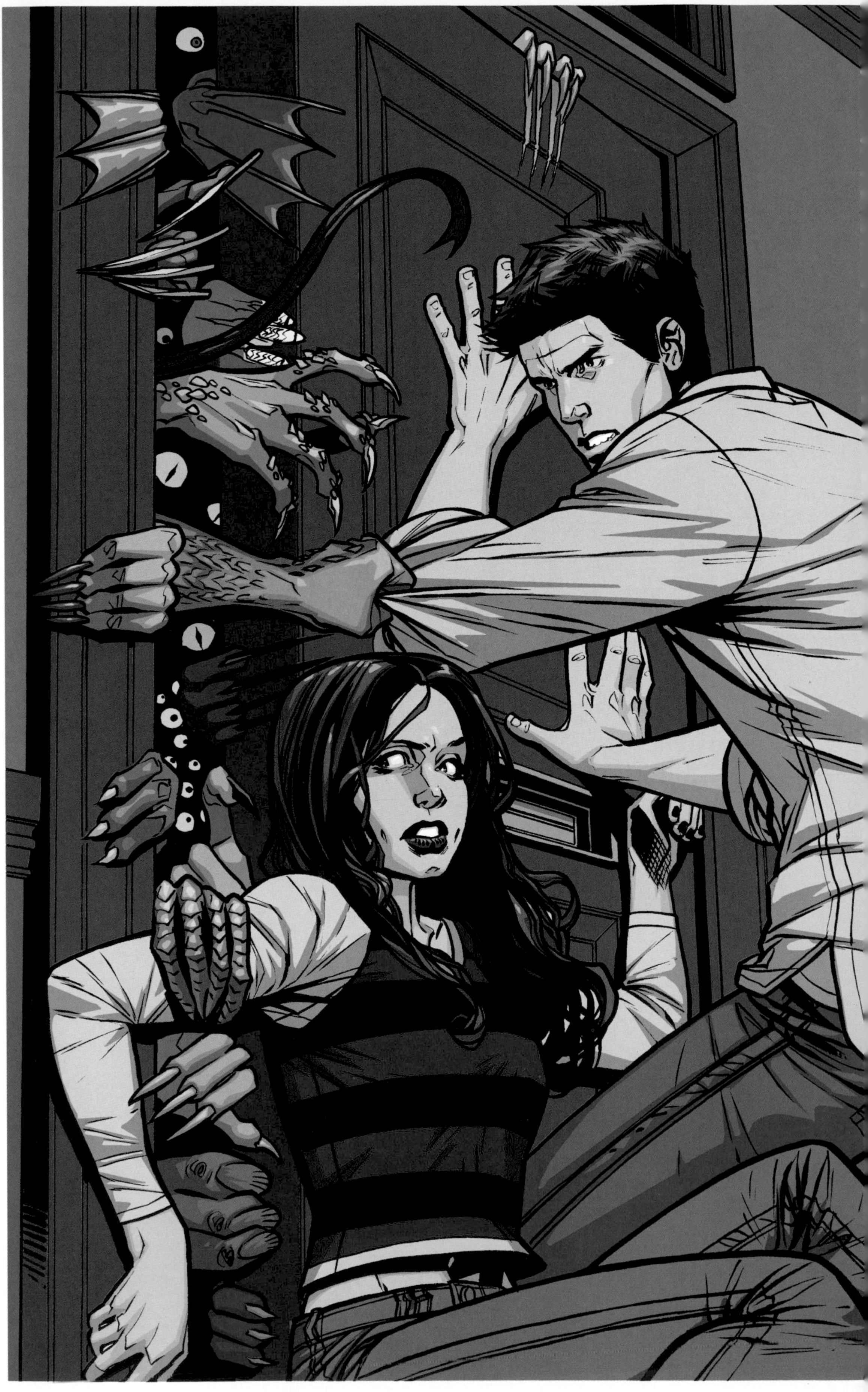

FROM JOSS WHEDON

BUFFY THE VAMPIRE SLAYER SEASON 8

VOLUME 1: THE LONG WAY HOME
Joss Whedon and Georges Jeanty
ISBN 978-1-59307-822-5 | $15.99

VOLUME 2: NO FUTURE FOR YOU
Brian K. Vaughan, Georges Jeanty, and Joss Whedon
ISBN 978-1-59307-963-5 | $15.99

VOLUME 3: WOLVES AT THE GATE
Drew Goddard, Georges Jeanty, and Joss Whedon
ISBN 978-1-59582-165-2 | $15.99

VOLUME 4: TIME OF YOUR LIFE
Joss Whedon, Jeph Loeb, Georges Jeanty, and others
ISBN 978-1-59582-310-6 | $15.99

VOLUME 5: PREDATORS AND PREY
Joss Whedon, Jane Espenson, Georges Jeanty, Cliff Richards, and others
ISBN 978-1-59582-342-7 | $15.99

VOLUME 6: RETREAT
Joss Whedon, Jane Espenson, Georges Jeanty, Karl Moline, and others
ISBN 978-1-59582-415-8 | $15.99

VOLUME 7: TWILIGHT
Joss Whedon, Brad Meltzer, and Georges Jeanty
ISBN 978-1-59582-558-2 | $16.99

VOLUME 8: LAST GLEAMING
Joss Whedon, Scott Allie, and Georges Jeanty
ISBN 978-1-59582-610-7 | $16.99

BUFFY THE VAMPIRE SLAYER SEASON 8 LIBRARY EDITION

VOLUME 1
ISBN 978-1-59582-888-0 | $29.99

VOLUME 2
ISBN 978-1-59582-935-1 | $29.99

VOLUME 3
ISBN 978-1-59582-978-8 | $29.99

BUFFY THE VAMPIRE SLAYER SEASON 9

VOLUME 1: FREEFALL
Joss Whedon, Andrew Chambliss, Georges Jeanty, and others
ISBN 978-1-59582-922-1 | $17.99

ANGEL & FAITH

ANGEL & FAITH VOLUME 1: LIVE THROUGH THIS
Christos Gage, Rebekah Isaacs, and Phil Noto
ISBN 978-1-59582-887-3 | $17.99

ANGEL & FAITH VOLUME 2: DADDY ISSUES
Christos Gage, Rebekah Isaacs, and Chris Samnee
ISBN 978-1-59582-960-3 | $17.99

DARK HORSE BOOKS

ALSO FROM JOSS WHEDON

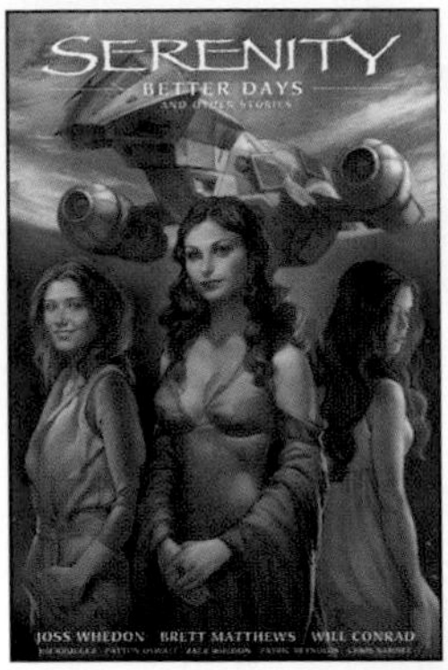
SERENITY
BETTER DAYS
JOSS WHEDON · BRETT MATTHEWS · WILL CONRAD

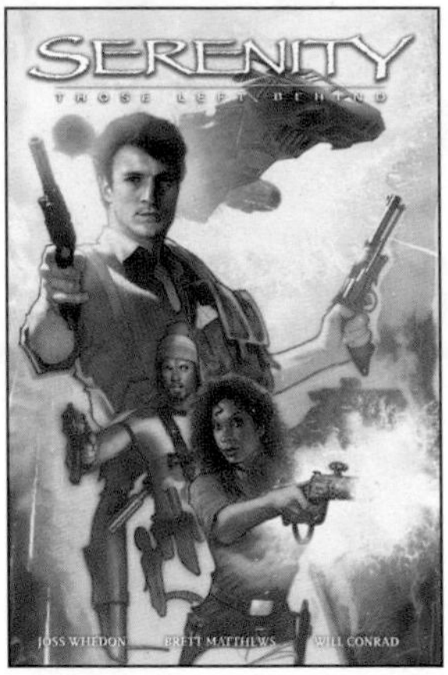
SERENITY
JOSS WHEDON
BRETT MATTHEWS
WILL CONRAD

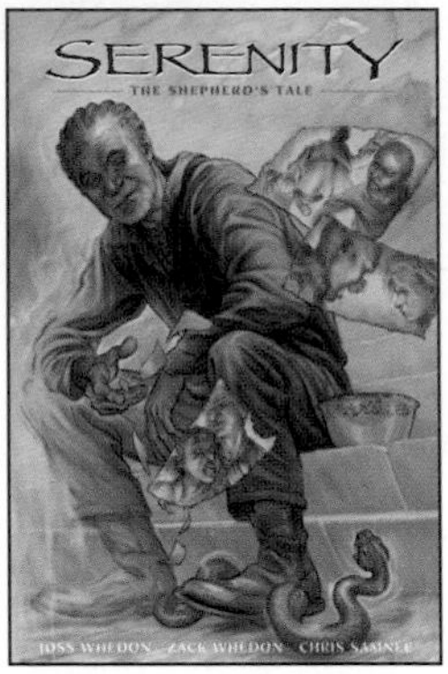
SERENITY
THE SHEPHERD'S TALE
JOSS WHEDON · ZACK WHEDON · CHRIS SAMNEE

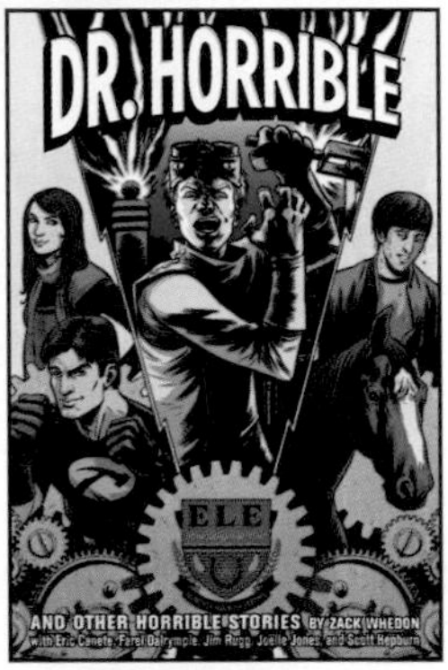
DR. HORRIBLE
ELE
AND OTHER HORRIBLE STORIES BY ZACK WHEDON

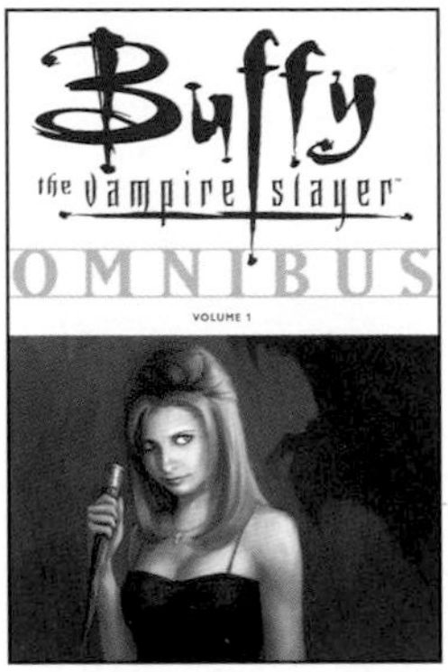
Buffy
the vampire slayer
OMNIBUS
VOLUME 1

BUFFY THE VAMPIRE SLAYER OMNIBUS
VOLUME 1
ISBN 978-1-59307-784-6 | $24.99
VOLUME 2
ISBN 978-1-59307-826-3 | $24.99
VOLUME 3
ISBN 978-1-59307-885-0 | $24.99
VOLUME 4
ISBN 978-1-59307-968-0 | $24.99
VOLUME 5
ISBN 978-1-59582-225-3 | $24.99
VOLUME 6
ISBN 978-1-59582-242-0 | $24.99
VOLUME 7
ISBN 978-1-59582-331-1 | $24.99

BUFFY THE VAMPIRE SLAYER: PANEL TO PANEL
ISBN 978-1-59307-836-2 | $19.99

ANGEL OMNIBUS
Christopher Golden, Eric Powell, and others
ISBN 978-1-59582-706-7 | $24.99

TALES OF THE SLAYERS
Joss Whedon, Amber Benson, Gene Colan, P. Craig Russell, Tim Sale, and others
ISBN 978-1-56971-605-2 | $14.99

TALES OF THE VAMPIRES
Joss Whedon, Brett Matthews, Cameron Stewart, and others
ISBN 978-1-56971-749-3 | $15.99

BUFFY THE VAMPIRE SLAYER: TALES HARDCOVER
ISBN 978-1-59582-644-2 | $29.99

FRAY: FUTURE SLAYER
Joss Whedon and Karl Moline
ISBN 978-1-56971-751-6 | $19.99

SERENITY VOLUME 1: THOSE LEFT BEHIND SECOND EDITION HARDCOVER
Joss Whedon, Brett Matthews, and Will Conrad
ISBN 978-1-59582-914-6 | $17.99

SERENITY VOLUME 2: BETTER DAYS AND OTHER STORIES HARDCOVER
Joss Whedon, Patton Oswalt, Zack Whedon, Patric Reynolds, and others
ISBN 978-1-59582-739-5 | $19.99

SERENITY VOLUME 3: THE SHEPHERD'S TALE HARDCOVER
Joss Whedon, Zack Whedon, and Chris Samnee
ISBN 978-1-59582-561-2 | $14.99

DR. HORRIBLE AND OTHER HORRIBLE STORIES
Joss Whedon, Zack Whedon, Joëlle Jones, and others
ISBN 978-1-59582-577-3 | $9.99

DOLLHOUSE VOLUME 1: EPITAPHS
Andrew Chambliss, Jed Whedon, Maurissa Tancharoen, and Cliff Richards
ISBN 978-1-59582-863-7 | $18.99